DISPUTE RESOLUTION
IN SPECIAL EDUCATION

Special Education Law, Policy, and Practice

Series Editors
Mitchell L. Yell, PhD, University of South Carolina
David F. Bateman, PhD, American Institutes for Research

The *Special Education Law, Policy, and Practice* series highlights current trends and legal issues in the education of students with disabilities. The books in this series link legal requirements with evidence-based instruction and highlight practical applications for working with students with disabilities. The titles in the *Special Education Law, Policy, and Practices* series are designed not only to be required textbooks for general education and special education preservice teacher education programs but are also designed for practicing teachers, education administrators, principals, school counselors, school psychologists, parents, and others interested in improving the lives of students with disabilities. The *Special Education Law, Policy, and Practice* series is committed to research-based practices working to provide appropriate and meaningful educational programming for students with disabilities and their families.

Titles in Series:

DISPUTE RESOLUTION IN SPECIAL EDUCATION

UNDERSTANDING, AVOIDING, AND MANAGING SPECIAL EDUCATION DISPUTES

DAVID F. BATEMAN
American Institutes for Research

MITCHELL L. YELL
University of South Carolina

JONAS S. DOREGO
Guam Department of Education (retired)

ROWMAN & LITTLEFIELD
Lanham • Boulder • New York • London

Associate Acquisitions Editor: Courtney Packard
Assistant Acquisitions Editor: Sarah Rinehart
Sales and Marketing Inquiries: textbooks@rowman.com

Published by Rowman & Littlefield
An imprint of The Rowman & Littlefield Publishing Group, Inc.
4501 Forbes Boulevard, Suite 200, Lanham, Maryland 20706
www.rowman.com

86-90 Paul Street, London EC2A 4NE

British Library Cataloguing in Publication Information Available

Library of Congress Cataloging-in-Publication Data

Includes bibliographic references and index.
ISBN: 978-1-5381-5615-5 (cloth)
ISBN: 978-1-5381-5616-2 (paperback)
ISBN: 978-1-5381-5617-9 (electronic)

∞™ The paper used in this publication meets the minimum requirements of American National Standard for Information Sciences—Permanence of Paper for Printed Library Materials, ANSI/NISO Z39.48-1992.

Disclaimer

The information in *Dispute Resolution in Special Education* does not constitute legal advice. Additionally, information in this text may be affected by state laws, regulations, and policies and local rules and policies. In situations involving legal issues, the advice of an attorney should be secured.

Brief Contents

Contents

Acknowledgments

We wish to thank the below reviewers whose thoughtful comments and expertise guided our writing and revisions for the development of this book. As always, any errors and omissions are our own.

Kaitlin Bundock, *Utah State University*
Kyena Cornelius, *Minnesota State University, Mankato*
Brittany Hott, *University of Oklahoma*
Timothy Letzring, *University of Central Florida*
Michelle McKnight, *Utah State University*
Elizabeth Lugg, *Illinois State University*
Kristin Murphy, *University of Massachusetts-Boston*
Ruby Owiny, *Minnesota State University, Mankato*
Barbara Qualls, *Stephen F. Austin State University*
Joseph "Rocky" Wallace, *Campbellsville University*
Carol Willard, *State University of New York–Oswego*

Introduction

Writing the majority opinion in the 1943 ruling from the U.S. Supreme Court in *McNabb v. United States*, Felix Frankfurter wrote, "The history of liberty has largely been the history of the observance of procedural safeguards (*McNabb v. United States*, 1943, p. 334). Basic fairness is the primary concept of contemporary procedural due process, which underlies every decision made by a government entity, such as a public school (Vacca, 2017).

The concept of due process originated in the Fourteenth Amendment to the U.S. Constitution. Although the primary purpose of this amendment was to protect individuals from the state, it has also been applied in numerous other areas. One such area was regarding students with disabilities in public schools.

Until the mid 1970s, students with disabilities were often excluded from receiving an education in the public schools. Sometimes they were educated in settings that did not meet their needs. As Chief Justice William Rehnquist wrote in the majority opinion in the first special education case heard by the U.S. Supreme Court too often students with disabilities were "left to fend for themselves in classrooms designed for education of their nonhandicapped peers" (*Board of Education of the Hendrick Hudson School District v. Rowley*, 1982, p. 191).

To response to the poor educational programming that their children with disabilities had to endure in school as well as the increasing exclusion of children with disabilities from school, parents began to band together to advocate for their children's education rights. The efforts of parents and parent advocacy groups, and the inability of individual states to ameliorate these problems, led to increasing federal involvement in efforts to pass law to ensure the education of students with disabilities.

When Congress passed the Education for All Handicapped Children Act of 1975, renamed the Individuals with Disabilities Act (IDEA) in 1990, the authors of the law believed that developing a system of procedural safeguard was absolutely essential in ensuring that students with disabilities received a free appropriate public education (FAPE). In fact, Senator Robert Stafford (1978), wrote that "where . . . administrative appeal procedures are in operation, they afford a timely, fair system for resolving conflicts" (p. 78).

The procedural safeguards in the IDEA are designed to protects the rights of students and their parents by ensuring that parents are to be (a) involved in all special education meetings involving their child; (b) be informed of any proposals to change a student's identification, evaluation, placement, or program, and (c) provide informed consent before their child can be evaluated for, or placed in, a special education program. The procedural safeguards also include mechanisms by which disputes between a student's parents and school district personnel can be settled, which are referred to as dispute resolution procedures. These dispute resolution procedures include mediation, resolution meetings, due process, and even litigation in state or federal courts.

School district personnel and parents find dispute resolution confusing, complex, and challenging. Our purpose in this text is to bring clarity to the dispute resolution procedures of the IDEA. The authors are experts in special education law and bring a wealth of experience in conducting due process hearings at the local and state levels.

References

McNabb v. United States, 318 U.S. 332 (1943).

Stafford, R. T. (1978). Education for the Handicapped: A senator's perspective. *Vermont Law Review*, 37, 71–82.

Vacca, R. S. (2017). Student discipline hearings and due process. In J. R. Decker, M. M. Lewis, E. A. Shaver, A. E. Blankenship-Knox, & M. A. Paige (Eds.). *The principal's legal handbook* (6th ed.). (pp. 1–14). Education Law Association.

CHAPTER 1

An Overview of the Individuals with Disabilities Education Act and Dispute Resolution

Advance Organizers

* What is the history of special education?
* What court cases led to the due process protections?
* What is the Education for All Handicapped Children's Act?
* What are the components of the Individuals with Disabilities Education Act?
* What is dispute resolution?

The purpose of this book is to provide guidance to administrators, teachers, and parents on the dispute resolution system of the Individuals with Disabilities Education Act (IDEA). These dispute resolution procedures and information in the IDEA are only for students with disabilities. These procedures do not apply to students who are not disabled under the IDEA.

In this chapter we begin by briefly reviewing the legal development of special education, including the court cases that led to the IDEA. We then cover the specifics of the IDEA and highlight the main components of the law that are often the subject of dispute resolution. Finally, we provide an overview of the IDEA's dispute resolution system.

The Legal Development of Special Education

Historically students with disabilities could be legally prevented from attending school in most states (Martin, 2013). As recently as 1973, the state of Virginia allowed for the exclusion for students physically or mentally incapacitated for school (Code of Virginia, 1973). Unfortunately, the history of educational services for students with disabilities is filled with stories and examples of wholesale exclusion and denials of appropriate educational services. Often, the best that a parent could hope for was some form of educational service in a state-run institution (Gerber, 2017) or inappropriate educational services provided in a public school (Martin et al., 1996). Moreover, there was no legal way for a parent to appeal school district officials' decisions to prohibit students with disabilities from attending their public school.

According to Burch (2009), parents and advocates begin promoting educational services for students with disabilities in the early nineteenth century. It was not until the 1960s and 1970s, however, that state legislators, federal courts, and the U.S. Congress began to address the educational rights of students with disabilities (Martin et al., 1996).

The Courts and Special Education

Two court cases set the groundwork for much of special education in the United States. We next examine these cases, *Pennsylvania Association for Retarded Citizens v. Pennsylvania* (1972) and *Mills v. Board of Education* (1972).

Pennsylvania Association for Retarded Citizens v. Pennsylvania (1972)

In 1969, the Pennsylvania Association for Retarded Children (PARC) filed a class-action lawsuit against the Commonwealth of Pennsylvania arguing students with mental retardation were not receiving publicly supported education, a violation of state statutes, specifically the compulsory attendance laws, and the students' rights under the Equal Protection of the Laws clause of the Fourteenth Amendment of the U.S. Constitution. In 1972, a consent decree was signed guaranteeing a free public education be provided to all children with mental retardation between the ages of six and twenty-one. The decree also established the Right to Education Office (REO). REO was the office where complaints were filed regarding any aspect of the student's education, and later was where due process hearings were administratively housed in Pennsylvania. Parents could file a complaint and someone from outside of the local school district would come investigate.

Mills v. Board of Education (1972)

In 1972, parents and guardians of seven children of school age filed a class-action suit against the District of Columbia Public Schools to resolve denial of a publicly supported education and to compel the defendants to provide the children with an immediate and adequate education. Like the PARC lawsuit, *Mills v. Board of Education* (hereinafter *Mills*; 1972) was based on the Fourteenth Amendment, and alleged students were improperly excluded from school without due process of law. The court ruled students with disabilities must be given a public education even if the students are unable to pay for the cost of the education and required the District of Columbia Board of Education to establish the following due process safeguards for labeling, placing, and excluding students with disabilities (Yell, 2017; Zettel & Ballard, 1982):

- The right to a hearing with representation, a verbatim record of the hearing, and an impartial hearing officer;
- The right to an appeal;

* The right to have access to records; and
* The requirement of written notice at all stages of the special education decision-making process.

These safeguards became the basis of due process provisions included in subsequent special education laws.

The *PARC* and *Mills* decisions was followed by similar cases throughout the country. In the two and a half years following the *PARC* and *Mills* decisions, forty-six right-to-education cases were filed on behalf of children with disabilities in twenty-eight states (Zettel & Ballard, 1982). The ruling in the right-to-education cases led to many states passing laws requiring students with disabilities receive a public education. Unfortunately, these laws varied substantially and resulted in uneven attempts to provide education to students. Martin (2103) asserted that despite the successes in these cases and state legislatures many students with disabilities continued to be denied an appropriate public education.

> In local school programs, children were frequently subjected to substandard services in poor facilities. Parents reported classes in basements, janitor's rooms, condemned buildings, and similar sites. Children were often placed in classes inappropriate for their needs . . . (Programs) were frequently trained teachers, and instructors generally had to create their own curriculum and materials . . . not a single state even pretended to educate all its children with disabilities. Even states that had mandatory laws did not enforce them (Martin, 2013, pp. 30–31).

These problems led many to advocate for the passage of federal laws to bring an end to these uneven efforts to provide appropriate educational programming to students with disabilities.

Congress and Special Education

In 1974, Congress held hearings on the educational problems experienced by students with disabilities and more generally all persons with disabilities. Two notable statements from Congressional findings about persons with disabilities were as follows:

> The long-range implications of these statistics are that public agencies and taxpayers will spend billions of dollars over the lifetimes of these individuals to maintain such persons as dependents and in a minimally acceptable lifestyle. With proper education services, many would be able to become productive citizens, contributing to society instead of being forced to remain burdens. Others, through such services, would increase their independence, thus reducing their dependence on society (U.S.C.C.A.N, 1975, p. 1433).

Additionally:

> Providing educational services will ensure against persons needlessly being forced into institutional settings. One need only look at public residential

institutions to find thousands of persons whose families are no longer able to care for them and who themselves have received no educational services. Billions of dollars are expended each year to maintain persons in these sub-human conditions (U.S.C.C.A.N, 1975, p. 1433).

In these congressional hearings, witnesses before the Senate and House committees, including parents, educators, advocates of disability rights, state legislators, program specialists, and governors, testified:

- A significant proportion of school-aged students with disabilities were either not receiving appropriate educational services or not receiving any educational services.
- Many states were considering or had recently adopted legislation mandating a free appropriate public education of all students with disabilities, some in response to court decisions.
- States varied widely in the extent to which they were providing appropriate special education programming to students with disabilities.
- Despite new mandates in a number of states to serve students with disabilities in public schools, increased state funding for students with disabilities, and good intentions of state program administrators, many students with disabilities were not receiving comprehensive services.
- Expanded funding for educational services for students with disabilities was believed to be a sound investment because, by some estimates, 90 percent of the population of persons with disabilities would become self-sufficient and taxpayers if they were properly educated.

Results of Congressional hearings convinced members that a federal standard was needed to help students with disabilities and bring uniformity to the states in providing educational services to students with disabilities. In 1975, Congress passed the Education of All Handicapped Children Act (EAHCA), renamed the IDEA in 1990. The EAHCA contained an educational bill of right for students with eligible students and provided federal financial incentives to assist states to provide special education programming. One of components included in the EAHCA was a dispute resolution system.

Education for All Handicapped Children Act of 1975 (EAHCA)

The EAHCA was passed by Congress in 1975. The law, which was often referred to as PL 94-142 (i.e., the 142 public law signed by the president in the 94th Congress), mandated that students with disabilities be provided special education and related services that conferred a free appropriate public education to eligible students between the ages of three and twenty-one. The primary objectives of the law were as follows:

1. To assure all children with disabilities have available to them a free appropriate public education.
2. To assure the rights of children with disabilities and their parents are protected.

3. To assist states and localities to provide for the education of children with disabilities; and
4. To assess and assure the effectiveness of efforts to educate children with disabilities.

As noted above, the IDEA is a law that was created because parents, advocacy groups, and professionals were dissatisfied with certain conditions and brought them to the attention of legislators. Congress found:

* More than eight million children with disabilities (from birth to age twenty-one) were living in the United States, and that more than half of them were not receiving an appropriate education.
* More than one million children with disabilities were excluded entirely from the educational system, and that many others were enrolled in regular education classes where, because their disabilities were undetected, they were not learning as much as could be expected.
* Families were being forced to find services outside the public schools because the educational services within the schools were inadequate.

The law requires states to have a plan that fully describes the policies and procedures used to ensure a free, appropriate education for all students with disabilities between the ages of three and twenty-one, and to have procedures in place for identifying all students with disabilities. States that failed to comply with these procedures would not receive federal IDEA funds.

Primary Components of the IDEA

Four primary components of the IDEA not only provide guidance to the persons who work with eligible students with disabilities and their families but also have been issues that have frequently been litigated, first in due process hearings and eventually in federal courts. These four areas involve (a) evaluation, both for eligibility and instructional planning; (b) FAPE, including the individualized education programs (IEPs); (c) least restrictive environment (LRE); and (d) procedural safeguards, including the dispute resolution process. Because FAPE is the primary obligation of special educators and the most frequently litigated area, we begin with a brief examination of this component.

Free Appropriate Public Education

The primary mandate of the IDEA and essential obligation of special educators is to develop a student's program of special education that confers a FAPE. The IDEA defines FAPE as special education and related services that

A. are provided at public expense, under public supervision and direction, and without charge,
B. meet standards of the state educational agency,
C. include an appropriate preschool, elementary, or secondary school education in the state involved, and

D. are provided in conformity with the individualized education program. (IDEA, 20 U.S.C. § 1401 [a][18]).

Congressional authors of the EAHCA included a number of procedural requirements in the law which were meant to ensure a student's parents were involved in the development of their child's program of special education. The law contained little in the way of substantive requirements or educational outcomes that fulfilling a FAPE would require. Because of this statutory gap, the federal court were left to clarify the distinction between the procedural and substantive requirements of the EAHCA. The primary case that clarified the procedural and substantive requirements was heard by the U.S. Supreme Court in 1982, *Board of Education v. Rowley* (hereinafter *Rowley*).

In *Rowley*, the high court created a two-part test for hearing officers and courts to use to determine if a school district had met the FAPE obligation of the federal law. The first part of the *Rowley* test was procedural and required that a hearing officer or judge decide if a school district had met the procedural requirements of the law. The second part of the *Rowley* test was substantive and required that a hearing officer or judge decide if a school district's IEP was reasonably calculated to enable a student to receive educational benefit. In 2017, the U.S. Supreme Court clarified the second part of the *Rowley* test in *Endrew F. v. Douglas County School District* (hereinafter *Endrew F.*). The new substantive standard developed in *Endrew F.* required that when a hearing officer or judge ruled on whether a school district's IEP had confirmed a FAPE, they would need to determine if a student's IEP was reasonably calculated to enable a student make progress appropriate in light of the student's circumstances. Under the Supreme Court's substantive standard, the content of a student's IEP must be sufficient in terms of the actual or likely results so that the student will achieve meaningful academic and/or behavioral progress (Berney & Gilsbach, 2017; Yell et al., 2021; Zirkel, 2017).

In the 2004 reauthorization of the IDEA, the Individual with Disabilities Education Improvement Act, Congress added language to the law which required that when ruling on a FAPE case, a hearing officer is to make his or her decision "on substantive grounds based on a determination of whether a child received a free appropriate public education" (20 U.S.C. § 1415[f][3][i]). Additionally, "In matters alleging a procedural violation, a hearing officer may only find that a child did not receive a free appropriate public education if the procedural violations resulted in substantive harm" (20 U.S.C. § 1415[f][3][ii]). The only procedural violations that may lead to substantive harm are violations that (a) impedes a student's right to a FAPE, (b) impedes the parents' opportunity to participate in the decision-making process regarding their child's FAPE, or (c) causes a deprivation of educational benefit. Procedural violations that are "merely technical violation of the IDEA" may not result in substantive harm, thus not violating the IDEA (Berney & Gilsbach, 2012, p. 7). When IEP team make multiple procedural errors, the cumulative effect of the errors may be a denial of FAPE, even when the errors when committed by themselves would not amount to a denial of a FAPE (Yell et al., 2021).

Although the lack of a definition of substantive benefits in the EAHCA/ IDEA resulted in the courts having to interpret FAPE with little in the way of statutory interpretation, this was not a congressional oversight. In fact, Senator Robert Stafford, a co-sponsor of the EAHCA, wrote that congressional authors "did not attempt to define 'appropriate' but instead we established a base-line mechanism, a written document called the Individualized Education Program (IEP)" (Stafford, 1978, p. 75). Thus, the IEP, developed collaboratively between a student's parents and school personnel, was the basis for determining if the educational program offered to a student with disabilities was appropriate for that student (Martin, 2013).

The IEP is a written document that describes:

* The student's present levels of functioning.
* The annual goals and short-term objectives of the program.
* The services to be provided and the extent of regular programming.
* The starting date and expected duration of services.
* Evaluation procedures and criteria for monitoring progress.

The IEP is the product of a thorough evaluation that begins with information about the child gathered from parents, teachers, and formal and informal assessments, and ends with a review by a team of professionals. The instructional goals specified in a student's IEP must be measurable, observable, and lead to and measure a student's progress. A student's IEP also contains the specific special education services, related services, and supplementary services a student is to receive. The IEP serves somewhat like a written contract between school personnel and a student's parents regarding the services that will be provided. The IEP is unlike a contract in that it doesn't guarantee results.

The FAPE requirements of the law are frequently litigated in due process hearings. In fact, Gerl (2014) estimated that 80 percent to 90 percent of all due process hearings involve FAPE issues. Because most FAPE hearings will involve an analysis of a student's IEP it is extremely important that the IEP be developed and implemented correctly. When a hearing officer or court rules in a FAPE case they will use the two part test as originally devised in *Rowley* and clarified in *Endrew F.*

An important aspect in understanding FAPE, which will be examined throughout this book, is the IDEA's and the Supreme Court's division of FAPE into two dimensions, the procedural dimension and the substantive dimension. As previously discussed, the procedural dimension obligates school district personnel to know and follow the various procedural requirements of the law, such as the notice and consent requirements, members required on a student's IEP team, and components that must be included in the IEP. The substantive dimension requires that students' IEP teams develop a program of special education and related services that enable a student to make progress appropriate in light of his or her circumstances, the *Endrew F.* standard. There is also a third dimension that must be considered when discussing a school district's responsibility when providing FAPE: the implementation dimension.

The IDEA's definition of a FAPE requires that a FAPE is "provided in conformity" with a student's IEP (IDEA Regulations, 34 C.F.R. 300.17[d], 2006). In a ruling of the U.S. Courts of Appeals for the Ninth Circuit in *M.C. v. Antelope Valley Union High School District* (2017; hereinafter *Antelope Valley*), the court noted that "an IEP, like a contract . . . embodies a binding commitment and provides notice to both parties as to what services will be provided to the student during the period covered by the IEP" (*Antelope Valley*, 2017, p. 1197). The IEP is not a contract in the sense that it is not a guarantee that a student will achieve all the goals written in the IEP; rather, it is a contract because school personnel are obligated to provide the services agreed to by parents and school personnel in the IEP (Yell et al., 2021). If a student's IEP is not implemented as written, it could be a denial of FAPE, and thus violate the IDEA. We return to an examination of these three dimensions in chapter 2 on avoiding dispute resolution.

Evaluation

To qualify for special education, students must be evaluated and determined eligible for special education services in one or more of thirteen disability categories. The IDEA includes specific procedural requirements regarding evaluation. Prior to conducting an initial evaluation for eligibility, a school district must receive informed written consent from a student's parents. Within sixty days of receiving parental consent, school district personnel must conduct an evaluation to (a) determine if a student has a disability and (b) determine the educational needs of the student for planning his or her IEP. If states have timelines less than the sixty days required the by IDEA, school personnel must adhere to those guidelines.

Specifically, the procedural requirements for conducting an evaluation obligate school district personnel to the following:

- Complete a full and individual evaluation of a student's needs prior to placing the student in special education.
- Administer tests in the child's native language or other mode of communication.
- Administer tests that are valid for the specific purpose for which they are used.
- Use trained personnel to administer tests in accordance with the instructions provided by their producer.
- Ensure that tests and other evaluation materials are relevant to specific areas of educational needs and are not designed to yield a single general IQ score.
- Ensure that the results of tests administered to students who have impaired sensory, manual, or speaking skills reflect aptitude or achievement and not the impairment.
- Do not determine special education placement on the basis of a single procedure.

- Ensure that evaluations for special education placement are made by a multidisciplinary team, including a student's parents and at least one teacher or other specialist with knowledge in the area of suspected disability.
- Assess all areas related to their suspected disability, including general health, vision, hearing, behavior, general intelligence, motor abilities, academic performance, and language abilities.

Although evaluating a student for eligibility purposes is obviously an extremely important requirement of the IDEA, and the key to providing special education services, it is not the only function of evaluation. A very important purpose is instructional planning. The content of a student's IEP is based on the evaluation, which must include information relating to enabling a student to be involved in and progress in the general education curriculum (IDEA Regulations, 34 C.F.R. § 300.304[b][ii]). A required participant on the IEP team is "an individual who can interpret the instructional implications of the evaluation results" (IDEA Regulations, 34 C.F.R. §300.321[a][5], 2006). This person on the team is crucial, because the information he or she provides form the basis of the student's "statement of . . . present levels of academic achievement and functional performance" (IDEA Regulations, 34 C.F.R. §300.320[a][1], 2006), which leads to the "statement of measurable annual goals, including academic and functional goals" (IDEA Regulations C.F.R. §300.320[a][2][i], 2006) and "statement of special education and related services and supplementary aids and services . . . and a statement of program modifications or supports for school personnel" (IDEA Regulations 34 C.F.R. §300.320[a][2][i], 2006).

The evaluation procedures are often the subject of due process hearings because to the extent that evaluations are incomplete, inaccurate, or outdated, the IEP will be inadequate to provide a FAPE (Bateman, 2017). In *Kirby v. Cabell County Board of Education* (2006), a district court judge wrote about the importance of the evaluation in the IEP process:

> If the IEP fails to assess the "child's present levels of academic achievement and functional performance" the IEP does not comply with § 1414 [IDEA]. This deficiency goes to the heart of the IEP; the child's level of academic achievement and functional performance is the foundation on which the IEP must be built. Without a clear identification of [the child's] present levels, the IEP cannot set measurable goals, evaluate the child's progress and determine which educational and related services are needed (*Kirby v. Cabell County Board of Education*, 2006, p. 694).

Least Restrictive Environment

Placement decisions must be based on a student's IEP (IDEA Regulations, 34 C.F.R. § 300.116[b], 2006). The placement decision is not technically part of the IEP process, although the IEP team usually makes the placement decision (Bateman, 2017). This practice is acceptable, because parents are participating members of both teams and most IEP teams also meet the placement team requirements. Both teams are comprised of persons knowledgeable about the child, the meaning of the evaluation data and the placement options (IDEA Regulations, 34 C.F.R. § 300.116[a][1], 2006).

Although there are several placement requirements in the IDEA, the requirement that is frequently the subject of due process hearings is the LRE component of the law.

The IDEA requires that eligible students with disabilities be placed in the LRE in which the student will receive an appropriate education. The definition of LRE in the IDEA requires that:

> to the maximum extent appropriate, children with disabilities, including children in public or private institutions or other care facilities, are educated with children who are not disabled, and that special classes, separate schooling, or other removal of children with disabilities from the regular educational environment occurs only when the nature or severity of the disability is such that education in regular classes with the use of supplementary aids and services cannot be achieved satisfactorily (IDEA, 20 U.S.C. § 1412).

The definition of LRE contains two parts. The first part details the presumptive right of all students with disabilities to be educated with students who are not disabled. This presumptive right means placement teams must make good faith efforts to place and maintain students with disabilities in less restrictive settings (Yell et al., 2020). The second part of the LRE definitions sets the terms by which the presumption that all students with disabilities are to be educated in the general education classroom can be rebutted or overturned. This part of the LRE requirement allows for the education of some students with disabilities in more restrictive settings, when appropriate, but only in situations in which educating a student in general education classrooms with the use of supplementary aids and services will not result in the student receiving an appropriate education.

To ensure students with disabilities are educated in the least restrictive and most appropriate environment, the IDEA requires school districts to offer a range or continuum of alternative placement options to meet student's unique academic and functional needs. The regulations require that:

a. Each [school district] shall ensure that a continuum of alternative placements is available to meet the needs of children with disabilities for special education and related services.
b. The continuum required must:
    1. Include the alternative placements (instruction in regular classes, special classes, special schools, home instruction, and instruction in hospitals and institutions); and
    2. Make provision for supplementary services (such as resource room or itinerant instruction) to be provided in conjunction with regular class placement (IDEA Regulations, 34 C.F.R. § 300.551, 2006).

The purpose of the continuum is to allow school personnel, in consultation with a student's parents, to choose from a number of options in determining the

LRE that was most appropriate for the student. School districts must also provide supplementary aids and services (e.g., resource room, itinerant instruction), if these services will allow a student to receive a FAPE in the general education placement.

States are to have policies and procedures in place to ensure students with disabilities are educated with children without disabilities, and that students are removed from the general education environment only when the severity of a disability is such that instruction in regular classes with the use of supplementary aids and services is not effective. Placements on the continuum are generally deemed more restrictive the less they resemble the general education classroom (Champagne, 1993).

Procedural Safeguards

When the EAHCA was passed in 1975, Congress sought to ensure that students with disabilities would be treated fairly and provided with a FAPE. Congress accomplished this by providing students and their parents with procedural protections to ensure that they would be meaningfully involved with school districts when special education programs were being planned and implemented. The procedural protections in the IDEA were based on the due process clauses of the 5th and 14th amendments to the U.S. Constitution, which prohibit states from depriving any person of life, liberty, or property without due process of law. According to the U.S. Supreme Court, Congress established the system of procedural safeguards to "guarantee parents both an opportunity for meaningful input into all decisions affecting their child's education and the right to seek review of any decisions they think inappropriate" (*Honig v. Doe*, 1988, p. 598).

The procedural safeguards requirements of the IDEA include (a) notice and consent requirements, (b) the right to examine relevant records, (c) procedures to protect the rights of a student when parents are unavailable, (d) the independent educational evaluation (IEE), (e) discipline provisions, (f) mediation, (g) the opportunity to present a complaint to the state educational agency (SEA), and (h) the due process hearing. Textbox 1.1 lists and describes these procedural safeguards.

Textbox 1.1.   Procedural Safeguards

- An opportunity for to examine their child's educational records.
- An opportunity to participate in meetings regarding their child's education.
- Consent requirements in which parents understand and agree in writing for the activity in question. This must include consent for initial evaluation, reevaluation, the initial provision of special education, and other activities as required by a state.
- A student's parents may revoke consent at any time.

- Procedures to protect the rights of a student when his or her parents are not known, the parents cannot be located, or the student is a ward of the state.
- The right to receive prior written notice (PWN) whenever the district proposes to or refuses to initiate or change their child's identification, evaluation, or educational placement, or the provision of FAPE.
- Procedures designed to ensure that notices are provided in the native language of the parents unless it is clearly not feasible to do so.
- An opportunity for parents to go to mediation (see chapter 4).
- An opportunity for parents to obtain an independent educational evaluation.
- An opportunity for parents to file a state complaint (federal regulations only, see chapter 3).
- Procedures that require SEAs to develop model forms to assist parents in filing a complaint
- Procedures that allow either party to file a due process complaint (see chapter 7).
- Due process hearing rights that include (a) having the student who is the subject of the hearing present, (b) open the hearing to the public, (c) being accompanied and advised by counsel, (d) presenting evidence, (e) examining and cross-examining witnesses, (f) prohibit the introduction of evidence that was not disclosed five days prior to the hearing, (g) obtain a written or electronic transcript of the hearing, (h) obtain a written or electronic findings of fact and decision at no cost, (i) the right of the losing party to bring a civil action in state or federal court with respect to the due process action.
- During the pendency of an administrative complaint, unless the parents and school district personnel agree otherwise, the student must remain in his or her current educational placement (also called the stay put rule).

We will address the following dispute resolution procedures in later chapters of this textbook: state complaints, mediation, and due process. We will review one of IDEA's procedural safeguards that is a frequent issue in due process hearings, the discipline of students with disabilities.

The legal issues of disciplining students with disabilities receiving special services under the IDEA have presented unique problems to school district administrators since the law's passage in 1975. This is because administrators need to balance the need to ensure a safe environment conducive to learning and the rights of students with disabilities under the IDEA. The primary IDEA problems arose when eligible students were suspended or expelled from school.

When the EAHCA was passed in 1975, there was no specific guidance regarding discipline so it fell to the federal courts to interpret how discipline of students with disabilities should look in practice. One of the highest-level courts to first rule on discipline and the IDEA was the U.S. Court of Appeals for the Fifth Circuit in *S-1 v. Turlington* (1981). In this ruling, the circuit court ruled that (a) schools could not expel students for misbehavior that was related their disability, (b) this determination must be made for students with any IDEA covered disability and not just emotional disturbance, and (c) a termination of services caused by an expulsion amounted to a change in placement and only a student's IEP teams can make such decisions. In 1988, the U.S. Supreme Court heard a case involving the discipline of students with disabilities, *Honig v. Doe* (hereinafter *Honig*).

In *Honig*, the Supreme Court held that Congress had intended to strip schools of their unilateral authority to exclude students with disabilities from school. Moreover, the High Court declined to read a dangerousness exception into the law. The court ruled that during the pendency of any review meetings, the student must remain in the then-current placement (i.e., the stay-put rule) unless school officials and parents agree otherwise. The court also held that expulsion constituted a change in placement, but noted that the IDEA did not leave educators "hamstrung" regarding the use of disciplinary procedures. Procedures such as time-outs, the use of study carrels, detention, restriction of privileges, and suspension for up to ten days could still be used without violated the law.

In the IDEA Amendments of 1997, Congress added a section to the procedural safeguards of the IDEA that addressed discipline issues. In doing so, Congress sought to strike a balance between school officials' duty to ensure that schools are safe and conducive to learning and their continuing obligation to ensure that students with disabilities receive a FAPE. The IDEA provides students with disabilities with a shield of procedural safeguards that are not available to students who are not disabled. In the IDEA Amendments of 2004, the Individuals with Disabilities Education Improvement Act, the disciplinary requirements were modified. The procedural rights of students with disabilities when faced with disciplinary infractions are depicted in textbox 1.2.

Textbox 1.2. Procedural Rights of Special Educations Students When Disciplined (IDEA Regulations, 34 C.F.R.§ 530 to 534)

- All public school students, disabled and not disabled, have procedural protections when suspended from school. These procedures, which were first announced in the Supreme Court's ruling in *Goss v. Lopez* (1975), apply to all suspension, including those less than ten or fewer days. Many states incorporate these safeguards into state law. These procedural rights include (a) an oral or written notice of the charges against the student and (b) an explanation of the evidence school officials have and an opportunity for the student to present his or her version of the incident.

- School authorities may consider any unique circumstances on a case-by-case basis when determining whether a change in placement is appropriate for a student with disabilities who violates a code of student conduct.
- A student with disabilities protected by the IDEA may be removed from his or her current placement to an appropriate interim educational setting, another setting, or suspended for violating a code of conduct.
- Such removal must not be for more than ten consecutive school days (to the extent that these procedures are applied to students without disabilities) and for additional removals of not more than ten consecutive school days in that same school year for separate incidences of misconduct as long as these removals do not constitute a change of placement.
- After a student has been removed from his or her current placement for ten school days in the same school year the student must be provided educational services, including participation in the general education curriculum (although in another setting), and an opportunity to make progress toward the goals set out in the child's IEP.
- In the disciplinary procedure changes a student's placement, within ten school days, school must conduct a manifestation determination to evaluate whether a student's misconduct is a manifestation of a student's disability.
- To determine if a student's misconduct is a manifestation of his or her disability, the district, the parents, and relevant members of the student's IEP team must determine if the conduct in question was (a) caused by or had a direct and substantial relationship to a student's disability or (b) was the district's failure to implement a student's IEP (in this situation the school district must take immediate steps to remedy these deficiencies).
- When a student's manifestation review team concludes that the student's misconduct was related to his or her disability, school personnel must conduct a functional behavioral assessment (FBA) and develop or revise a student's behavioral intervention plan (BIP).
- If a school district concludes that student's misconduct was not related to a student's disability, the school district may impose disciplinary sanctions.
- If a school district includes that a student's misconduct was related to a student's disability, the IEP team must either conduct a functional behavioral assessment and implement or revise a behavior intervention plan for a student.

- Return the student to his or her previous placement unless the parent and school district have agreed to a change of placement as part of the modification of the behavioral intervention plan.
- If a decision is made to change a student's placement, the student's parents must be provided with a notice of procedural safeguards.
- If a student's misconduct involves bringing a weapon or drugs to a school or a school function, or if the misconduct involved serious bodily injury, a student can be unilaterally removed for up to forty-five school days.
- When a student is removed for weapons, drugs, or serious bodily injury, he or she must, as appropriate, receive a functional behavioral assessment and a behavior intervention plan.
- A student's parents may appeal the results of a disciplinary placement or a manifestation determination in an expedited due process hearing.

The use of discipline with IDEA eligible students with disabilities remains an area in which dispute resolution continues to occur.

What Is the Dispute Resolution System of the IDEA?

In passing the EAHCA in 1975, congressional authors included processes in the law that parents could use to resolve disputes when they disagree with a school district's special education identification, evaluation, programing, or placement. Regulations to the IDEA further expand on these dispute resolutions processes. Furthermore, in 2013 officials in the U.S. Department of Education's Office of Special Education Programs (OSEP) released an updated guidance document titled, "Dispute Resolution Procedures Under Part B of the Individuals with Disabilities Education Act (Part B)." According to the guidance document, "the IDEA and its implementing regulations provide specific for resolving disputes between parents and public school districts (school districts), which can be used in a manner consistent with our shared goals of improving results and achieving better outcomes for children with disabilities" (OSEP, 2013, p. 1).

When a student's parents and school personnel disagree about the special education services provided to a student, the IDEA and implementing regulations provide the less formal dispute resolution systems of mediation (see chapter 3) and resolutions sessions (see chapter 4) and the more formal procedures of the complaint resolution system and the due process hearing as means to settle these disputes. Zirkel (2016) referred to the IDEA's more formal dispute resolution systems as adjudicative and investigative.

The adjudicative avenue refers to the due process hearing system, which is the procedure created legislatively in the IDEA. This avenue is the more legalistic of the formal procedures with an impartial due process hearing officer presiding over a hearing in which both sides in the dispute are often represented by attorneys. Evidence is introduced in the hearing and witness are examined and cross-examined. The hearing officer determines the facts, decides on the prevailing party, and issues a ruling in the dispute. We address due process hearings in chapter 4.

The investigative avenue refers to the state complaint procedure, which is outlined in the regulations implementing the IDEA. The regulations require that state educational agencies implement a procedure in which a parent may submit a complaint to the state agency regarding a possible violation of the IDEA. When the complaint is received, state personnel must investigate and issue a written decision. We address state complaints in chapter 3.

Conclusion

Our purpose in this chapter was to provide basic information about the history of special education, the primary components of the IDEA, and the dispute resolution procedures of the IDEA and its implementing regulations. We emphasized the FAPE, evaluation, LRE, and procedural safeguards of the law. We also reviewed a specific procedural requirement of the IDEA, the disciplinary provisions. An understanding of the components of the IDEA is important because it lays the foundation for the subsequent chapters and the primary components of the law that will often be litigated in special education due process hearings.

References

Bateman, B. D. (2017). Individualized education programs. In J. M. Kauffman, D. P. Hallahan, & P. C. Pullen (Eds.), *Handbook of Special Education* (2nd ed.). Routledge.

Bateman, D. F., & Cline, J. L. (2019). *Special Education Leadership: Building Effective Programming in Schools.* Routledge/Taylor and Francis Group.

Berney, D. J., & Gilsbach, T. (2017). Substantive vs. procedural violations under the IDE. Retrieved January 11, 2020 from http:/www.berneylaw .com/2017/11/12/substantive-vs-procedural -violations-idea/.

Board of the Hendrick Hudson Central School District v. Rowley, 458 U.S. 176 (1982).

Burch, S. (2009). *Encyclopedia of American Disability History.* Infobase Publishing.

Champagne, J. F. (1993). Decisions in sequence: How to make placements in the least restrictive environment. *EdLaw Briefing Paper, 9 & 10,* 1–16.

Code of Virginia, Section 22.275.3 (1973).

Endrew F. v Douglas County School District, 137 S. Ct. 988 (2017).

Gerber, M. M. (2017). The history of special education, in J. M. Kauffman, D. P. Hallahan, & P. C. Pullen (Eds.), *Handbook of Special Education* (2nd ed.). Routledge.

Gerl, J. (2014). Hot button issues in special education law. Presentation at the annual Tri-State Special Education Law Conference. Omaha, NE.

Goss v. Lopez (1975). 419 U.S. 565 (1975).

Honig v. Doe, 479 U.S. 1084 (1988).

Individuals with Disabilities Education Act, 20 U.S.C. § 1401 et seq., 2004.

Individuals with Disabilities Education Act Regulations, 34 C.F.R. § 300.1 et seq. 2006.

Kirby v. Cabell County Board of Education, 46 IDELR 149 (S.D WV 2006).

Martin, E. (2013). *Breakthrough: Special Education Legislation 1965–1981.* Bardolf & Company.

Martin, E. W., Martin, R., & Terman, D. L. (1996). The legislative and litigative history of special education. *The Future of Children: Special Education for Students with Disabilities*, 6 (1), 25–39.

Mills v. Board of Education of the District of Columbia, 348 F. Supp. 866 (D.D.C. 1972).

Pennsylvania Association for Retarded Citizens (PARC) v. Commonwealth of Pennsylvania, 343 F. Supp. 279 (E.D. Pa. 1972).

Stafford, R. T. (1978). Education for the handicapped: A senator's perspective. *Vermont Law Review, 3*, 71–82.

United States Code Congressional and Administrative News 1975 (U.S.C.C.A.N. 1975).

Yell, M. L. (2017). *The Law and Special Education* (5th ed.). Pearson.

Yell, M. L., Bateman, D.F., Shriner, J.G. (2021). *Developing Educationally Meaningful and Legally Correct IEPs.* Rowman and Littlefield.

Zettel, J. J., & Ballard, J. (1982). The Education for All Handicapped Children Act of 1975 (P.L. 94–142): Its history, origins, and concepts. In J. Ballard, B. Ramirez, & F. Weintraub (Eds.), *Special Education in America: Its Legal and Governmental Foundations* (pp. 11–22). Reston, VA: Council for Exceptional Children.

CHAPTER 2

Avoiding Dispute Resolution

Advance Organizers

* What strategies have proven successful in collaborating successfully with parents?
* What factors often lead to conflicts been parents and IEP team members?
* What are alternative dispute resolution strategies?

According to former associate justice of the U.S. Supreme Court, Sandra Day O'Conner, "The courts of this country should not be the places where resolution of disputes begins. They should be the places where the disputes end after alternative methods of resolving disputes have been considered and tried" (McFeatters, 2006, p. 157). In this chapter, we examine the most effective method for handling conflict: Prevention. Specifically, we review (a) how parents and school personnel can avoid formal dispute resolution processes through developing meaningful relationships with parents, (b) recognizing the signs of potential conflict, and (c) resolving serious conflicts by using alternative dispute resolution procedures.

The Critical Importance of a Good Parent–School Partnership

The most basic of all the procedural requirements of the IDEA is that a student's parents are full and equal participants with school district personnel in the development of their child's IEP (Bateman, 2017). In 2017, Barbara Bateman asserted that

> IDEA makes parental participation central in all decisions regarding the child's program and placement and when full and equal parent participation is abridged or denied, a denial of FAPE will most likely be found. Few, if any, of IDEA's procedural rights are more vigorously protected by courts (Bateman, 2017, p. 91).

According to the IDEA Amendments of 2004, hearing officers may find a denial of a free appropriate public education (FAPE) if procedural violations "significantly impeded the parent's opportunity to participate in the decision-making process regarding the provision of FAPE to the parent's child" (IDEA Regulations, 34 C.F.R. § 300.513[a][2], 2006). Similarly, the U.S. Court of Appeals for the Ninth Circuit stated, "procedural violations that interfere with parental participation in the IEP formulation process undermine the very essence of the IDEA" (*Amanda J. v. Clark County School District*, 2001, p. 892). Clearly, it is imperative that all special and general education administrators and teachers need to understand their important responsibilities to collaborate with a student's parents throughout the special education process. In fact, according to Turnbull et al. (2021), meaningful collaboration with a student's parents lead to compliance with the IDEA and compliance with the IDEA supports the student to achieve.

We are strong advocates of parents and school personnel collaborating and working together to prevent and resolve potential problems before they occur, thus avoiding the dispute resolution procedures of state complaints and due process hearings. Most of our suggestions, therefore, relate to better communication and making good-faith efforts to establish good working relationship with the parents. Establishing good relations with a student's parents has the potential to (a) enhance student's learning and achievement, (b) support positive student behavior and school attendance, (c) improve instruction and increase teacher's efficacy, (d) improve parent satisfactory and parenting skills, and (e) reduce levels of stress of parents (Francis et al., 2016). Even when conflicts develop, as they sometimes will, it is more likely to be resolved in an environment of open communication, shared power, and trust between the parties (Lake et al., 2019).

Unfortunately, sometimes parent–school partnerships are characterized by a lack of trust and ongoing, sometimes contentions disputes. Even in these instances, we can avoid the formal dispute resolution mechanisms of the IDEA if we recognize and respond to such situations appropriately. In this chapter we first examine factors that contribute to meaningful parent–school partnerships. Second, we address how administrators and IEP members can recognize factors that contribute to parent–school conflicts in special education and how we can respond effectively. Third, we review alternative methods of resolving disputes before they reach IDEA's formal dispute resolution procedures.

Factors that Contribute to Establishing Meaningful Parent–School Partnerships in Special Education

School personnel should establish meaningful collaborative partnerships with a student's parents. Preventing disputes with parents begins with the proactive development of strong parent–school partnerships (Lake et al., 2019). Moreover, when both parties view each other as reliable allies and a student's parents have multiple opportunities for meaningful participation in the development of their child's special education program, the likelihood of developing meaningful partnerships is enhanced (Francis et al., 2016).

Martha Blue-Banning and her colleagues conducted thirty-three focus groups and thirty-two individual interviews to ascertain what school-based professional behaviors facilitated collaborative relationships with parents (Blue-Banning et al., 2004). In conducting this research, Blue-Banning and her colleagues sought to "create a profile of partnership components that identified common themes across a wide range of cultural, geographic, and socioeconomic points of view" (p. 170). The profile of partnership these researchers developed included the following common themes: (a) communication, (b) commitment, (c) equality, (d) skills, (e) trust, and (f) respect.

Communication

The first component that Blue-Banning et al. (2004) identified was communication. Participants in the research emphasized the importance of good communication as essential to forming positive collaborative relationships. The quality of communication needs to be positive, understandable, and respectful. Five specific attributes led to effective communication between school-based professionals and a student's parent: Be friendly, listen, be clear, be honest, and provide and coordinated information.

Be Friendly

First, being friendly in interactions with a student's parents will help parents to feel comfortable enough to share information about their child (Turnbull et al., 2021). Friend (2007) shared the advice of an early intervention provider who noted the first requirement in working with parents was to establish rapport and show parents that you are an advocate for them and their child.

Listen

According to Blue-Banning et al. (2004) parents want school-based professionals to be empathetic listeners, which means being nonjudgmental and understanding the parent's point of view. Parents of students with disabilities have reported that school-based professionals' refusal to listen can escalate conflicts, which can lead to mediation or due process hearings (Lake & Billingsley, 2000).

It is important to listen to all the options and consider what is appropriate for a student. It is also important that IEP team members act in a respectful manner and avoid inappropriate responses to parental requests. Listening is critical to understanding each party's thinking regarding various issues that arise in an IEP meeting (Lake et al., 2019).

Be Clear

The third behavior that parents identified as necessary to effective communication was being clear. We know that special education is filled with acronyms and complicated concepts and that school-based team members too often use such terms and concepts. It is likely that such terms and concepts will not be understood by parents who do not have formal training in special education. Turnbull et al. (2021) advised that school-based personnel should avoid jargon and technical terms and instead use several words to explain concepts and terms that special educators have reduced to a single word (e.g., LRE). If you use technical terms, clearly explain the meaning of these terms.

Additionally, IEPs should be written in uncomplicated and easily executable language. Ensure that the portion of the IEP that is to be implemented in the general education classroom is clear and the general teachers understand their role in implementation.

A good way to end an IEP is to summarize the primary components of the document and ask a student's parent for their comments and questions. Ensure that the student's parents and everyone on the IEP is clear on their responsibilities in implementing the student's special education program.

Be Honest

The fourth behavior involves being honest with a parent, which requires being direct but tactful. When we need to share information that may be difficult, we must do so in ways that are sensitive to how a parent may react. School-based personnel should never blame parents; however, we may offer suggestions in a tactful and sensitive manner. Additionally, if parents ask a question and we are unsure of the answer, it is best to admit we do not know the answer but that we will find the answer to the question and get back to the parents as soon as possible.

In the research conducting by Blue-Banning and her colleagues, parents interviewed "stressed that communication should be honest and open, with no hidden information or 'candy-coating' of bad news" (p. 173). In these situations, we need to be tactful and sensitive but we always should remember that the primary responsibility is to develop an IEP that confers a FAPE and enable our students to make progress appropriate in light of a student's circumstances (*Endrew F. v. Douglas County School District*, 2017).

Provide and Coordinate Information

A student's parents should be informed of, and participate in, the assessment process, IEP development, placement, and progress-monitoring of their child. Parental participation throughout the special education process is essential. Following the procedures required by the IDEA, such as providing sufficient notice of meetings and sending prior written notice before making a change, or refusing to make a change, in their child's evaluation, placement, or provision of a FAPE will help to engage parents in their child's education. To ensure that this procedural involvement is meaningful, we should adopt strategies to ensure full and ongoing participation by a student's parents, which include (a) providing a draft of their child's IEP to the parents, (b) opening the IEP meeting by having the parents talk about their child, and (c) encouraging parental participation by eliciting their participation through questioning and soliciting their opinions regarding the draft IEP.

The requirement to provide a student's parents with information does not end with the development of their child's IEP but also includes monitoring of their child's program of special education and related services. Regulations to the IDEA require that the IEP includes a description of how their child's progress toward his or her annual goals will be measured and

> when periodic reports on the progress the child is making toward meeting the annual goals (such as through the use of quarterly or other periodic reports, concurrent with the issuance of report cards) will be provided. (IDEA Regulations, 34 C.F.R. § 300.320 [3][ii])

In *M.C. v. Antelope Valley Union High* (2017), the U.S. Court of Appeals for the Ninth Circuit noted the following:

> In enacting the IDEA, Congress was as concerned with parental participation in the *enforcement* of the IEP as it was in its *formation* . . . parental participation doesn't end when the parent signs the IEP. Parents must be able to use the IEP to monitor and enforce the services that their child is to receive (*M.C. v. Antelope Valley Union High* 2017, p. 1198).

In this section of the ruling, the circuit court pointed to the importance of parental participation in monitoring their child's progress. Thus, it is important that the IEP schedule regular progress monitoring reporting to a student's parents. Teachers need to collect data on student progress toward their academic and/or functional goals and frequently share this data with a student's parents. Teachers should also keep detailed records that include numerical data that provides evidence of their child's progress toward the goals in the IEP. If the data indicates that the student may not meet his or her goals, the IEP team should meet to determine what can be changed to help the student achieve the goals. In such situations, the discussions should be documented and the teacher should implement the changes and continue to collect data and report it regularly. If improvement is still not noted despite the changes, the team should consider reevaluating the student.

Commitment

The second component identified by Blue-Banning et al. (2004) as being critical to establish effective parent–professional partnerships was commitment. Parents emphasized that they wanted school-based professionals to demonstrate (a) a commitment and dedication to their work, (b) the importance of working to help their child to succeed, and (c) recognition of the importance of collaborating with parents. If a student's parents believe that school-based personnel are committed to their child and providing their best efforts to meet the child's goals, the parent–school partnership will be enhanced. School personnel should strive to demonstrate commitment, which they can do by being flexible, consistent, and sensitive.

Demonstrating commitment includes fully considering all request made by a student's parent. The student's IEP team should always be willing to compromise and consider other alternatives, although the student's needs must remain paramount in all decisions made by the team. Perhaps the team can provide the requested service or an alternative service.

The IEP team members, therefore, should examine and carefully consider all information provided by parents and discuss all requests that they make; however, all decisions should be made on the basis of whether the service requested is necessary for the student to receive a FAPE. If a service, support, or modification is necessary, then it should be provided. If it is not necessary, the team should clearly and respectfully inform parents that the IEP team believes the service is not necessary for the child to receive a FAPE. In situations in which an IEP team declines to provide a parentally request service, support, or modification, a prior written notice (PWN) must be given to the parent. Again, the purpose of a PWN is to provide the student's parents with information as to the reasoning behind the team's refusal (or proposal) to change a student's identification, evaluation, educational placement, or provision of FAPE to the student. The goal of this requirement is to afford parents the opportunity to consider and possibly respond to the school district's action prior to the district implementing or refusing to implement the particular action (Tatgenhorst et al. 2014). Textbox 2.1 includes requirements of the PWN.

Textbox 2.1. Important Elements of Prior Written Notice

Prior written notice is a written notice that must be given to the parents of a student with disability a reasonable time before the school district proposes to initiate or change the identification, evaluation, placement, or provision of FAPE to a student.

Content of the notice

- A description of the action proposed or refused by the school district.
- An explanation of why the school district proposes or refuses to take the action.
- A description of each evaluation procedure, assessment, or record, or report the school district used as a basis for the proposed or refused action.
- A statement of the student's procedural protections.
- Sources for parents to contact to obtain assistance in understanding these provisions.
- A description of other options that the IEP team considered and the reasons why those options were rejected.

The PWN must be written in language that is understandable to the general public and provided in the native language or other mode of communication used by the parent.

Equality

Attending an IEP meeting can be intimidated for a student's parents, especially for parents who are attending their first IEP meeting. Usually, parents will be surrounded by a team of professionals, who too often use terms with which they may be unfamiliar and rush through the presentation of the child's special education program. Blue-Banning and her colleagues found that parents reported that there must be an equal partnership between them and the professionals on the IEP team and that an equal partnership included an ease in the relationship. Moreover, establishing this partnership requires that the professionals work to promote and empower the parents by actively encouraging the parents' participation and acknowledging the validity of their point of view.

Skills

The school-based personnel who provide special education services should have expertise in collecting and analyzing student data, using evidence-based educational procedures, and adapting instruction to meet a student's needs in response to the data. Along with this expertise comes confidence that will be apparent in IEP meetings. According to Blue-Banning and her colleagues, parents admired teachers who were willing to learn and kept up with the technology of their field. On the other hand, parents also admired professionals who were not afraid to admit when they didn't know something, but were willing to find out and report back to them.

Clearly, to establish effective and collaborative parent–school partnerships administrators and teachers need to know and understand the evidence-base in their fields. Additionally, the IDEA requires that special education services in a student's IEP be based on peer-reviewed research. According to the language of the law, "A statement of the special education and related services and supplementary aids and services, based on peer-reviewed research to the extent practicable—that will be provided to the child" (IDEA, 20 U.S.C. § 1414[d] [1][A][i][IV]). In the final regulations to the IDEA, issued on August 14, 2006, the U.S. Department of Education defined peer-reviewed research in the commentary as generally referring "to research that is reviewed by qualified and independent reviewers to ensure that the quality of the information meets the standards of the field before the research is published" (Federal Register, 2006, p. 46664). Thus, when developing a student's special education program, the IEP team must base the programming on educational research to the extent that such research is available.

Because the knowledge base in our field changes so rapidly, school district officials should adopt mechanisms to provide ongoing continuing education in evidence-based practices for their staff. In addition to on-site training, there are many excellent resources available to special educators to keep them abreast of new developments in their fields. Table 2.1 lists a few of these resources. Teachers should receive funding to attend reputable conferences on evidence-based practices and to subscribe to reputable professional journals.

Table 2.1. **Resources on Evidence-Based Practices**

Name	URL	Description
Best Evidence Encyclopedia	www.bestevidence.org	The Center is intended to give educators and researchers information about the evidence base of various educational programs.
Council for Exceptional Children (CEC)	exceptionalchildren.org	The largest international association dedicated to improving the success of students with disabilities. Publishes the preeminent journals in special education.
IRIS Center	https://iris.peabody.vanderbilt.edu/	The IRIS Center for training enhancement is a free online resource that translates research on the education of students with disabilities into practice.
Center on Positive Behavioral Interventions & Supports (PBIS)	pbis.org	The Center on Positive Behavioral Interventions and Supports is devoted to giving schools information and technical assistance for identifying, adapting, and sustaining effective school-wide disciplinary practices.
National Center on Intensive Interventions (NCII)	intensiveintervention.org	NCII builds the capacity of state and local education agencies, universities, practitioners, and other stakeholders to support implementation of intensive intervention in literacy, mathematics, and behavior. NCII's approach to intensive intervention is data-based individualization (DBI).
National Technical Assistance Center on Transition (NTACT)	www.transitionta.org	The National Technical Assistance Center on Transition (NTACT) is dedicated to ensuring full implementation of the IDEA and helping youth with disabilities achieve desired post-school outcomes.
Progress Center	promotingprogress.org	The Center provides information, resources, and support for local educators and leaders responsible for the development and implementation of high-quality educational programming for students with disabilities that ensures access to free appropriate public education (FAPE) and progress toward appropriately ambitious goals.

Trust

According to Blue-Banning and her colleagues, the parents in their research acknowledged that trust was a very important element in developing a positive working relationship but referred to three specific dimensions of trust. The first dimension of trust involved reliability of school-based professionals. That is, administrators and teachers could be depended upon to follow through with an action they said they were going to do. The second dimension of trust occurs when parents could depend on the child's teachers to keep their child safe, include ensuring that their child was treated with dignity. The third dimension of trust involved discretion, which meant that professionals could be trusted not to divulge confidential and private information.

Of course, educational professionals are prohibited from releasing confidential student information by the *Family Educational Rights and Privacy Act* (FERPA). The regulations implementing FERPA can be found in 34 C.F.R. Part 99 (https://www.ecfr.gov/current/title-34/subtitle-A/part-99).

According to Stoner et al. (2005) every interaction between parents and school-based personnel has the potential to either enhance or reduce trust. Because of the importance of trust to the parent–school partnership, we must always seek to enhance it.

Respect

The final component that Blue-Banning and her colleagues found was essential to establishing a positive and collaborative working parent-school partnership was respect. To many of the parents in the study, respect meant that school personnel valued their child as a person instead of as a diagnostic or disability label. Parents need to know that their thoughts and opinions are valued. Additionally, respect can be shown through simple courtesies such as (a) calling parents "Mr." or "Mrs." unless given permission to use their first name, (b) being on time for meetings, (c) not allowing attendees to come and go during a meeting, and (d) acknowledging a parent's contributions and efforts. Respect is showing common courtesy toward parents.

Summary: Factors that Contribute to Establishing Meaningful Parent-School Partnerships in Special Education

The most important aspect to which we should attend in order to prevent disputes was perhaps best summed up by Blue-Banning et al. (2004), "The results of this study underscore the point that common sense and ordinary human decency are at the heart of positive partnerships between families and professionals serving children with disabilities" (p. 181). Common courtesy is inexpensive but can pay long-term dividends in working with parents. Parents in the Blue-Banning et al. study emphasized that meaningful partnerships with school personnel improved their quality of life and the quality of life of their children with disabilities. Because the majority of parent–school dispute involve decisions made and actions taken during and after the IEP meeting, administrators, teachers, and other personnel should develop their skills in involving parents in meaningful collaboration (Lake et al., 2019).

Factors that Contribute to Parent-School Conflicts in Special Education

We began this chapter by examining factors that contribute to establishing meaningful parent-school partnerships in special education. The surest way to avoid dispute resolution is to prevent it from occurring in the first place. Additionally, common courtesy, tact, and respect go a long way to establishing good parent–school partnership. Moreover, there are specific actions that special education administrators and IEP team members can take to ensure the establishment of good relationships.

Despite our best attempts, disputes may still occur. It is important that we are aware of what factors may lead to disputes and when they occur, how to address these factors in a thoughtful, respectful, and constructive manner (Lake et al., 2019). Furthermore, addressing conflict in such a way as soon as it arises may help school personnel to protect the trusting relationship they have developed with parents (Lake & Billingsley, 2000). Conflict is inevitable; the way we handle conflict is not. We next examine several strategies for addressing conflict before it leads to the IDEA's formal dispute resolution systems.

Strategy #1: Provide Training to Administrators and Teachers on Conflict Resolution Procedures

Martin (2001) recognized that inept handling of parental concerns by school staff often leads to a steady loss of trust and a deteriorating relationship with a student's parents that may culminate in a due process hearing. He also asserted that the "best strategy for dispute resolution with parents is not allowing a concern or issue to escalate to the point that it becomes a full-blown dispute" (p. 5). Martin contended, however, that school personnel with no training on handing complaints and conflicts will not learn basic conflict resolution skills on the job and that such inept handling of potential conflict may reasonably be expected to occur. He suggested that to avoid such problems, school officials should provide staff training on conflict resolution procedures that can drastically reduce the possibility of an issue escalating to formal dispute resolution procedures. Martin further noted that training in conflict resolution is readily available in many communities and should be explored as a proactive step to preventing more formal dispute resolution procedures. According to Martin, conflict resolution training would "pay for itself many times over if it helps avoid just one due process hearing" (p. 5).

Strategy #2: Recognize Situations that Lead to Parent-School Conflicts

Lake and Billingsley (2000) conducted research to understand factors that tend to escalate and deescalate conflict. The research conducted forty-four in-depth telephone interviews with parents, administrators, and mediators. From these interviews, Lake and Billingsley identified eight factors that escalated special education conflict and extrapolated principles to prevent and handle such conflict. When school personnel are properly trained in conflict resolution procedures, recognizing these eight factors can help to ensure that escalation of conflict is avoided.

Discrepant View of a Child or a Child's Needs

Ninety percent of the respondents to Lake and Billingsley (2000) identified a major source of conflict as a difference in the view of a child or a child's needs between school-based personnel and a student's parents. The parents who were interviewed perceived two major areas of conflict regarding discrepant views. First, a major source of conflict occurs when parents do not believe school-based personnel see their child as an individual with unique abilities and strengths. As one parent told Lake and Billingsley, "the most important thing is to find a school that will recognize your child as an individual" (p. 244). Second, another source of conflict occurs when school-based personnel describe a parent's child from a deficit-model perspective. They concluded that the conflict source in this area was the different lenses though which parents and school-based personnel viewed a child. When school-based personnel communicate that they view a child through the deficit lens, parents may view that the school personnel focus on a child's weaknesses and shortcomings and do not consider the whole child. An obvious implication is to resist the temptation to view a child from a deficit-perspective and not to communicate just the child's weaknesses, but to also consider the child's strengths. Clearly listening to parents' concerns, discussing their suggestions, and possibly incorporating their suggestions into students' IEPs will help to narrow these discrepant views.

Lack of Problem-Solving Knowledge

Lake and Billingsley also included special education mediators in their interviews. The mediators interviewed indicated that school-based personnel's lack of problem-solving knowledge and poor communication strategies often escalated minor conflicts into major conflicts. Mediators and parents also acknowledged that when parents, administrators, and teachers were more knowledgeable about special education, evidence-based practices, and the child, conflicts could be more quickly be prevented or contained. An imbalance of knowledge about special education between parents and school-based personnel can also be a source of frustration. A way to defuse a knowledge gap is to have someone on staff act as a parent liaison. Martin (2001) suggested that school officials should consider pairing all parents of special education students with a parent mentor to assist the parents, and especially parents who are new to the IEP process. Such actions could help to resolve knowledge-based conflicts.

Service Delivery

Parents reported the school-based personnel's failure to substantiate or sufficiently answer their questions about the special education services was an indicator "that something was amiss with how services were actually being given to a child" (Lake & Billingsley, 200, p. 245). No such conflicts should arise when the services are planned during the IEP meeting and the administrator and all involved teachers and related service personnel understand and implement the IEP as originally developed. It is important that general education teachers be informed of their IEP responsibilities. School officials should develop a procedure in which the implementation of the IEP is checked systematically and frequently to ensure fidelity of implementation (Yell et al., 2022). Moreover, parents need to be regularly apprised of their child's progress in his or her program.

Constraints on Resources

Lake and Billingsley (2000) found that when parents believe that IEP decisions are made or services are not included in an IEP because of constraints of resources (e.g., time, money, personnel, materials), conflicts are likely to occur. Furthermore, parents mentioned that sometimes when a good reason for denying services is not given by school-based personnel, parents may suspect that the real reason that services were denied is not being provided because school personnel are hiding the real reason. If the child needs the service in order to receive a FAPE, the service should be provided. We should never decide not to provide services based on a lack of resources. The only exception to this is if there are two services or devices that will provide a FAPE, we can choose the less expensive. All services decisions need to be made with the interests of the child in mind. If a service is necessary, then it should be provided. If it is not necessary, the team should state the service is not necessary for the child to receive a FAPE and write a PWN denying the service.

Devaluation of the Parent–School Partnership

The researchers heard from parents that when they feel devalued by a member or members of the IEP team or their child is devalued, conflicts are more likely to occur. Thus, being valued as a partner who is playing a meaningful role in the entire special education process is important to parents. Parents also reported being treated in a condescending manner as a source of conflict. Clearly, we need to value and encourage parental participation at all stages of the special education process from evaluation to progress monitoring. When we provide opportunities for parents to discuss their child and their hopes for their child, preferably at the beginning of an IEP meeting, and include these perceptions in the planning process, it is much more likely that parents will feel valued.

Reciprocal Power

Participants in the Lake and Billingsley study indicated that power is used by both parents and school-based personnel in an attempt to resolve conflicts after they occur in an attempt to get what they wanted. Unfortunately, the participants recognized that the costs of using power in this way was a breakdown in trust and the parent–school partnership. Many studies have examined the imbalance of power between parents and school-based personnel (Crockett et al., 2019). Nonetheless, we must avoid the use of this power in attempts to force parents into decisions.

Trust and Communication

The final two factors that Lake and Billingsley found can lead to conflict are when trust and communication between the parties break down. When trust is intact, parents have a certain sense of predictability and security regarding the actions of school-based personnel and were able to tolerate negative events occasionally and did not attach too much importance to any one event. When trust was intact, parents believed that school-based personnel were professionally capable and were considerate of their children's needs. On the other hand, when the trusting relationship was not intact, parents had difficulty accepting school-based personnel's suggestions and they were less satisfied with the school and the special education process. Moreover, they expected fewer positive outcomes and viewed school-based personnel as unresponsive and uncaring about their children's needs. It was at this point that the parents were more likely to seek out-of-school placements or to rely on the IDEA's dispute resolution procedures.

Similarly, a diminished frequency of communication, total lack of communication, lack of promised follow-up, or misunderstood communications were frequently triggers for escalating conflicts. Lack of communication was often seen by parents as withholding information, which also escalated the possibility of conflict. Interestingly enough, Lake and Billingsley found that sometimes parents found having many school-based personnel at meetings could be a deterrent for full communication, because parents felt intimidated.

Clearly trust and clear communication are important factors in avoiding conflict and when either trust or communication breaks down it is more likely that conflict will follow. As Lake and Billingsley aptly wrote, "educators who develop strong, reciprocal relationships with children and parents and use good communication skills provide a foundation for satisfying and productive relationships" (p. 249). In such relationship, parents feel valued and respected and conflicts are more easily addressed or avoided all together.

Summary: Factors that Contribute to Parent–School Conflicts in Special Education

Lake and Billingsley (2000) identified factors that contributed to and escalated parent–school conflicts. Identifying and understanding these factors will help us to avoid these situations. Nevertheless, sometimes conflict cannot be avoided and sometimes parents and school-based personnel act in a way that makes it difficult to avoid conflict. In such situations it is useful to have alternative methods to resolve disputes without relying on the IDEA's formal dispute resolution mechanisms.

Alternative Dispute Resolution Mechanisms

When parent–school conflict has escalated and it seems that being involved in a state complaint or due process hearing is unavoidable, there are alternative dispute resolution strategies that may be used in an attempt to resolve conflict without going to a due process hearing. We next review alternative methods of conflict resolution.

Strategy #1: Be Prepared for Possible Contentions IEP Meetings

When school personnel become aware of a conflict that may lead to the IDEA's dispute resolution, school administrators should assess the situation that led to the conflict. Martin (2001) suggested that school personnel should prepare for the potentially contentious IEP as if they were preparing for a formal mediation session, which includes (a) convening pre-meeting staff session, (b) developing a meeting agenda, (c) anticipating potential problem areas, (d) reviewing assessment data, (e) gathering relevant data, (f) brainstorming possible proposals and contingency plans, and (g) preparing documentation of student progress. It is important proper notice of the meeting has been sent to the parents and ensure that all IEP team members and participants attend the entire meeting if possible. Martin (2001) also warned that in such meetings if team members arrive late, documentation has to be searched for, or the meeting is disorganized, parents may perceive that neither they nor their child are important, which may only worsen the conflict. Although a pre-meeting staff planning session is appropriate, finalizing any decisions should only made in the meeting in which parents are present.

Strategy #2: Listen Carefully and Be Willing to Resolve the Dispute

Martin (2001) asserted that as soon as school personnel know that a student's parents have retained an attorney, the school's attorney should be contacted and given a copy of the student's educational file to review. The school's attorney can then assess potential problem areas. During this process, the school attorney may interview school staff to provide him or her information about the student and the file. It is likely that the school attorney may contact the parent's attorney. If there is a potential problem, an informal way to settle the dispute may be suggested. Martin (2001) suggested that the attorneys for both sides and IEP team members may decide to draft a written settlement that disposed of the issue or issues in dispute with going to a due process hearing.

Strategy #3: Use an Ombudsperson

Another option that many states have available to possibly settle IEP disputes before they go to due process is an ombudsperson. An ombudsperson is usually a third party who investigates a complaint, proposes solutions, and negotiates with the parties (The Center for Appropriate Dispute Resolution in Special Education [CADRE], 2017). Most states have ombudspersons in their State Departments of Education and many states have an ombudsperson in their office of special education (e.g., New Jersey, South Carolina, Virginia, Washington, D.C.). The role of the ombudsperson may be slightly different from state to state so it is important that individuals contact their own state ombudsperson to determine what services are provided.

The New Jersey Department of Education and South Carolina Office of Special Education Services have special education ombudspersons who serve as a resource for parents, students, and educators to help them better navigate the special education process and proactively attempt to resolve disputes between parents and school district. The URL to the New Jersey Ombudsperson website is https://www.nj.gov/education/specialed/parents/index.shtml and the South Carolina Ombudsman website is https://ed.sc.gov/districts-schools/special-education-services/parent-resources/dispute-resolution-information/ombudsman/.

If your state does not have an ombudsman, school district officials may want to appoint a staff person (e.g., a school counselor who is not directly involved in IEP teams) to assist parents and acts a parent liaisons throughout the IEP process. According to Martin (2001), if disputes arise, this person would be unrelated to the actual dispute and bring objectivity and fresh ideas to potential disputes. Ideally, this person would have had extensive training in conflict resolution.

Strategy #4: Use IEP Facilitation

IEP facilitation usually involves a person trained in facilitating meetings between parents and school staff, who is appointed to encourage communication between parties in a special education dispute. According to the CADRE Center (2017), all meetings can benefit from having skilled and capable facilitators who can assist IEP team in crafting agreements that lead to educational programs with beneficial outcomes for students with disabilities. When IEP teams reach an impasse, or meetings are expected to be contentious, an independent, trained facilitator may help guide the IEP team through the process by helping member communicate more effectively. A facilitator helps keep members of the IEP team focused on the development of the IEP while addressing conflicts and disagreements that may have occurred before the IEP meeting or emerge during the meeting (CADRE, 2017). IEP facilitation has been shown to (a) decrease the use of IDEA's formal dispute resolution process, (b) improve relationships between school personnel and families, and (c) increase the capacity of IEP teams for solving conflicts as they observe how facilitators conduct meetings successfully (CADRE, 2017). A number of states have persons trained as IEP facilitators who can come to IEP meeting in which conflicts have arisen. For example, the South Carolina Office of Special Education Services have trained IEP facilitators who are available to attend IEP meetings if requested to do so by school administrators and parents (South

Carolina Department of Education, 2022). The services, which are voluntary, are available at no cost to parents or school districts. The URL to the South Carolina IEP facilitation website is https://ed.sc.gov/districts-schools /special-education-services/parent-resources/dispute-resolution-information /facilitated-individualized-education-program-fiep-team-meeting/.

Summary: Alternative Dispute Resolution Mechanisms

We can collaborate with parents and attempt to form a good relationship between parents and school-based personnel; nonetheless, conflicts may occur during IEP meetings. We should always try to recognize the issue or issues over which the conflict is occurring but often we may need to use alternative dispute resolution mechanisms in an attempt to solve a conflict before a due process hearing request is made. Two alternative methods are using an ombudsperson and IEP facilitation. Hopefully, these strategies and alternative methods will help to reduce use of the formal IDEA dispute resolution system.

Conclusion

Our best advice to administrators and special educators regarding IDEA's formal dispute resolution system, especially due process hearings, is to avoid them whenever possible! As will be explained in the following chapters, formal dispute resolution can be expensive, time-consuming, and may irretrievably damage any opportunity for a productive parent–school relationship. Perhaps the most important way to avoid dispute resolution is to prevent conflicts through having IEP team members be effective communicators and collaborators. Unfortunately, one of the surest ways to exacerbate conflict is through negative communications and inept handling of parental concerns. Thus, we suggest that administrators and teachers who will be involved in IEP meetings receive training in communication, collaboration, and conflict resolution. If an IEP looks like it is headed for a due process hearing, attempt to use alternative dispute resolution systems and bring your school district attorney in to review the situation.

The Center for Appropriate Dispute Resolution in Special Education or CADRE, which is funded by the Office of Special Education (OSEP) in the U.S. Department of Education has fabulous resources on dispute resolution. The URL of the center is https://www.cadreworks.org/. We suggest that readers explore the CADRE resources.

References

Amanda J. v. Clark County School District, 260 F.3d 1106 (9th Cir. 2001).

Blue-Banning, M., Summers, J. A., Frankland, H. C., Nelson, L. L., & Beegle, G. (2004). Dimension of family and professional partnerships: Constructive guidelines for collaboration. *Exceptional Children, 70*(2), 167–184.

Center for Appropriate Dispute Resolution in Special education (CADRE), (2017). *Ombudsperson*, Available at https://www.cadreworks.org/continuum/ombudsperson?page=1.

Crockett, J. B. Billingsley, B., & Boscardin, M. L. (2019). *Handbook of Leadership and Administration for Special Education*. Routledge.

Endrew F. v. Douglas County School District, 137 S.Ct. 988; 580 U.S. ___ (2017).

Family Educational Rights and Privacy Act (FERPA), 34 C.F.R Part 99.

Federal Register, (2006), Vol. 71, n. 156, page 46664.

Francis, G. L., Hill, C., Blue-Banning M., Turnbull, A. P., Haines, S. J., & Gross, J. (2016). Culture in inclusive schools: Parental perspectives on trusting family-professional partnerships. *Education and Training and Autism and Developmental Disabilities*, *31*(1), 281–293.

Friend, M. (2007). The co-teaching partnership. *Educational Leadership*, *64*(5), 48–52.

IDEA, 20 U.S.C. § 1401 et seq. (2004).

IDEA Regulations, 34 C.F.R. § 300 et seq. (2006).

Lake, J. F., & Billingsley, B. (2000). An analysis of the factors that contribute to parent-school conflict in special education. *Exceptional Children*, *21*(4), 240–251.

Lake, B. J., Billingsley, B., & Stewart A. (2019). Building trust and responding to parent-school conflict. In J. B. Crockett, B. Billingsley, & M. L. Boscardin, *Handbook of Leadership and Administration for Special Education* (pp. 265–278). Routledge.

M.C. v. Antelope Valley Union High, 858 F.3d 1189 (9th Cir. 2001).

Martin, J. L. (2001). *Effective Strategies to Resolve Special Education Disputes Without Due Process*. LRP.

McFeatters, A. C. (2006). *Sandra Day O'Connor: Justice in the Balance*. University of New Mexico Press.

South Carolina Department of Education, Office of Special Education Services (2022). Facilitated Individual Education Program (FIEP) team meeting. Available at https://ed.sc.gov/districts-schools/special-education-services/parent-resources/dispute-resolution-information/facilitated-individualized-education-program-fiep-team-meeting/.

Stoner, J. B., Bock, S. J., Thompson, J. R., Angell, M. E., Heyl, B. S., & Crowley, E. P. (2005). Welcome to our world: Parent perspectives of interaction between parents of young children with ASD and education professionals. *Focus on Autism and Other Developmental Disabilities*, *20*(1), 39–51.

Tatgenhorst, A., Norlin, A., & Gorn, S. (2014). *What Do I Do When . . . The Answer Book on Special Education Law*. LRP.

Turnbull, A., Turnbull, H. R., Francis, G. L., Burke, M. M., Haines, S., Gershwin, T., Shepard, K. Holdren, N., & Singer, G. H. (2021). *Families and Professionals: Trusting Partnerships in General and Special Education* (8th ed.). Pearson.

CHAPTER 3

State Complaints

Advance Organizers

* What is a state complaint?
* Why are states required to establish complaint procedures when such procedures are not required in the IDEA?
* Who may file a state complaint?
* What information should be included in a state complaint?
* What are possible remedies from a state complaint?
* What are the differences between a state complaint and a due process hearing?

A due process hearing is not the only way a parent may seek a remedy to a perceived violation of the Individuals with Disabilities Education Act (IDEA), such as a denial of a student's free appropriate public education (FAPE) or violation of the law's least restrictive environment (LRE) mandate. A parent, representative of a child, or an organization may file a complaint with a state education agency (SEA) about a potential IDEA violation. In this chapter, we cover the basics of a state complaint, describing the process, the requirements of the complaint, and the possible remedies if it is determined a school district violated the IDEA. Additionally, the chapter includes a sample state complaint for readers to review. Much of the information we used in compiling the information we provide in this chapter comes from the regulations to the IDEA (34 C.F.R.§§ 300.152–300.153), a document published by the Office of Special Education Programs in 2013, Dispute Resolution Procedures under Part B of the Individuals with Disabilities Education Act (2009), and "IDEA Special Education Written State Complaints" developed by the OSEP-funded Center for Appropriate Dispute Resolution in Special Education or the CADRE center (CADRE, 2014).

Why Are States Required to Develop and Implement Complaint Procedures?

The IDEA includes requirements regarding due process hearings but does not address state requirements for developing and implementing a state complaint procedure (SCP). Nonetheless, the U.S. Department of Education has determined that states must develop, offer, and implement a SCP system. According to officials in the department:

> Although Congress did not specifically detail a State complaint process in the Act, we believe that the State complaint process is fully supported by the Act and necessary for the proper implementation of the Act and these regulations. We believe a strong State complaint system provides parents and other individuals an opportunity to resolve disputes early without having to file a due process complaint and without having to go to a due process hearing. (Federal Register, v. 71, n. 156, p. 46600, 2006)

Furthermore, the IDEA requires that funding provided by the federal government shall be used for monitoring, enforcement, and complaint investigation (IDEA, 20 U.S.C. § 1411 [E][2][B][I]). The statute also prohibits a state from preventing a parent from filing a complaint regarding staff qualifications (IDEA, 20 U.S.C. § 1412 [a][14][E]). The IDEA also clarifies that nothing in the statute's due process provisions should be construed as affecting the rights of parents to file a complaint with their SEA, 20 U.S.C. § 1415[f][3][F]). Thus, in writing the IDEA, officials in the U.S. Department of Education believed that Congress anticipated that SEAs would implement their own complaint processes.

The regulations to the IDEA require each state to establish and implement written procedures for resolving any complaint that meets the definition of state complaint set forth in the regulations. It is, therefore, very important that readers consult their states regulations on state complaints. The IDEA requires that a state's complaint procedure be widely communicated to parents and others by including information on the complaint process in the procedural safeguards notice provided to parents (34 C.F.R. § 300.151[a][2]).

What Is a State Complaint?

The SCP involves a parent or organization writing a letter to the SEA to report a possible violation of a student's or students' special education rights and requesting that state investigate the issue. Complainants can raise broad systemic issues or focus on individual student issues (Lake, 2019). The letter of complaint is also sent to the local education agency (LEA). State personnel are then responsible for investigating and deciding about the complaint, although sometimes the SEA may settle a complaint without doing a full investigation.

Who May File a State Complaint?

Any organization or individual, including one from another state, may file a signed, written state complaint that meets the requirements in 34 CFR §§ 300.151 through 300.152 (see section on "What Should Be Included in a Complaint?" below). More parties may file for a SCP then may file for a due process hearing (OSEP, 2013). School district officials, however, may not file a state complaint. This contrasts to a due process hearing because either a parent or a school district may file a due process complaint. Similarly, while a parent has the option of filing a state complaint or requesting a due process hearing, an organization or individual, other than a child's parent, may not file a request for a due process hearing.

State complaints must be filed within one year of the alleged violation. States may increase this statute of limitations. States, however, cannot shorten the statute of limitations (OSEP, 2009). Textbox 3.1 lists information that should be included in a state complaint.

Textbox 3.1. What Should Be Included in a Complaint?

An organization or individual may file a signed written complaint under the procedures described in 34 CFR 300.151–300.152. The complaint must include:

- A statement that a public agency has violated a requirement of Part B of the Act or of Part 300;
- The facts on which the statement is based;
- The signature and contact information for the complainant; and
- If alleging violations with respect to a specific child:
  - The name and address of the residence of the child;
  - The name of the school the child is attending;
  - In the case of a homeless child or youth (within the meaning of section 725(2) of the McKinney-Vento Homeless Assistance Act (42 U.S.C. 11434a(2)), available contact information for the child, and the name of the school the child is attending;
- A description of the nature of the problem of the child, including facts relating to the problem; and
- A proposed resolution of the problem to the extent known and available to the party at the time the complaint is filed.

The party filing the complaint must forward a copy of the complaint to the local educational agency (LEA) or public agency serving the child at the same time the party files the complaint with the SEA.
[34 CFR 300.153(b) and 300.153(d)] [20 U.S.C. 1221e-3]

A regulation to the IDEA prohibits any issue that is part of a due process hearing from being considered during a state complaint (34. C.F.R. § 300.152[c][1]). Thus, if a parent makes an allegation in a hearing, that issue or issues may not be part of a state complaint. However, any decision by a hearing officer will be binding on any SEA's complaint procedure (34. C.F.R. § 300.152[c][2]).

The Advantages of Filing a State Complaint

There are a number of advantages to parents in filing a state complaint. First, SCPs are usually a less costly method available to parents. In due process hearings both parties will often be represented by attorneys in the hearing, which will likely involve considerable expense parents will accrue as the attorney prepares for the hearing and participates in it. Additionally, attorneys will typically suggest the use of expert witnesses in the hearing, which also likely will involve additional up front expenses for the parents. These expenses are not present in filing a state complaint because attorneys are seldom involved in a SCP. Moreover, the parent's involvement is usually limited in the SCP to filing and/or amending the complaint. The SCP does not involve the full procedural protections that are available in a due process hearing such as the right to confront and cross examine witnesses (OSEP, 2013).

A second advantage in submitting a SCP is that complaint process must be completed more quickly than a due process hearing. In a state complaint, the final report by of the investigation is due sixty days after the complaint is filed. A due process hearing decision is rendered in seventy-five days.

A third advantage that the SCP may often be stricter on school districts when school personnel commit procedural errors than a due process hearing officer will be (Zirkel & McGuire, 2010). This is because there is no requirement in FAPE complaints made to SEAs, as there are in due process hearings, that the procedural errors made by school personnel must result in substantive harm to a student before a violation is found. Similarly, SEAs may be stricter on substantive violations of the IDEA and remedies for such violations.

A fourth advantage is that the SCP may find and address systemic problems in a school district if uncovered during an investigation. For example, if SEA investigators are looking into a complaint that a school district has not collected, analyzed, and/or reacted to progress monitoring data on a particular student and they find that the failure to collect progress monitoring data is a system-wide problem, state personnel could require that the school district officials undertake a school district–wide training program in data collection. A hearing officer could not order system-wide remedies such as this because hearing officers are "powerless . . . to require structural relief" (*New Jersey Protection & Advocacy, Inc. v. New Jersey Department of Education*, 2008, p. 488). Similarly, a complainant could file an SCP that a school district failed to provide FAPE to an individual student or that the district has failed to provide FAPE to a group of students. If the latter is the case, an SEA would likely investigate system-wide issues in the school district. Additionally, officials at OSEP have noted that SCPs are a powerful tool to enable SEA officials to fulfill their general supervisory responsibilities to monitor IDEA Part B requirements (Office of Special Education Programs, 2013).

Tips on Completing a State Complaint

The regulations to the IDEA require states develop model forms that assist parents to fill out complaints, although parents are not required to use these forms (IDEA Regulations, 34 C.F.R. § 300.509). When alleging that a school violated a requirement of the IDEA, it is required that parents provide facts that support their allegations by providing as much information as possible that relates to the issues being reporting.

According to the IDEA regulations at § 300.153, the complaint must include (a) a statement that the school district has violated the IDEA, including the facts on which the allegation is based; (b) the signature and address of the person or organization filing the complaint; (c) the name and address of the student and the name of the school he or she is attending; (d) a description of the problem the student exhibits; and (e) a proposed solution. The following are examples in which good information is given to support an allegation:

Statement of violation of the IDEA: My child's school is not providing speech and language services as required by my child's IEP.

Facts that form the basis of the statement: My child's IEP, which was dated September 21, 2020, requires speech and language services for thirty minutes weekly. Since September 21, 2020, my child has not received any speech and language services. I have confirmed this with Mr. John, the school administrator.

The parent usually is given an opportunity to make a proposed resolution to the problem.

Proposed Resolution: Implement speech and language services as required by my child's IEP as soon as possible, and provide compensatory speech and language services since September 21, 2020.

A few additional suggestions tips for filing and reacting to a state complaint are depicted in textbox 3.2. Textbox 3.3 contains possible allegations of violations of the IDEA that could be the basis of a state complaint.

Textbox 3.2.   Tips for filing and Reacting to State Complaints

Parents:

1. Include detailed information so the state can verify your allegations.
2. Be specific on how you want the matter resolved.
3. Give the school/agency an opportunity to respond to the complaint.

School District:

1. Review all allegations included in the complaint.
2. Review all information related to each allegation.
3. Give parent/complainant an opportunity to provide additional information.
4. Provide a comprehensive explanation of the reason(s) for final decision.

Textbox 3.3. Possible Allegation in a State Complaint

- *I was not part of my child's IEP meeting* (Possible failure to include parent in the development of the IEP).
- *My child was not provided speech services as required by her IEP* (Possible failure to implement related services included in the IEP).
- *My child has not been reevaluated for the past four years* (Possible failure to complete Tri-annual evaluation).
- *My child, who is in special education, has been expelled from his school* (Possible violations of the disciplinary requirements of the IDEA).
- *I made a request with my child's school principal to have him evaluated for special education, but I've had no response for several weeks* (Possible failure to provide prior written notice, possible child find violation).
- *I disagree with the school district's decision regarding my child's eligibility for special education services* (possible failure to properly conduct or consider the evaluation results)
- *The services listed in my child's IEP were not provided* (Possible failure to implement an IEP).

The SEA Complaint Resolution Process

Upon receiving a state complaint, if SEA officials determine that a full investigation is necessary then the investigation must be conducted onsite. The SEA has sixty calendar days from the date of receipt of the complaint to conduct its investigation and issue the written decision unless extenuating circumstances exist. The regulations to the IDEA specify two allowable reasons for extending the sixty-day time limit for the CPR resolution. Under 34 CFR §300.152(b)(1), the SEA may extend this time limit only if: (1) exceptional circumstances exist with respect to a particular complaint; or (2) the parent is engaged in mediation or in another alternative means of dispute resolution, which are available under a state procedures and the involved school district officials agree to extend the time to engage in mediation or other alternative means of dispute resolution. States officials need to determine, on a case by case basis, whether it is appropriate to extend the sixty-day resolution time limit for a particular complaint due to such exceptional circumstances.

When investigating a school district, SEA personnel must review all relevant information and make an independent determination as to whether a school has violated a requirement of the IDEA. State personnel must allow personnel in the school district to respond to the complaint. Additionally, a parent must be given an opportunity to add additional information or to amend a complaint. Moreover, regulations to the IDEA require that voluntary mediation be offered to both parties involved in the complaint (34 C.F.R. § 300.152[a][3][ii]). Following the investigation, the SEA must issue a written decision that addresses each of the allegations in the complaint and include findings of fact and conclusions, and the reasoning behind the final decision.

If the SCP ends with a decision that a school district violated the IDEA, the SEA must address the failure of the school district and prescribe corrective remedial actions (34 C.F.R. 300.151[b][1]). Such remedial actions could include compensatory services, monetary reimbursement, and appropriate future provision of services for all students with disabilities (34 C.F.R. § 300.151[b][1]). An SEA, pursuant to its general supervisory authority, has broad flexibility to determine appropriate remedies to address the denial of appropriate services to an individual child or group of children. Tatgenhorst et al. (2017) asserted that SEA's may award any remedy for a violation that a court or hearing officer may award. The final report completed by state personnel must also include procedures to assist school districts to effectively implement the SEA's corrective actions, which may include technical assistance activities and actions to achieve compliance.

If an SEA fails to implement a corrective action related to a state complaint, parents have the option to file a request for due process hearing on the same issue as alleged in the state complaint. But before resorting to the due process hearing option, parents are encouraged to work with the school district to implement the corrective actions in the state complaint. Whether the SEA's resolution of a complaint is subject to appeal to a state or federal court is a matter of state law. Hearing officers do not have the jurisdiction to review or enforce the state's CRP decision (Zirkel & McGuire, 2010). Nonetheless, the SEA's decision in the CRP is enforceable in court (*Beth V. v. Carroll*, 1996).

Textbox 3.4 is a sample complaint investigation report.

Textbox 3.4.   Special Education Compliant Investigation Report—Complaint Decision

On October 20, 2020, the Department of Education, Office of Special Education (OSE) received a special education complaint filed by a parent on behalf of her son. The complaint alleged that public school, which is under the jurisdiction of the ED, violated the Individuals with Disabilities Education Act (IDEA). Pursuant to the Code of Federal Regulations 34 CFR §§ 300.151 through 300.153 implementing the IDEA, the OSE conducted an investigation into the allegations in this complaint. Consistent with the IDEA and federal regulations, the OSE issues the following Findings of Fact, Conclusions, and Decision.

Complaint Issues: Whether the school district followed the procedures required by the IDEA, specifically—whether the school district provided special education services (speech and language) consistent with the IEP pursuant to 34 CFR § 323.

Investigatory Process:
Documents reviewed include:

1. Original State Complaint document; and
2. IEP document submitted by the District.

Interviews were conducted with the following:

1. Parent; and
2. District Director of student services.

The OSE provided the School District and the Parent the opportunity to submit additional information for consideration during the investigation of this complaint.

Applicable Federal Regulations or State Rules: 34 CFR § 323, When IEPs must be in effect.

Relevant Time Period: Pursuant to CFR 34 CFR § 151(c), the OSE has the authority to investigate allegations of violations that occurred not more than one year from the date the complaint was received. In light of this limitation, the investigation will be limited to the period of time from October 20, 2019, to October 20, 2020, for the purpose of determining if a violation of the IDEA occurred.

Findings of Fact:

1. The student was nine years old, in the fourth grade. The student is eligible to receive special education services as a student with a speech and language impairment.
2. On September 21, 2020, the IEP team determined that the student should receive direct speech and language services for thirty minutes weekly.
3. The District Director of student services confirmed that the student has not received speech and language direct services as required by the student's IEP dated September 21, 2020, due to no Speech Therapist available to provided direct speech services.
4. On December 14, 2020, a Speech Therapist was hired to provide speech services for the District.
5. The student did not receive speech and language services for twelve weeks.

Conclusions: The student did not receive direct speech and language services for twelve weeks as required by his September 21, 2020, IEP.

Decision: The investigation revealed a violation of the IDEA—The District failed to provided speech and language services pursuant to the student's IEP.

Reason for the Final Decision: The IDEA requires that as soon as possible following the development of the IEP, each public agency shall make special education and related services available to the child in accordance with the child's IEP (34 CFR § 323).

Differences Between a State Complaint and a Due Process Hearing

In chapter 1, we addressed Zirkel's (2016) division of two of the IDEA's various options for dispute resolution into (a) the adjudicative route (i.e., the due process hearing, possibly culminating in review in state or federal court), and (b) the investigative route (i.e., state complaint). The investigative route is not as legalistic as the adjudicative route and does not require the use of attorneys, case preparation, or face-to-face confrontation (Zirkel, 2016). This avenue of dispute resolution involves an investigation by a state official or a team of state officials of a complaint and may end with a corrective action.

There are a number of additional differences between the state complaint route and the due process route. We are already addressed the financial differences between the complaint and the hearing; the involvement of attorneys in due process hearings can be considerably more costly to parents and school districts. According to the U.S. Department of Education, the SCP tends to be less adversarial than the due process hearing and the department has rejected requests to allow parties to (a) provide evidence under the threat of perjury, (b) permit parties to review submissions, and (c) allowing one party to cross examine the other party because these actions are "contrary to the intent of the State complaint process" (Federal Register, 71, 46605, 2006). As hearing officers, we can attest to the notion that being involved in a hearing is very much like being involved in a court case. A judge presides over the case, in this situation a hearing officer or administrative law judge (ALJ), usually a court reporter is present, and often both sides are represented by attorneys who submit evidence, and examine and cross-examine witnesses. In the state complaint, the parent submits the complaint to the SEA and then waits for the investigation to proceed. Although the parent may amend the complaint, that tends to be the extent of parental involvement in the procedure while the state team investigates the complaint.

Zirkel (2016) noted that the SCP tends to be stricter in their interpretation of school districts' procedural and implementation requirements under the IDEA. We believe this may also be the case when school districts commit substantive violations of the IDEA. In fact, Zirkel (2020) also asserted that parents' success rate in the SCP is much greater than it is in due process hearings.

Conclusion

Parents and school district personnel have a number of dispute resolution options available to them through the IDEA. One such option open to a student's parents, but not school districts, is to file a complaint with an SEA. States are required by regulations to the IDEA to develop complaint procedures when parents disagree with a school district regarding IDEA matters. The complaints must be filed within one year of the occurrence of the violation and can be filed on any issues. In such a state complaint, a parent alleges that the school has violated the IDEA. When parents file a complaint with an SEA, they must also notify the LEA that they are filing the complaint.

If state officials determine that an investigation is needed, state personnel then have sixty days to conduct an onsite investigation of the complaint. Prior to conducting the investigation, state officials must allow the parents to submit additional information and also allow school district personnel to respond to the complaint. The school district must be given a similar opportunity. School district personnel are also allowed to propose a solution to the complaint. If the SCP ends with a decision that a school district violated the IDEA, the SEA must address the failure of the school district and prescribe corrective remedial actions, such as compensatory services, monetary reimbursement, and appropriate future provision of services for students with disabilities

References

Beth V. v. Carroll, 87 F.3d 80 (3rd Cir. 1986).

Center for Appropriate Dispute Resolution in Special Education (CADRE; 2014). *IDEA Special Education Written State Complaints*, Available at https://www.cadreworks.org/sites/default/files/resources/Written%20State %20Complaint%20Parent%20Guide%202014_0.pdf

Federal Register, Volume 71, 46600, 2(006).

IDEA Regulations, 34 C.F.R. § 300.01 et seq.

Lake, S. E. (2019). *What Do I Do When . . . The Answer Book on Special Education Practices and Procedures* (2nd ed.). LRP Publications.

New Jersey Protection & Advocacy, Inc. v. New Jersey Department of Education, 563 F. Supp. 2d 474 (D.N.J. 2008).

Office of Special Education Programs (2009). Questions and answers on procedural safeguards and due process procedures for parents and children with disabilities. Available at https://www2.ed.gov/policy/speced/guid/idea/pro cedural-safeguards-q-a.pdf

Tatgenhorst A., Norlin, J. W., & Gorn, S. (2014). *What Do I Do When . . . The Answer B ook on Special Education Law* (6th ed.). LRP Publications.

U. S. Department of Education, Office of Special Education Programs (2013). Questions and answers on IDEA Part B dispute resolution procedures (Revised 2013). Available at https://sites.ed.gov/idea/files/idea/policy/speced /guid/idea/memosdcltrs/acccombinedosersdisputeresolutionqafinalmemo -7-23-13.pdf

Zirkel, P.A. (2016). A comparison of IDEA's complaint resolution processes: Complaint resolution and impartial hearings. *Education Law Reporter*, *326*, 1–8.

Zirkel, P. A. (2008). Legal boundaries for the IDEA complaint resolution process. *West's Education Law Reporter*, *237*, 565–570.

Zirkel, P.A. (2020). Questionable initiations of both decisional dispute resolution processes under the IDEA: Proposed regulatory interpretations. *Journal of Law and Education*, *49*(1), 99–109.

Zirkel, P. A., & McGuire, B. L. (2010). A roadmap for legal dispute resolution for students with disabilities. *Journal of Special Education Leadership*, *23*(2), 100–112.

CHAPTER 4

Mediation

Advance Organizers

* What is mediation?
* What is the process of mediation?
* What are the rules for mediation?
* Why chose mediation?
* How does one prepare for mediation?
* What are examples of effective mediation practices?

A question-and-answer memorandum on dispute resolution issued by the Office of Special Education Programs (OSEP) in the U.S. Department of Education addressed the importance of collaboration between parents and school personnel. In introducing the document, officials at OSEP wrote,

> The Office of Special Education Programs (OSEP) encourages parents and local educational agencies (LEAs) to work collaboratively, in the best interests of children, to resolve the disagreements that may occur when working to provide a positive educational experiences for all children including children with disabilities. To this end, the IDEA and its implementing regulation provide specific options for one for resolving disputes between parents and public agencies, which can be used in a manner consistent with our shared goals of improving results and achieving better outcomes for children with disabilities (Office of Special Education Programs, 2013, p. 1).

The purpose of the OSEP memorandum was to answer frequently asked questions to assist states facilitate to implement the dispute resolution procedures of the Individuals with Disabilities Act (IDEA).

The use of mediation to address IDEA disputes has long been used in states. Although the Education for All Handicapped Children Act, renamed the IDEA in 1990, did not include mediation as a dispute resolution system, the initial regulations to the law noted the success of mediation in many states and suggested the use of the procedure prior to due process hearings (Office of Special Education Programs, 2013). In the 1997 amendments to the IDEA, mediation was added to the law. In the 2004 amendments to the IDEA, language in the IDEA required states to resolve disputes concerning any matters arising under Part B of the IDEA using mediation.

Our purpose in this chapter is to examine the mediation requirement of the IDEA. Information about mediation is provided to parents in the procedural safeguards notice. Even though mediation may not lead to a final decision, it is an important proceeding and should be taken very seriously. In this chapter we cover the important steps and procedures of mediation. A settlement reached in mediation could have far-reaching consequences for a student, his or her family, and the school district.

What Is Mediation?

Mediation is a voluntary process that brings together parties that have a dispute concerning any matter arising under Part B of the IDEA to have confidential discussions with a qualified and impartial mediator. Mediation is available to resolve disagreements whether it is related to a due process hearing or not. This means that mediation is also available to resolve disputes before a due process hearing or filing a state complaint. Additionally, a parent may opt to use mediation in lieu of the resolution meeting (see chapter 5 on due process hearings for an examination of the resolution session).

The goal of mediation is for the parties to resolve the dispute without having to file a state complaint or request a due process hearing. Successful mediation culminates in a legally binding written agreement reflecting the resolution of the mediation. Mediation may not be used to deny or delay a parent's right to a hearing on the parent's due process complaint, or to deny any other rights afforded under Part B of the IDEA (34 CFR §300.506[b][1] and [8]). Thus, states are required to offer voluntary mediation but neither states nor school districts can require parents to go through mediation prior to a state complaint or due process hearing. The benefits of mediation are described in textbox 4.1.

Textbox 4.1. Benefits of Mediation

Parents:

1. The mediation process is facilitated by an impartial third party who is trained to open the lines of communication between parents and the school district with the goal to resolve disputes, resulting in a legally binding written agreement.
2. The mediation process is less adversarial and maintains relationships with teachers and staff that work with the student.
3. Participation in mediation is no cost to the parent. Note that this is not the case if an attorney is involved.
4. You may get your dispute resolved faster by participating in a mediation rather than a due process hearing which may take months. Mediation meetings must be held as soon as possible and are usually held within several weeks.

5. If the dispute is not resolved through mediation, you may proceed with the due process hearing or file a due process hearing request.

School District:

1. Using the mediation process to resolve special education disputes with parents is cost effective.
2. An opportunity to listen to parents' concern regarding student programming, and how they would like their issues to be resolved.
3. The mediation process maintains relationship with parents.
4. Using an impartial mediator can help establish trust that may have been lost with parents.

Mediation as a Process

The purpose of mediation is to provide an opportunity for parents and a representative of the school district to reach an agreement about any area of dispute under Part B of the IDEA or any other matter under the regulations to the IDEA. Mediation can also be used to resolve issues that cannot be addressed in due process hearings, such as the qualifications of teachers (Lake, 2019; Office of Special Education Programs, 2013).

The mediation session is facilitated by an outside person who serves as a neutral third party—the mediator. The mediator has the role of trying to get agreement and should have professional training for that role. Although neither the IDEA nor its regulations require that mediators be certified, officials at OSEP have noted that mediators should be trained in effective mediation techniques although any such requirements should be left to the states (*Letter to Chief State School Officers*, 2000). The IDEA regulations do require that mediators must be impartial and have no personal or professional interests that conflict with their objectivity (34 C.F.R. § 300.506[c][1][ii]). The mediator cannot be an employee of the school district or state educational agency (SEA) that is involved in the education or care of the student about who the dispute concerns. Thus, the mediator does not represent the district or the parents. Additionally, mediators must be knowledgeable in the laws and regulations related to the provision of special education and related services. States can use IDEA funds to recruit and train mediators and pay the mediator and the costs of the meeting space in which the mediation is held. States must maintain a list of qualified mediators and when a mediator is requested to resolve a dispute, state personnel must select the mediator from the list on a random, rotational, or some other impartial means (34 C.F.R. § 300.506[b][3][ii]).

The mediator works to build trust, and to help both sides find a way to agree on the child's education plan. Mediation sessions can last from two to eight hours. Some disputes may require multiple mediation sessions. Again, the purpose is to come to agreement about the programming for a student.

Neither party can be required to attend mediation. It is completely voluntary, and either party can leave at any time they believe progress is not being made toward an agreement. In some states attorneys are allowed to attend mediation but in other states attorneys are not allowed to attend. The IDEA and regulations are silent regarding who is allowed to attend mediation sessions so the decision on who may attend is up to the parties and/or state law (Lake, 2019). If an attorney attends a mediation, all parties should be informed of the attorney's presence ahead of time, so the other party may also bring an attorney. According to OSEP, "because successful mediation often requires that both parties understand and feel satisfied with the plan for conducting a mediation session it is best practice to discuss and disclose who, if anyone, will be accompanying the party at the mediation session prior to that session" (Office of Special Education Programs, 2013, A-12).

Mediation is different from a state complaint or a due process hearing. All dispute resolution systems have the same general goal, to resolve a dispute regarding special education, and all systems usually involve parents and school district personnel. Mediation is different than a due process hearing because it less formal and legalistic, is less expensive to parents, and is often less adversarial. Most often attorneys are not involved in mediation. In fact, school districts cannot have attorneys at a mediation unless the parents brings an attorney to the meeting.

In a mediation session both sides present their viewpoints and then to come to agreement about the issue(s) and what the next steps should be. Mediation does not always work because either the parties are (a) too far apart in what they think is necessary, (b) cannot agree on the specifics of what the dispute is, or (c) cannot agree on the remedy that is being sought is one that cannot be delivered by the mediator. States vary in their requirements regarding mediation; therefore, readers should consult their state's regulations regarding mediation.

Mediation typically starts around a table, where the mediator lays out the ground rules and discusses the issue(s). Most mediators spend time at the beginning of the mediation to clarify expectations and discuss rules for participants. The following in textbox 4.2 are rules of mediation to which participants should adhere.

Textbox 4.2. Rules of Mediation

Most mediators spend time at the beginning of the mediation clarifying expectations and discuss rules for participants. The following are important aspects of mediation to which participants should agree.

- The mediator is an impartial third party and has no authority to compel any action by either party.

- The mediation session will only be recorded if both parties agree in writing to recording the session.
- Information discussed in mediation is not admissible in a due process hearing or civil procedure.
- The mediation is confidential. The information discussed should not be shared with others.
- As the mediator goes from room to room, everything said to the mediator can be shared with the other party.
- All information shall be disclosed to all parties, including the mediator.
- Technical jargon in legal documents should be simplified to the fullest extent possible to ensure understanding from all parties.
- Participants will refrain from personal attacks.
- Participants will treat all parties involved with respect and will agree to talking turns to speak allowing them an opportunity to present their ideas and solutions without being interrupted.
- All information shall be disclosed to all parties, including the mediator.
- Participants will ask questions of each other for the purposes of gaining clarity and understanding and not as attacks.
- Participants will listen to what others say about the situation.
- Participants will not interrupt each other. If someone is saying something you believe requires a comment, write your comment down, and contribute following the contribution.
- Each person should be prepared and offer ideas for solutions to the problem.
- Participants will work to understand what the other person is saying.
- Participants will speak up if something is not working for them in the mediation.
- Participants may request a break when needed.
- Participants will follow the instructions of the mediator.
- Parties can request a caucus at any appropriate time.
- Participants will seek to avoid dwelling on things that did not work in the past, and instead focus on the future.
- Participants will agree to make a conscious, sincere effort to refrain from unproductive arguing, venting, and narration and agree to use their time in mediation to work toward what to be the most constructive agreement possible.
- Participants will point out if we they believe the mediator is not impartial or neutral.
- The mediator will terminate the mediation at any point the mediator believes that a resolution or agreement is not possible.

Mediation is typically conducted in two different rooms with the mediator going back and forth between the rooms.

Why Choose Mediation?

Mediation is a less adversarial procedure than the other dispute resolution systems and is often completed more quickly. Although there are no specific timelines by which mediation must occur, the process is intended to facilitate prompt resolution of issues (Office of Special Education Programs, 2013, A-10). Moreover, the length of the mediation process will depend on the number and complexity of the areas of dispute. Mediation often only takes several hours, as opposed to a due process hearing, which might take multiple days over several weeks or a state complaint, which has a sixty-day time limit. Additionally, states bear the costs of mediation under the IDEA (34 C.F.R. § 300.506[b][2]). When either party chooses mediation, it also does not prevent them from later filing a due process hearing on the same issue(s), so nothing is lost by choosing mediation. If the parties come to agreement, it is legally binding.

Just bringing in a person from the outside to hear the issues clarifies the seriousness of the dispute. For some this is all that is needed, and they then take it very seriously because the parents view the outside person as a check on the system. This is important when trust has broken down when clarifying the educational program of a child. We next address the steps that are often followed in a mediation session.

Step One: The Beginning of a Mediation Session

As noted above, mediation is typically done with all the participants present, often seated around a table. The mediator often begins by having everyone introduce themselves, clarifying the issue(s), and then discussing the goals of the mediation. The mediator will also explain the format of the mediation session, which may involve two rooms, with the mediator going back and forth between the rooms.

Step Two: The Specifics of the Issue Being Mediated

In step one the mediator states in broad terms the issues that are to be discussed. In step two, the party that filed the complaint addresses the specifics about the issue as they see it. Think of this as an opening statement. Parents should state specifically why they think the school district is not addressing their child's needs, and what they believe is necessary to address their concerns. School personnel should then explain why they have offered a particular program for the student and why they believe the program is necessary and appropriate.

The mediator may give the party who made the first statement an opportunity to respond or to clarify statements made. The mediator will then review what they believe the issues for the mediation are and seek confirmation from both parties that these are indeed the issues of dispute. The mediator will then confirm what will happen next in the session and clarify where everyone will be located during the private discussions.

Step Three: Conduct the Mediation Session

After the opening statements both parties will often go to separate rooms. The mediator will choose one of the rooms and spend time clarifying the specifics of either the complaint or the specifics of the offer. Mediators often go to both rooms multiple times, often with further clarifying questions based on the information that is received. This often takes several hours, and the group waiting for the mediator to come back and discuss the issues should be prepared that it might seem like a long time before the mediator returns.

The purpose of the mediator going back and forth is to allow private discussions and to seek a resolution for the issue. The mediator may provide private guidance to both parties about the merits of their case, and help each party understand where there is agreement, and what areas of disagreement remain. Just a reminder, what is said in mediation remains private and confidential and may not be used as evidence in a subsequent due process hearing or civil action (34 C.F.R. § .300.506[b][8]), although the mediator may ask permission to reference specific statements that would help clarify the issue(s) being mediated.

Preparation for Mediation

Although mediation is considered less adversarial and not as formal as a due process hearing, one should prepare for the session. The following steps can help tailor the presentation of information and help others understand the issue from your perspective. Often mediation is scheduled fairly shortly after it is requested (within two weeks) so the time to prepare is often very short. That is why all documents should be kept in an orderly fashion so they are readily accessible when needed. In mediation, parents and school district personnel work together to solve a dispute with the help of someone who does not take sides—a mediator. These tips can help you get ready for the meeting.

First: Focus on Purpose

In preparation for the mediation, it is important to remember the purpose is to obtain an agreement on the programming and/or placement for a student with a disability. The purpose is not to win, not to "stick it" to the other side, but to come to an amicable agreement about the programming. Keep that in mind.

Second: Clarify the Issues

If the parents are the ones who have requested mediation, the next step is ensuring they spend time before the mediation to clarify the issue. When clarifying the issue also think about what a desirable outcome from the mediation would be. Outline the issue(s) and what the important documents are related to this issue.

Third: Develop an Index of Documents

The individuals who have the most problems with mediation are the ones that are not organized and cannot find a relevant file or record. The school district should have copies of all the necessary documents. Parents can request a copy of any file or record of a student and should strongly consider doing this before the mediation is requested to ensure they have the necessary files and they then also have the time to review the files.

The best way to prepare is to take every document and place in chronological order and then number them. Take the documents and write the numbers on a separate sheet with a title of the document that will serve as an index. Also, on your index sheet write anything that would be important from that document. This index will help find documents in a hurry while meeting with the mediator and discussing issues with the opposing party.

The most important documents are the ones that relate to the issue, so typical documents used are Individualized Education Programs (IEPs), evaluations, letters, report cards, and the regular progress reports. Other documents that might be of importance include discipline records, notes from teachers, statements from transition personnel, statements from transportation personnel, any notes from observations. The critical part of this step is to develop the index of all the documents that can help with quick access when necessary.

Fourth: Develop a Summary

After the documents are placed in chronological order and the index is developed, the next step is to develop a sense of familiarity with each document. This is a time-consuming part of the process. All the documents need to be read with a brief summary developed for each. Many of the documents will be fairly straightforward, such a note from a teacher or a suspension. Other documents will be long and involved like the IEP or evaluation information. They both will take a while to review, but it is necessary to understand them to the greatest extent possible.

For the longer documents it is often helpful to put page numbers on each document and to include those when doing the summary. Some also find it helpful to use sticky notes when there are important phrases, statements, or programming that needs to be addressed. This step is necessary to further prepare the documents and to clarify the issues so that when sitting down with the mediator one can focus on the issue(s) and not on spending all of their time at the meeting looking for a document.

Fifth: State Your Issues

Prepare the case by developing an opening statement about what the issue is from your perspective and what you are seeking as a resolution. Clarify the documents that are important related to the specific issue(s) that are to be addressed. This is different than the above step of placing all the documents in order. This step clarifies the documents related to the specific issue. For example, if there are problems related to transportation, clarify any evidence of transportation needs, any statements in the IEP related to transportation, and any comments or notes from the bus driver, transportation officials, or principals on this topic.

If the issue is a failure to implement all of or a portion of the IEP, then the IEP and notes reflecting teacher's comments related to the IEP should be included. Pay attention to all the documents because there may be some documents that are immediately not viewed as necessary or important but will help clarify the specifics later—like notes from teachers or testing information from related services personnel.

Understanding the documents and the issues will make it easier to respond during mediation and allow the discussion to focus on the issue and possible resolution. Remember the purpose of the mediation is to come to agreement on the program for a student with disability. Preparing will allow the resolution to be the focus instead of spending all the time looking at documents.

Evidence is an important part of your case. Start by marking helpful documents that you want to show at the meeting. For example, if the student's IEP goal report indicates that the school's program is not working, you will want to highlight that. Other evidence may include report cards, test scores, and evaluations. Also look out for evidence that may not be as obvious, such as discipline reports and letters or emails from teachers. Use the documents to help you prepare to respond to the school's arguments.

Sixth: Plan Sufficient Time for the Process

Mediation is to occur at a mutually agreeable time and place. As noted above, mediation typically starts in one room with everyone sitting around a table. Plan for mediation to take multiple hours as it typically takes time for the mediator to learn both sides and to go back and forth on the issues. Sometimes the issue for mediation is a very narrow one that does not take long, but that is often not the case. Mediations with complex or multiple issues can last an entire day, so check that the scheduled time is long enough. Multiple mediation sessions may be needed. Make sure to set aside enough time for the scheduled session. For school districts this may involve hiring substitute teachers or cancelling other meetings that day. For parents, this may involve taking time off from work or hiring sitters for their children.

Set aside the time. This allows for a focus on the issue(s) instead of worrying about who will cover your class or who will watch your children.

Seventh: Attendees at the Mediation

If the mediator is scheduled during a school day, the district will likely have to hire substitute teachers and administrators will have to cancel other meetings that are scheduled in order to attend. School officials should schedule the mediation in a timely manner, although what constitutes a timely manner is not defined in the regulations. Parents may have to take time off from work.

School districts should make sure they have an individual who has the authority to commit funds for programming in attendance. It would be very frustrating to develop an agreement and then not have someone with that authority from the district to be able to sign at the end. Typically, it is a special education director or supervisor who attends.

Parents may want to bring an educational advocate or expert who has worked with the child or understands the specifics around the issues. Often these individuals are not volunteering and may need payment for their time and services.

Some states have regulations related to whether attorneys can attend. If a parent is bringing an attorney, they should inform school district officials. Parents should be informed that if they do bring an attorney to mediation, the IDEA does not allow an award of attorney's fees in preparation or participation in mediation, unless mediation was ordered by a court or by the state (20 U.S.C. § 1415[1][3][D][ii]). Thus, if parents bring an attorney, they will assume responsibility for paying the fees.

Eighth: Review the Procedural Safeguards

Parents should review the procedural safeguards notice provided by the district. This will help clarify some of the obligations a district has toward providing an appropriate education. District representatives should ensure they have a plan that is tied to the specifics of the student's needs—not to the student's disability label. The program offered is individualized based on the needs highlighted as a part of the evaluation, and that the student is making progress on their goals and objectives.

Ninth: Focus on Your Goals

Keep in mind the goal of the mediation is to come to agreement. Both parties often attend mediation with a goal or expectation but both should also be open to suggestions from the mediator and understand there may a different or better way to solve the issue. Keep in mind the overall focus of what the end result should be but realize there may be different ways of getting to that result.

What Makes for an Effective Mediation?

According to OSEP (2013), the success of a mediation depends on (a) the mediator's ability to obtain the trust of both parties and (b) the commitment of the parties to the process. A mediator who is fair, impartial, and knowledgeable about the law will help to establish a trusting relationship between the parties. The OSEP-funded Center for Appropriate Dispute Resolution in Special Education (CADRE; cadreworks.org) includes information on various dispute resolution practices in states, including innovative ways for conducting effective mediations. These effective practices can be found on the CADRE website at https://www.cadreworks.org/continuum/mediation.

Mediation Agreements

When mediation is successful, the parties must implement a legally binding settlement agreement that includes the resolution terms of the mediation. The agreement must also commit to the confidentiality of the entire mediation process and ensure that any discussions will not be used as evidence in any due process hearing or court action (Lake, 2019). The agreement must be signed by the parent and the representative of the school district (34 C.F.R. §300.506[b][6][ii]). Textbox 4.3 is a sample mediation agreement.

If there is an agreement after the mediator has been going back and forth, then the mediator will bring both parties together to clarify the agreement. They typically restate the reason for the mediation, and then clarify the specifics of the agreement, which he or she will have discussed in private sessions prior to bringing everyone back into the same room. If everyone agrees, then they will have both parties sign their notes and then provide a hard copy for both parties.

States vary in their timelines about allowing the parties to reconsider the results of the mediation. Readers should check with their state regulations on this. Typically, both parties have three days to think about the negotiated agreement before it is considered final. This should be explained by the mediator to everyone prior to leaving the room for the final times.

Not every mediation results in agreement. It may narrow the issue(s) and clarify positions, but there still may be an outstanding dispute. If agreement is not reached the mediator will bring everyone back together and clarify the next steps which may include another mediation session. The mediator will clarify any agreement or progress. There may be partial agreement to move forward on one aspect of a child's education with others still in dispute. If the mediator believes the parties are too far apart for agreement, they may make recommendations for a due process hearing.

These steps may be different than the specific steps used in your state. However, the goal of mediation remains the same—to get to an agreement about an area of contention so that the student who is eligible for special education and related services can receive an appropriate education. It would be great if everyone walked away from mediation happy—but that is not the goal. There may need to be concessions in order to reach agreement. The goal of mediation is agreement. Keep that in mind.

Conclusion

The use of mediation is encouraged as a less adversarial method of resolving the issues related to the education of an eligible child. The purpose of mediation is to come to an agreement on how to move forward. Preparation for mediation is vital in order to facilitate a better understanding of not only the issues, but also potential alternatives for settlement. Mediation can move a contentious process forward, avoid the more formal dispute resolution avenues of state complaints and due process hearings, and assist a student with disabilities to receive an appropriate education.

Textbox 4.3. Sample Mediation Agreement

Date:

Student Name:

Parent's Name:

School District Representative:

Mediator:

We, the undersigned, participated in mediation on (DATE HERE) and being satisfied that the plan agreed to by both parties is fair and reasonable, we hereby agree to abide by and complete the following:

1. The district will complete a new reading evaluation of (STUDENT). The evaluation will consist of batteries from the Woodcock Johnson Psychological Examination, the WIAT. There will be observations of the student in reading class by the special education teachers, a school psychologist, and a reading specialist. This will be completed within the next thirty days.
2. An IEP meeting will be held ten days after the completion of the new evaluation.
3. A parent will have the opportunity to observe the classroom(s) recommended by the district after the completion of the IEP. This will occur within five days after the IEP meeting.
4. The IEP team will reconvene after the parent visit to determine the specific placement for the implementation of the IEP. This will occur within five days after the observation(s) of the parent are completed.
5. If the parent is unable to visit the classrooms the pendent program for the student is the second grade classroom with thirty minutes/day of support for reading in the special education classroom.
6. If no agreement can be reached about the placement for the student after the observations, both parties agree to a second mediation which will be held as soon as possible.

We agree that the discussions during this mediation will remain confidential and shall not be used as evidence in a due process hearing or civil action.

Signatures

School District Representative: _____

Parents: _____

Mediator: _____

References

IDEA, 20 U.S.C. § 14.01 et seq., 2004.

IDEA Regulations, 34 C.F.R. 300.1 et seq., 2006.

Lake, S. E. (2019). *What Do I Do When . . . The Answer Book on Special Education Practices and Procedures* (2nd ed.) LRP Publications.

Letter to Chief State School Officers, 2000.

Office of Special Education Programs (2009). Questions and answers on procedural safeguards and due process procedures for parents and children with disabilities.   https://www2.ed.gov/policy/speced/guid/idea/procedural-safeguards-q-a.pdf

U. S. Department of Education, Office of Special Education Programs (2013). Questions and answers on IDEA part b dispute resolution procedures (Revised 2013). Available at https://sites.ed.gov/idea/files/idea/policy/speced/guid/idea/memosdcltrs/acccombinedosersdisputeresolutionqafinalmemo-7-23-13.pdf

CHAPTER 5

The Resolution Meeting

Advance Organizers

* What is a resolution meeting?
* What are the benefits of a resolution meeting?
* What is the process of resolution meeting?
* How to prepare for a resolution meeting.

The 2004 amendments to the IDEA made a significant change to due process procedures by prohibiting parents from filing a complaint and going directly to a due process hearing without first going through a thirty-day resolution period (IDEA, 20 U.S.C. 1415[f][1][B][i]). Officials in the U.S. Department of Education, Office of Special Education Programs (OSEP) explained the reasoning behind the change as follows:

> The purpose of the resolution process is to attempt to achieve a prompt resolution of the parent's due process complaint as early as possible at the local level and to avoid the need for a more costly, adversarial, and time-consuming due process proceeding and the potential for civil litigation. (U.S. Department of Education, 2013, Question D-1)

When parents file a due process hearing request with the state educational agency (SEA), a school district must schedule the resolution meeting within fifteen calendar days, even if school is not in session or if a holiday occurs within these fifteen days. If school officials fail to hold the resolution meeting within fifteen days of receiving the due process complaint, the student's parents may request that the due process hearing officer begin the due process hearing timeline (IDEA Regulations, 34 C.F.R. § 300.510[b][5]).

As is the case when scheduling an IEP meeting, school district personnel must try to hold the meeting at a time and place in which all participants can attend. If the school district does not schedule the resolution meeting, the parents may ask a due process hearing officer to schedule the hearing.

Resolution Meetings

The IDEA 20 U.S.C. § 1415(f)(1)(B) and the implementing regulations (34 C.F.R. § 300.510) require that prior to a parent's due process hearing going forward, the resolution meeting must be held. There are only two situations in which a resolution session is not required: (a) when the parents and district officials mutually agree to waive the resolution session (34 C.F.R § [a][3][i]) or (b) when the parents and district officials use mediation instead of a resolution session in an attempt to solve the problems (34 C.F.R § [a][3][ii]).

There is not, however, a similar requirement to hold a resolution meeting when the school district is the party that files for a due process hearing. The explanation for this disparity was included in the Department of Education's 2006 Analysis of Comments and Changes that accompanying the Part B Regulations, "there is no provision requiring a resolution meeting when an LEA (Local Educational Agency) is the complaining party. The Department's experience has shown that LEAs rarely initiate due process proceedings" (Federal Register, vol. 71, n. 156, p. 46700, 2006).

During the meeting, the student's parents present the reasons they filed for a due process hearing and the facts leading to their decision to file. The LEA then attempts to resolve the issues leading to the complaint without the need to proceed to a due process hearing. There is no required agenda for a resolution meeting. In fact, the regulations to the IDEA leave the format, conduct, and structure of the resolution meeting to the participants. In response to comments to the proposed IDEA 2006 regulations, officials in the U.S. Department of Education commented that the resolution meeting was an opportunity to discuss the concerns raised by the parents who filed the due process complaint and how those concerns might be addressed, so:

> We do not believe it is necessary or appropriate to regulate on the specific structure or protocol for resolution meetings as doing so could interfere with the LEA and the parents in their efforts to resolve the complaint in the resolution meeting. (Federal Register, v. 71, n. 156, p. 46701, 2006)

Thus, a student's parents and school district personnel should spend time prior to the resolution meeting discussing when and where the meeting will occur, who will be involved, the meeting agenda, and what should be discussed during the meeting. In *Clark County School District* (2007), a hearing officer held that a reasonable interpretation of participation in a resolution meeting involves a student's parents actually engaging rather than just attending the meeting. According to Lake (2019), the goal of the resolution meeting is sound, has proven to be worthwhile, and is well worth the investments of time and personnel.

Unlike mediations, the deliberations of the resolution meeting are not confidential unless the parent and school district personnel agree to keep the deliberations confidential. In such situations, a confidential agreement may be signed by all parties. School district personal may not, however, require a student's parents to sign a confidentiality agreement. Moreover, a parent may not condition their participation in a resolution meeting on a school district's agreeing to sign a confidentiality agreement.

Another difference between mediation and resolution meetings is that the discussion during the resolution meeting may be brought up at a due process hearing or court proceeding. A resolution meeting has timelines that must be adhered to when conducting the meeting. The resolution meeting's timelines are included in textbox 5.1.

Textbox 5.1. Timelines for the Resolution Meeting

- 15 calendar days—Within 15 days of receiving notice of a parent's due process complaint, the school district must convene a resolution meeting with the parents and relevant members of the IEP team unless both parties agree in writing to waive the meeting. In an expedited hearing the school must convene a resolution meeting,
- 30 calendar days—If the school district has not resolved to the parents' satisfaction the due process complaint within 30 days, the due process hearing may occur.
- 3 business days—Either party has three business days to void the agreements reached in a resolution meeting.
- 45 calendar days—A hearing officer or ALJ must issue his or her ruling within 45 calendar days after the after the conclusion of the 30-day resolution meeting.

The Courts and Resolution Meeting

Hearing officers, administrative law judges, and courts have strictly enforced the resolutions meeting requirements of the IDEA. In *Matthews v. Douglas County School District RE 1* (2001), the U.S. District Court for the District of Colorado ruled that a parent's failure to cooperate with the LEAs efforts to schedule a resolution led to the parent being unable to hold the district responsible for failing to hold the resolution meeting. In this case the parents would not cooperate with the LEAs efforts to schedule a resolution meeting within thirty days. The district kept thorough documentation of their multiple efforts to schedule the meeting. According to the court, "The record reflects that the District made several attempts to schedule a resolution meeting consonant with the (parents') availability, and that it was the (parent's) insistence on irrelevant or unreasonable conditions that prevented the meeting from occurring" (*Matthews v. Douglas County School District RE 1*, 2001, p. 5). Because the parents had refused the school district's multiple attempts to schedule the resolution meeting, the administrative law judge (ALJ) dismissed the parent's due process compliant. The court upheld the ALJ's dismissal of the complaint.

In *Marinette School District* (2007), an ALJ ruled that a Wisconsin school district's refusal to sign a confidentiality agreement prior to a resolution meeting did not justify the parent's refusal to participate in the meeting. The ALJ, finding that the parents had not acted in good faith and the school had maintained documentation of all efforts to schedule the meeting, granted the school district's motion to dismiss the parent's due process complaint. Similarly, in *Washington Township Board of Education* (2007), an ALJ dismissed a student's parents request for a due process hearing when they did not participate in the resolution meeting. In *Spencer v. District of Columbia* (2006), a student's parent requested a due process hearing and the school district scheduled the resolution meeting. The parent then withdrew the request for the hearing and filed another hearing request. The school district then scheduled another resolution meeting but the student's mother argued that because the district had not held the first resolution meeting, she was entitled to go straight to a due process hearing without holding a resolution meeting. A federal district court rejected the mother's request for due process hearing, ruling that the parent had failed to exhaust her administrative remedies.

These decisions and others clearly should that because the resolution meeting is required by the IDEA, all parties must participate meaningfully in the process. If the parent or the school district fail to participate in the resolution meeting, the part that attempted to participate may seek the intervention of a hearing officer to either dismiss the due process complaint or begin the hearing.

Participants in the Resolution Meeting

Participants in the resolution meeting should include the parent, someone from the LEA who can make decisions on behalf of the school, and members of the IEP team who have knowledge about the issue raised in the due process complaint. Neither the IDEA nor regulations specify how the school district personnel or parents are to determine who the relevant members of the IEP team who attend the resolution meeting will be. Parents may also choose to bring an advocate, family friends, or other support person to the resolution meeting.

Although the rights of parents to bring other persons are not included in the regulations, officials in the OSEP have written that "such individuals could attend the resolution meeting if the LEA or parent determined that such individuals are relevant members of the IEP team" (Federal Register, V. 71, N. 156, p. 46701, 2006). The department further urged that "LEAs and parents act cooperatively in determining who will attend the resolution meeting" because a resolution meeting unlikely to result in any resolution of the dispute if the parties cannot agree on who should attend (71 Federal Register, V. 71, N.156, p. 46701, 2006). If a student's parents believe certain personnel, such as their child's teacher or related service provider, be present at the resolution meeting they should make this request prior to the meeting.

The resolution meeting is informal; therefore, the LEA may not have an attorney attend the meeting unless the parent brings an attorney. If the parents chose to bring an attorney, it is permissible for the school district to have an attorney at the meeting. In such situations, parents will be responsible for paying their attorney's fees. Attorney's fees for a resolution meeting are not reimbursable.

Some states allow facilitators to attend a resolution meeting if both parents and school district participants agree (Center for Appropriate Dispute Resolution in Special Education, 2014). Officials at the Center for Appropriate Dispute Resolution in Special Education (CADRE) suggested that if parents believe a facilitator is needed, they may want to request a mediation instead of a resolution meeting (Center for Appropriate Dispute Resolution in Special Education, 2014).

In circumstances when parents do not participate in a resolution meeting because of disagreement over who attends the meeting or other issues, a due process hearing office may dismiss the parents complain. As officials in the U.S. Department of Education have noted, "[T]here are no provisions that allow a parent or an LEA to unilaterally waive the resolution meeting" (71 Federal Register, v. 71, n. 156, p. 46701, 2006) and that furthermore, "if the LEA is still unable to convince the parent to participate in the resolution meeting, we believe that an LEA should be able to seek intervention by a hearing officer to dismiss the complaint" (71 Federal Register, v. 71, n. 156, p. 46701, 2006). Thus, even in situations in which the parent wants to waive the resolution meeting, if the school district does not likewise agree to waive the meeting, the parents need to participate. If they choose not to participate, a due process hearing officer may dismiss their complaint.

If there is an issue that could result in parents not participating in the resolution meeting, school district officials must always make good faith efforts to obtain parental participation (IDEA Regulations, 34 C.F.R. § 300.322[d]). Furthermore, school officials must take care to document the efforts to ensure that parents participate. Lake (2014) suggested maintaining (a) a record of telephone calls and the results of those call, (b) a log and keeping copies of correspondence send to student's parents and the results, (c) a record of visits made to the parent's home.

It is critical that the parents and school district personnel make good faith efforts to work out the issues in a cooperative manner. The resolution meeting offers a valuable opportunity to resolve any disputes before expending what can be considerable time and money in a due process hearing (Lake, 2014).

Reaching a Resolution Agreement

If the parent and LEA resolve the issues at the resolution meeting, they must put the agreement terms in writing, and both the parent and a representative of the LEA who has the authority to commit the LEA must sign the agreement. The agreement is a legally binding document and may be enforced by a court. If the school district has not resolved the issues to the parent's satisfaction within thirty days of the due process hearing complaint being filed, the due process hearing may occur.

Regulations issued prior to the issuance of the 2006 regulations noted that if a resolution meeting did not end in a resolving a dispute, a due process hearing "must" occur. In the 2006 regulations, the must was removed from the regulations and replace with the more permissive "may" because officials in the U.S. Department of Education believed that requiring a due process hearing may be unduly restrictive, especially if the parties had agreed to an extension of the resolution period (Federal Register, v. 71, n.156, p. 46701, 2006). When an agreement is not be reached during the thirty-day resolution meeting, parents may request a due process hearing officer for additional time to resolve the dispute or mediation could be pursued (CADRE, 2024).

If the parents do not attend the resolution meeting, despite good faith efforts being made by the school district to involve them, school district officials may request that a due process hearing officer dismiss the parents' complaint. In such situations, school personnel should document their efforts by keeping detailed records of telephone calls, email, home visits, copies of written correspondence (Letter to Walker, 2012). Similarly, if the school district fails to respond in a timely manner or fails to participate in the resolution meeting, the parent may request that the forty-five-day timeline for holding the hearing begin and that a due process hearing officer allow the hearing to commence.

States vary on specific requirements regarding resolution meetings, but like the agreements that are reached in mediation, either the parent or LEA may void the agreement within three business days of the date of the agreement (IDEA Regulations, 34 C.F.R. § 300.510[e]). After three days, the agreement is binding on both parties. If either party believes that an agreed upon resolution meeting settlement has been breached, that party may seek enforcement of the agreement in state or federal court (Lake, 2014).

Neither the law nor the regulations address what happens to the due process hearing if an agreement is reached during the resolution meeting. Presumably, the due process hearing is canceled but the law does not specify which party asks that the due process hearing complaint be withdrawn or dismissed after the three-business-day period in which either party may void the agreement. According to officials at OSEP, this is a matter best left to the hearing officer and the SEA (U.S. Department of Education, 2013).

Benefits of Resolution Meetings

The IDEA requires the use of resolution meetings prior to a due process hearing, when requested by a student's parents. In addition to the legal requirement, there are a number of advantages to participating in the resolution meeting.

First, although a resolution meeting can be stressful, it can also be an opportunity to collaborate and improve the relationship between parents and school personnel. Additionally, working together to resolve disputes can prevent the need for a due process hearing, which can have a negative effect on relationships between parents and school personnel.

Second, the resolution meeting keeps the final decision about the program and placement for the student between the parent and the school district; the individuals who know the student and the situation best. If a due process hearing occurs, the hearing officer makes the final decision about the program and placement for the student.

Third, the resolution meeting is less expensive than a due process hearing. According to officials at the U.S. Department of Education,

Because of the high cost of due process hearings and the low expected cost of conducting a resolution meeting, there would likely be some savings for all parties involved if resolution meetings were relatively successful in resolving disagreements. (Federal Register, v. 71, n. 156, p. 46,748, 2006)

Officials in the Department of Education also noted that the cost of a resolution meeting, estimated at $700 a day, was somewhat less than a mediation session, estimated at $600 to $1,800 a session, but far less than the estimated cost of due process of $10,000 to $12,000.

Preparing for a Resolution Meeting

It is important to work together to maintain a relationship between the parents and school district personnel. Given that, however, there should not be compromise just for the sake of compromise but parties should strive to find a resolution that will lead to a student receiving the appropriate education that will allow them to make progress.

When preparing for a resolution meeting it is important to attend to the following:

* Identify the issue(s) and all of the components of the issue(s) so that all relevant information and document can be identified and discussed.
* Identify all possible solutions for the issue(s). Think broadly. Make sure all solutions are related to providing the student FAPE. Personnel at the CADRE Center (2014) suggested that solutions that have proven to be effective in the past should be considered.
* Organize all of the necessary documents, write dates and notes on them (CADRE, 2014). Put the documents in order and develop an index of the documents. Bring the documents and the index to the meeting. If there is additional information that could be of assistance, that also should be brought to the resolution meeting. Textbox 5.2 includes documents that the Parent Advocacy Institute recommends that parents should consider bringing to the resolution meeting (Wettach, 2009).

Textbox 5.2. Documents That Parents Should Bring to the Resolution Meeting

* Report cards
* PWNs
* IEP progress reports
* IEPs
* Standardized test scores
* Independent evaluations
* Disciplinary records

- Discuss possible responses to the issues and think of possible solutions.
- Parents are encouraged to bring a friend, advocate, or parent mentor to the meeting. Having someone with them at the meeting may serve to increase confidence and help ensure a thorough discussion of the issues. School district personnel should bring everyone who is relevant to the issue including teachers, supervisors, necessary related services staff, and importantly a representative of those who make financial decisions and agree to any agreement.
- Someone from both parties in attendance should take detailed notes of the proceedings. The comments and discussion from the meeting may be helpful in prepared for a due process hearing should that be necessary.
- Because discussions at resolution meetings may become emotional, be prepared to deal these emotions if they should arise (CADRE, 2014).
- Always be respectful and considerate of the feelings of participants.
- Encourage all parties to participate in the discussion. If an interpreter is needed, CADRE suggests that the SEA be contacted (CADRE, 2014).

Conclusion

A resolution meeting is a mandatory meeting that the school district must convene within fifteen days of receiving the parents' due process complaint. The resolution meeting must occur when a student's parents request a due process hearing. There is no similar requirement, however, when an LEA files a due process complaint. This step was added to the IDEA in 2004 to encourage parents and school personnel to work out their differences prior to going to a due process hearing. Parents must attend the resolution meeting. If they do not, the due process hearing complaint may be dismissed. If an agreement is reached, it must be put into writing and signed. Either party may void the agreement within three business days. After the three days have expired, the agreement is enforceable in a court of law. If there is no agreement, the parties proceed to the due process hearing.

References

CADRE (2014). The center for appropriate dispute resolution in special education. Document available at https://www.cadreworks.org/sites/default/files/resources/Resolution%20Meeting%20Parent%20Guide%202014_0.pdf.

Federal Register, v. 71, n. 156, p. 46700 (2006).

IDEA, 20 U.S.C. § 14.01 et seq., 2004.

IDEA Regulations, 34 C.F.R. 300.1 et seq., 2006.

Lake, S. E. (2019). *What Do I Do When . . . The Answer Book on Special Education Practices and Procedures* (2nd ed.). LRP Publications.

Letter to Walker, 59 IDELR 262 (OSEP 2012).

Marinette School District, Wisconsin State Educational Agency. (2007) 114 LRP 27793.

Matthews et al. v. Douglas County School District RE1, No. 1:2017cv03163—Document 40 (D. Colo. 2018).

Spencer v. District of Columbia, 416 F. Supp 2d 5 (2006).

U.S. Department of Education, Office of Special Education Programs (2013). Questions and answers on IDEA part b dispute resolution procedures (Revised 2013). Available at https://sites.ed.gov/idea/files/idea/policy/speced/guid/idea/memosdcltrs/acccombinedosersdisputeresolutionqafinalmemo-7-23-13.pdf.

Washington Township Board of Education, New Jersey State Educational Agency (2007), 107 LRP 38312.

Wettach, J. R. (2009). Preparing for special education mediation and resolution sessions. The Advocacy Institute and the Duke Children's Law Clinic. Document available from https://www.advocacyinstitute.org/resources/Preparing.for.SpEd.Mediation.Resolution.Sessions.pdf.

CHAPTER 6

Settlement Agreements

Advance Organizers

* What is the purpose of a settlement agreement?
* What are the components of a settlement agreement?
* Can settlement agreements be enforced?

The goal of alternative dispute resolution procedures, such as mediation and resolution meetings, is to settle a dispute between a student's parents and a school district before the disagreement goes to a due process hearing. In mediation and resolution systems, the terms of the settlement should be written out and signed. When the settlement is memorialized in this way, it is less likely that there will be disputes over the terms of the settlement (Lake, 2014). In this chapter, we address the writing, signing, and enforcement of settlement agreements.

The Purpose of a Settlement Agreement

In this book, we have advocated that school district personnel and students' parents use non-judicial alternative dispute resolution dispute procedures in an attempt to settle contentious issues and avoid expensive, time-consuming, and emotionally difficult due process hearings. Not only do alternative dispute resolution procedures avoid these problems, but they also put the ultimate decision-making power where it rightly belongs, in the hands of these who know the student best: his or her parents, teachers, and principal.

The preferred result of non-judicial alternative dispute resolutions systems such as use of an ombudsman or IEP facilitation, which may be encouraged by states but are not required by the IDEA, and mediation and resolution meeting, which are required by the IDEA, are to settle disputed issues between school districts and parents. If an agreement is reached in these systems the result will be a written settlement agreement, which both parties agree to and sign. Settlements can also be reached by parents and school districts during the course of a due process hearing.

Parents and school districts have a great deal of flexibility when developing a settlement agreement (Granelli & Sims, 2018). We next examine settlement agreements arising out of mediation and resolution meetings.

Settlement Agreements and Mediation

When parents and school district official resolve a dispute as the result of mediation, the parties involved must sign a written settlement agreement.

> If the parties resolve through the mediation process, the parties must execute a legally binding agreement that sets forth that resolution and that— (i) (S)tates that all discussions that occurred during the mediation process will remain confidential and may not be used as evidence in any subsequent due process hearing or civil proceeding; and (ii) is signed by both the parent and a representative of the agency who has the authority to bind such agreement. (IDEA Regulations, 34 C.F.R. § 300.506[b][6][i–ii])

Moreover, "A written, signed mediation agreement . . . is enforceable in any state court of competent jurisdiction (i.e., has the authority to issue judgements over such disputes) or in a (federal) district court" (IDEA Regulations, 34 C.F.R. § 300.506[b][7]). According to officials at the Office of Special Education Programs (OSEP) in the U.S. Department of Education, the enforceability of this and other signed and binding settlement agreements is based on applicable state and federal law (OSEP, 2000). The requirement that the mediation settlement discussions remain confidential may not be used as evidence in a due process hearing is the only difference between settlement agreements in mediation and resolution meetings.

Settlement Agreements and Resolution Meetings

A resolution meeting is the final attempt at settling a dispute prior to going to a due process hearing. In chapter 5 we addressed the importance of the resolution meeting, which a school district must convene within fifteen calendar days of receiving a student's parents' due process complaint. Parents and school district officials must attend the resolution meeting unless the parents and school district officials mutually agree to wave it. If a school district has filed the due process complaint, a resolution meeting is not required.

The school district has thirty calendar days to settle the dispute. If it is not settled by that time, the due process hearing may proceed. If, however, the resolution meeting is successful and there is an agreement between parents and the school district, the parties must execute a signed written agreement.

> If a resolution to the dispute is reached at the meeting . . . the parties must execute agreement that is—(1) signed by both the parent and a representative of the (school district) who has the authority to bind the agency; and (2) (E)nforceable in any State court of competent jurisdiction or in a district court of the United States, or, by the SEA, if the State has other mechanisms or procedures that permit parties to seek enforcement of resolution agreements. (IDEA Regulations, 34 C.F.R. § 300.510[d][1–2])

Although parents and the school district may choose to include a confidentiality agreement as part of the final settle agreement, it is not required by the law (OSEP, 2008). However, school districts may not require that parents sign a confidentiality agreement as a condition for participating in the resolution meeting.

The Contents of a Settlement Agreement

In public comment period on the proposed 2006 IDEA regulations, one commenter asked that the U.S. Department of Education require that state educational agencies (SEAs) develop a model form to be used for settlement agreements. The department decided that because the terms of a settlement agreement will vary because of numerous factors "we do not believe that it is useful or practical to require SEAs to develop a model settlement agreement form" (Federal Register, v. 71, n. 156, p. 46704, 2006). Nonetheless, nothing prevents states or school districts from developing their own model forms. Any forms that are used must be legally sufficient to protect the interests of both parties because settlement agreements are legal binding and enforceable (Lake, 2014). Thus, it is a good idea to communicate with an attorney during negotiations because settlement agreements can be legally complex (Wyner & Tiffany, 2010).

Wyner and Tiffany (2010) explained that well-drafted settlement agreements can be very effective in resolving disputes and allowing the parties to move forward, whereas poorly drafted agreements can create more problems and sometimes lead to even more litigation. The key to a well-crafted settlement agreement is specificity (Wyner & Tiffany, 2010). The more specific the terms of the agreement are spelled out, the less likely it will be that parties will misinterpret and dispute the agreement.

Granelli and Sims (2018), Lake (2014), and Wyner and Tiffany (2010) noted that the terms of a settlement agreement will vary; nonetheless, they suggested that settlement agreements should include the following components:

- **The Title:** The title should identify (a) the dispute being settled, and (b) the nature of the agreement (Wyner & Tiffany , 2010).
- **A Whereas Clauses/Preamble:** This is a section that lists the basic facts of the agreement. It often includes the names of participants, the issues in dispute, and the time frame covered by the settlement (Granelli & Sims, 2018). Wyner and Tiffany (2010) suggested that in addition to the participants, the preamble should include language about the purpose of the agreement, including areas the agreement is intended to solve.
- **A Substantive Obligations Clause:** Granelli and Sims (2018) referred to the substantive obligations of the parties as the crux of the settlement agreement and Wyner and Tiffany (2010) called this section the heart of the agreement. Moreover, the more clearly these obligations are described, the likelihood of future litigation is decreased.

    The substantive obligations are the remedies or relief decided upon during the meeting and includes requirements such as (a) Tuition reimbursement for a private school or tutoring, (c) agreement to pay for the cost of an independent educational evaluation, (c) training for parents or staff (e.g., principal, teachers, related services providers), (d) technology hardware or software, (e) modifications to a student's IEP, (f) related service, (g) compensatory services, (h) transportation, (i) attorneys' fees, (j) prospective services, (k) development of a new IEP, (l) compensatory education, and (m) provision of ongoing services for the student to receive a FAPE.

- **A Reimbursement Clause:** Wyner and Tiffany (2010) noted that the agreement may also describe any reimbursements that are agreed upon during the meeting. They also noted that a reimbursement clause should carefully define the scope of reimbursements, documentation to support the reimbursement, and timelines for payment.

- **A Withdrawal of the Complaint and Release of Claims:** Granelli and Sims (2018) noted that from a school district's perspective this may be the most critical part of the settlement agreement because it generally requires the parents to withdraw any and all claims against the school district under the Individuals with Disabilities Education Act (IDEA), Section 504, the American with Disabilities Act (ADA) as well as claims for compensatory, tuition, or other damages. Lake (2014) observed that the complaining party, usually the parent, should agree not to file any more state or federal complaints, due process hearing requests, or legal proceedings related to these matters. According to Wyner and Tiffany (2010), careful consideration must be given before providing a release of claims, especially unknown claims.

- **A Stay-put Clause:** During the pendency of a hearing, a student must stay put in their current educational placement, unless the parents and school district officials agree otherwise (IDEA Regulations, 34 C.F.R. § 300.518). The purpose of the stay-put rule, sometimes referred to as the status-quo provision, is to protect students with disabilities from a unilateral disruption of their current program while disputes are being heard regarding programming or placement are being heard (Tchao, 1999). If parents and school officials agree otherwise regarding a student's placement, the new setting becomes the stay-put or status-quo placement. Tchao (1999) suggested that if a school district and a parent agree to a placement other than the current educational placement, the school district should ensure that the placement is temporary, and spell out the terms very clearly (e.g., specific date and time limitation of the placement), which is especially important if the temporary setting is a private school. If the new placement is in a private school, the school district should (a) include the date by which the school district's payment for the private school should end, (b) include the date by which the student will return to the school district, and (c) ensure the agreement clarifies that public school does not agree that the private school is necessary for the student to receive a FAPE but only for the settlement of claims (Tchao, 1999).

Although it is likely that the meeting will have resolved placement issues, it is a good idea to address the student's placement should another dispute occur (Granelli & Sims, 2018). Lake (2014) suggested that "(I)f the agreement is going to have any effect on the student's IEP or provide the student with additional services, it should address whether the change or additional services are intended to be part of the student's stay-put IEP" (Lake, 2014, p. 9:26). Furthermore, if the settlement agreement is intended to amend the student's IEP, the school district should attach a copy of his or her updated program into an amended IEP.

- **A Confidentiality Clause:** Settlement agreements from mediation meetings require confidentiality clauses. Additionally, Lake (2014) suggested that all settlement agreements include confidentiality clauses. He noted that the privacy of all parties involved, especially minor students, is very important and should be ensured. Lake (2014) further noted that a confidentiality clause can avoid bad press with the contents of settlement agreements if released to a newspaper. Because such agreement constitutes an educational record, they are also subject to the confidentiality requirements of the Family Educational Rights and Privacy Act (FERPA), which prevents school district from releasing the information without parental permission. According to Granelli and Sims (2018) confidentiality provisions should account for legal mechanisms, such as the Freedom of Information Act, that may permit access to these documents.

- **An Attorneys' Fees and No Admissions Clause:** According to Lake (2014), a clause should be inserted in the settlement agreement that requires that parties pay their own attorneys' fees and that a statement be included that there was no prevailing party in the resolution meeting. This can serve to prevent future litigation. Granelli and Sims (2018) noted that settlement give both parties the opportunity stipulate that there are no admissions of wrongdoing of any kind.

- **A Continued Residency Clause:** According to Lake (2014), a school district should include a provision that ties the terms of the agreement to the student's continued residency in a school district. By doing this it affirms that if the student moves out of the district, the school district is not responsible for meeting the terms of the agreement.

- **A Consents Clause:** Granelli and Sims (2018) suggested that a clause should be included in a settlement agreement that allows a school district to obtain consent from a student's parents for the release and exchange of information between the school district and a student's evaluators, tutors, private schools, and others.

- **A Standard Contract Clauses:** Granelli and Sims (2018) believed that a settlement agreement should also include standard contract provisions related to areas such as amending the agreement, governing laws, language construction, and authority to sign. Because the settlement agreement can be canceled by either party up to three days of that language could be included in this clause.

Enforcement of Settlement Agreements

A settlement agreement reached in both a mediation (IDEA Regulations, 34 C.F.R. 516[b][7]) and a resolution meeting (IDEA Regulations, 34 C.F.R. 510[d][2]) are enforceable in state of federal district court. However, neither the IDEA nor the regulations are clear regarding where this enforcement is to occur. In fact, a few courts have noted that there is a muddle of law on settlements in the IDEA context and while the IDEA clearly favors alternative dispute resolution the law is not clear on interpreting settlement agreements (*D.R. v. East Brunswick Board of Education*, 1997; *South Kingstown School Committee v. Joanna S.*, 2013, 2014). Wyner and Tiffany (2010) noted that a settlement agreement may be enforceable in state court as a breach of contract claim.

Generally, parents must go through the IDEA's administrative process before filing a claim in a court. However, an exemption to this rule may be when either party attempts to enforce a settlement agreement (*McClendon v. School District of Philadelphia*, 2004). The U.S. Courts of Appeals for the Sixth Circuit allowed parents to enforce a settlement agreement even though they had not exhausted their administrative remedies (*Hall v. Memphis City Schools*, 2014). Interestingly, in this case a student's parents had signed a settlement agreement that included a release of all IDEA and state law claims. The circuit court also allowed the parent's claim against a school district under Section 1983 (42 U.S.C. § 1983), a law that allows suits against governmental entities for Constitutional violations, to go forward. The circuit court also allowed the parents' lawsuit against the school district for breach of contract to go forward.

A state educational agency (SEA) may also enforce a settlement agreement. According to the 2006 federal regulations to the IDEA,

> there is nothing . . . that would prevent the SEA from using other mechanisms to seek enforcement of that agreement, providing the use of those mechanisms is not mandatory and does not delay or deny a party the right to seek enforcement of the written agreement in a state court . . . or in a district court of the United States. (IDEA Regulations, 34 C.F.R. §300.537)

Unless state law holds otherwise, hearing officers can probably not issue rulings on settlement agreements. According to OSEP "the IDEA does not specifically address enforcement by hearing officers of settlement agreement reached by the parties. Therefore, a state may have uniform rules relating to a hearing officer's authority or lack of authority to review and/or enforce settlement agreements" (*Letter to Shaw*, 2007, p. 2). Furthermore, the U.S. Court of Appeals for the Second Circuit in *H.C. v. Colton-Pierrepoint Central School District* (2009) held that a hearing officer does not have the authority to enforce a settlement agreement. If state law doesn't confer the authority to enforce settlement agreements to hearing officers, it may be prudent to consider that they do not possess the authority to enforce a settlement agreement.

Lake (2014) asserted that a settlement agreement may be vacated if the agreement (a) violated the IDEA, (b) denied the student a FAPE, (c) violated state law, (c) falsely stated the facts upon which the agreement was based, or (d) if the agreement was forced under duress. If a student's parents were to bring a lawsuit making such allegations, the parents would bear the burden of proof in challenging the agreement under the doctrine announced by the U.S. Supreme Court in *Schaffer v. Weast* (2005).

Conclusion

A settlement agreement is a procedure used by school districts and parents to memorialize the arrangement agreed upon by the parties to settle a special education dispute. It is a final step to solve issues that would otherwise lead to a due process hearing. A settlement agreement is legally binding and enforceable. A settlement agreement is a complex legal document. If it is drafted with care it can serve to resolve disputes, improve the education of students with disabilities, and prevent the need for future litigation. However, a poorly drafted settlement agreement may lead to misunderstanding and result future disputes, and even more litigation.

References

D.R. v. East Brunswick Board of Education, 109 F.3d 898 (3rd Cir. 1997). Available at https://casetext.com/case/dr-v-east-brunswick-bd-of-educ.

Federal Register, v. 71, n. 156, p. 46704, 2006.

Hall v. Memphis City Schools, 764 F.3d 638 (6th Cir. 2014)

H.C. v. Colton-Pierrepoint Central School District, 341 F. App'x 687 (2nd Cir. 2009). Available at https://casetext.com/pdf-downloaded?download_redirect=hc-v-colton-pierrepont-central-sch&utm_source=Iterable&utm_medium=email&utm_campaign=prospecting-emails&content=finalday&term=long.

Granelli, L. J., & Sims, B. L. (2018). Special education disputes litigate or settle: That is the question. Pre-conference workshop at the 22nd Annual School Law Conference, New York. Available at https://www.nyssba.org/clientuploads/nyssba_pdf/Events/precon-law-2018/06-special-ed-disputes-outline.pdf.

Lake, S. E. (2014). What Do I Do When . . . The Answer Book on Special Education Practice and Procedure (2nd ed.). LRP.

McClendon v. School District of Philadelphia, Civil Action No. 04-1250 (E.D. Pa. Oct. 29, 2004). Available at https://casetext.com/case/mcclendon-v-school-district-of-philadelphia-2.

Office of Special Education Programs (2000). Letter to Chief State School Officers, 33 LRP 6364.

Office of Special Education Programs (2008). Letter to Baglin, 53 53 IDELR 164.

South Kingstown School Committee v. Joanna S., (D. RI, 2013). Available at https://casetext.com/case/s-kingstown-sch-comm-v-joanna-s.

South Kingstown School Committee v. Joanna S., 773 F.3d 344 (1st Cir., 2014). Available at https://casetext.com/case/s-kingstown-sch-comm-v-southern-ex-rel-pjs.

Tchao, A. K. (1999). Special education settlement agreements pose challenges. *School Law Aadvisory*, *271*, 1. Available at https://schoollaw.com/wp-content/uploads/pdf/271.pdf.

Wyner, S., & Tiffany, M. (2010). *Demystifying settlement agreements*. Available at https://www.wrightslaw.com/law/art/wyner.tiffany.agreement.pdf.

CHAPTER 7

Due Process Hearings

Advance Organizers

- What is a due process hearing?
- What is the intent of due process hearings?
- Who may request a due process hearing?
- What are the contents of a due process hearing complaint?
- How does a due process proceed?

The Individuals with Disabilities Education Act (IDEA) allows parents or school districts to file a due process complaint on any matters related to the identification, evaluation, placement, or provision of a free appropriate public education (FAPE) of an IDEA-eligible student with a disability (IDEA Regulations, 34 C.F.R. § 507). The due process hearing is conducted either by a state educational agency (SEA) or the public school district (IDEA Regulations, 34 C.F.R. § 511[b]). The due process hearing has been a procedural safeguard in the IDEA since the law was first passed as the Education of All Handicapped Children Act in 1975.

This chapter provides an overview of the basic components of the due process hearing. Subsequent chapters will go into greater detail on the specific components of the due process hearing. After reading this chapter the reader will understand the basics of a resolution session and a due process hearing, including timelines, and the resulting actions. Because state educational agency (SEA) requirements regarding dispute resolution vary, we suggest that readers consult their state's requirements for further information on how due process hearings are conducted. Information on a state's dispute resolution process will usually be on the state's special education website.

Due Process Hearings

When school district personnel and parents meaningfully collaborate in developing a student's educationally meaningful individualized education program (IEP), school personnel collect data to monitor students' progress, and teachers share regular progress reports on students' progress with their parents, it is likely that dispute resolution can be avoided and there will be less need for due process hearings. In such situations there would be a clear understanding of the services a student would receive, thus preventing many disputes related to how students with disabilities should be educated. However, disputes do arise in response to the efforts of school personnel to provide special education services or disputes may arise as a result of school personnel being perceived as unresponsive to the needs of parents. A due process hearing is a formal presentation of facts before an impartial due process hearing officer.[1] The hearing officer hears both sides of a dispute, examines the issues, applies the law to the facts, and renders a decision.

One-Tier and Two-Tier Due Process Hearing Systems

States either have a one-tier hearing structure or a two-tier hearing structure. In one tier hearing states, a due process complaint is filed and following an unsuccessful resolution meeting (if the parents filed the complaint), a due process hearing is held. Following the hearing, the hearing officer's ruling may be appealed directly to state or federal court. In a tier two structure, the appeal is made to a review officer or a panel of reviewers at the SEA. The second-tier hearing officer reviews the first tier ruling and either affirms or over rules the decision. Either party may then appeal to state or federal court. Most states use a one tier due process hearing. In 1991, Katsiyannis and Klare (1991) reported twenty-five states used a one-tier system and twenty-six states used a two-tier system, the number of states using a two tier system has dropped to just seven states. We examined websites of SEA's special education sites and found that only the following seven states still use two tier systems: Kentucky, Kansas, Nevada, New York, Ohio, Oklahoma, and South Carolina. North Carolina was a two-tier state but the state assembly recently passed a law moving the state to a one tier due process system.

This section will describe important concepts associated with special education due process hearings and provide an overview of special education due process hearing terms and procedures. These concepts hold for either one or two-tier systems.

We provide an overview of rights afforded to parents or guardians by the IDEA and rights afforded to the school district officials involved in disputes with parents or guardians. We describe the due process hearing process, and what roles and responsibilities surface regarding special education due process hearing participants. Because states may have slightly different procedures, readers should consult their state's special education rules and procedures for specific processes to follow.

What Is Meant by Special Education Due Process?

The Fourteenth Amendment of the U.S. Constitution provides the basis of students and parents or guardians' educational rights to fair and appropriate

---

[1] For ease of description, due process hearing officer is the term that will be used throughout this book; however, states may have administrative law judges conducting due process hearings rather than impartial due process hearing officers.

treatment. Due process rights in special education, and other areas, stem from the rights guaranteed by the Fourteenth Amendment. Due process hearings in special education are formalized procedures occurring when there is a disagreement between parents and school districts concerning students who are eligible under the IDEA for special education and related services, or thought to be eligible. States may have specific additional rules related to who can hear the issue, a due process hearing officer or administrative law judge (ALJ), rules relating to presentation of evidence, and rules related to appeals. Some states have an appeals panel that will complete a de novo[2] review of the information from the hearing, whereas other states require persons to go directly to either state or federal court after a hearing. One important point that exists in all states is that in order to get to state or federal court on a special education issue there first needs to be a due process hearing with testimony, evidence, and a ruling by a hearing officer. This requirement to complete the hearing prior to appealing to a state or federal court is referred to as exhausting administrative remedies.

The intent of a due process hearing in special education is to resolve conflicts when the two parties are involved have disagreement regarding the identification, evaluation, placement, or provision of FAPE of an IDEA-eligible student and cannot solve the problems and arrive at workable solution. Moreover, mediation and the resolution meeting have not been successful. There are two parties at a special education due process hearing: (a) the parents or guardians[3] and (b) the school district responsible for delivering the educational services to the IDEA-eligible (or thought to be eligible) student. Federal law mandates both sides involved in the disagreement must be allowed to present complaints relating to students' identification, evaluation, or educational placement, or the right to FAPE. In addition, parties losing in special education due process hearings have the right of review of the due process hearing officer's ruling by appealing to a state or federal court any decision that they believe is incorrect (IDEA Regulations, 34 CFR § 300.510).

Federal law requires that each SEA ensure all school districts establish, maintain, and implement procedural safeguards that meet federal requirements of due process procedures (IDEA, 20 U.S.C. 1415 [a]). In essence, special education due process procedures protect both sides and afford equal protection in the educational conflict by offering an opportunity to be heard so that problems can be solved. Importantly, special education due process rights protect all students from unilateral decisions by school district personnel and/or parents or guardians that deny students access to FAPE.

The Qualifications and Independence of the Hearing Officer

The IDEA and regulations include specific information about who may serve as a hearing officer. The primary rule of persons who may serve in this role is that

---

[2] A de novo review is when a court or SEA decides an issue without giving deference to a previous ruling.

[3] Throughout this document we will refer to parents generically, but want to clarify that when we do so it represents parents, guardians, and those with educational custody of eligible students.

they must be impartial and independent and have no personal or professional interest that conflicts with their objectivity in the hearing (U.S. Department of Education, 2013, question C-15). The IDEA includes minimum qualifications that the hearing officer must meet (IDEA Regulations, 34 C.F.R § 300.511[c] [1]). The minimum qualifications are depicted in textbox 7.1.

Textbox 7.1. Minimum Qualifications of Hearing Officers

A hearing office must not be

- An employee of the SEA or the school district that is involved with the education or care of the child.
- A person having a personal or professional interest that conflicts with the person's objectivity in the hearing.

A hearing office must

- Possess knowledge of, and the ability to understand, the provisions of the IDEA, federal and state regulations pertaining to the IDEA, and legal interpretations of the IDEA by federal and state courts.
- Possess knowledge and ability to conduct hearings in accordance with appropriate standard legal practice.
- Possess the knowledge and ability to render and write decisions in accordance with appropriate standard legal practice.

Procedural and Substantive Issues

Due process hearings address both procedural and substantive issues. As noted in chapter 1, the Supreme Court's rulings in *Board of Education v. Rowley* (1982) and *Endrew F. v. Douglas County School District* (2017) confirmed the importance of addressing both procedural and substantive issues in special education matters. Moreover, when FAPE is an issue in which there is a conflict, due process hearing officers will consider both procedural and substantive issues.

In the 2004 amendments to the IDEA, Congress required that when hearing officers hear disputes about the provision of a FAPE to a student, the hearing officer is to base his or her decisions upon substantive grounds of whether a student received a FAPE (IDEA, 20 U.S.C § 1415 [f][3][E][i]). Thus, hearing officers will likely emphasize substantive violations over procedural violations. Nonetheless, some procedural requirements are so important that if they violated by school district personnel, the violation could result in a school district denying students a FAPE. These procedural violations included (a) impeding a student's right to a FAPE, (b) impeding a student's parents' opportunity to participate in the decision-making process regarding their child's FAPE, or (c) depriving a student of educational benefits (IDEA, 20 U.S.C § 1415 [f][3][E] [ii]).

The IDEA is less clear on substantive violations and does not clearly distinguish between what constitutes a procedural and a substantive violation (Berney & Gilsbach, 2017). Courts, especially the U.S. Supreme Court, have issued rulings that have clarified the procedural and substantive distinction of the IDEA. According to Zirkel (2017), the substantive dimension focuses on the adequacy of an IEP with respect to its likely or actual results. In the *Endrew F.* ruling, to meet the substantive requirements of the IDEA, a student's IEP must be reasonably calculated to make progress in light of his or her circumstances. There may be a dispute between the parties about how much progress a student is expected to make in their program (see chapter 2 for further explanations of procedural and substantive issues).

Who May Request a Due Process Hearing?

The parent or school district may request a due process hearing with respect to any matter relating to the identification, evaluation, or educational placement of the child or the provision of a FAPE by filing a due process complaint. Parents may request a due process hearing on educational decisions related to the following:

- their child was not identified and evaluated or was incorrectly identified and evaluated as a child with a disability,
- their child's IEP was not appropriate to meet his needs or was not implemented;
- their child's placement was not appropriate to meet his or her needs; or
- their child was otherwise being denied a FAPE.

School personnel may request a due process hearing if the parent refuses to consent to the evaluation or reevaluation of the child or for the provision of a FAPE for the child. Another example of when school personnel may request a due process hearing is when a parent requests an independent educational evaluation and the school district defends their evaluation of the student. One area in which school districts cannot request a due process hearing is whether the district has the permission to place a child in special education after the initial evaluation. Before initiating a due process hearing, all parties must be informed of the opportunity for voluntary mediation.

Timeline of a Due Process Hearing

States may have slightly different timelines so readers should consult their state's special education regulations. The parent or school district must request a due process hearing by filing a due process complaint within two years of the date the parent or the school district knew or should have known about the alleged action that forms the basis of the complaint. There are a few exceptions to this timeline, which include if the (a) parent was prevented from requesting the due process hearing due to the specific misrepresentations by the school district that it had resolved the problem forming the basis of the due process hearing request, and (b) school district withheld required information from the parent.

It is important that the date be included on the complaint. This date is important because the hearing officer must issue his or her decision within forty-five days of the complaint being received. Additionally, the resolution meeting must be offered with fifteen days on the complaint being received. Textbox 7.2 depicts required due process hearing timelines included in the IDEA or implementing regulations.

Textbox 7.2. Due Process Timelines (IDEA Regulations, 34 C.F.R § 300.508 et seq.)

- 5 calendar days—A hearing officer or ALJ may grant permission to amend a complaint no later than 5 days before the hearing begins.
- 5 calendar days—Within 5 days of the receiving the notice of insufficiency, the hearing officer or ALJ must decide if the due process complaint meets the requirements of the IDEA.
- 5 business days—At least 5 business days prior to the hearing, each party must disclose to all other parties all evaluation, recommendations that the party intends to use in the hearing.
- 10 school days—Within 10 school days, the hearing officer or ALJ must issue a decision in an expedited hearing.
- 10 calendar days—A party must file a response to a due process complaint.
- 15 calendar days—Within 15 days of the date of the hearing notice and before the start of the hearing, the school district must convene a resolution meeting.
- 20 school days—An expedited hearing must have been conducted within 20 days of the date the complaint was filed.
- 30 calendar days—If the resolution meeting has not been successful in producing an agreement, with 30 days of the receipt of the complaint, the due process hearing may begin.
- 45 calendar days—No later than 45 days after the expiration of the 30-day resolution period, the hearing officer or ALJ must issue and mail their final ruling.
- 90 calendar days—A party has 90 days from the date of the release of the hearing officer or ALJ ruling to file a civil action.
- 2 years—A parent of school district must request an impartial on their due process complaint within two years of the date the parent or school district knew or should have known of the alleged violation.

Notice of a Due Process Hearing

Most states have specific requirements about the content of the due process hearing complaint. This information is often included in the state's procedural safeguards notice provided to parents. A due process hearing will not proceed until all required information is provided in a written request for a due process hearing. States are required to develop model forms that may be used by parents and school district officials in filing a due process complaint (IDEA Regulations, 34 C.F.R § 300.509[a]).

When either party files a due process complaint that party must forward the request to the state body that coordinates hearings. At the same time the party filing the hearing request must forward a copy of that request to the other party. The following information is required to be in the complaint (IDEA Regulations, 34 C.F.R. § 300.508[b]).

* The name of the child.
* The address of the child.
* The name of the school the child is attending.
* If the child or youth is homeless, available contact information for the child and the name of the school the child is attending.
* A description of the nature of the problem, including facts relating to such problem; and
* A proposed resolution of the problem to the extent known and available to the party filing the complaint.

If the school district has not sent a prior written notice (PWN) to the parent regarding the subject matter contained in the parent's due process complaint, the district must send to the PWN to the parent, within ten days of receiving the due process complaint. The purpose of the PWN is to explain why the school district proposed or refused to take the action the parent raised in the complaint (Lake, 2014). The PWN includes the following information:

* An explanation of why the school district proposed or refused to take the action raised in the parent's due process hearing request;
* A description of other options the IEP Team considered and the reasons why those options were rejected;
* A description of each evaluation procedure, assessment, record, or report the LEA used as the basis for the proposed or refused action; and
* A description of the factors relevant to the LEA's proposal or refusal.

Filing this response to the parent's due process complaint does not prevent the school district from challenging the sufficiency of the complaint. If the school district has already sent PWN to the parent, or if the parent receiving the due process complaint, then a response to the due process complaint must be sent to the other side within ten days of receipt of the request. The response should specifically address the issues raised in the due process complaint.

Sufficiency Challenge

After receiving a complaint, the opposing party may file an objection to the complaint with the due process hearing officer if the party believes the complaint is insufficient, which means that the complaint does not include the required information required by the IDEA regulations at 34 C.F.R. § 300.508(b). This objection, called the Notice of Insufficiency, must be filed within fifteen days. The hearing officer then has five days to determine if the complaint is sufficient. The due process complaint will be considered to be sufficient unless the party receiving it notifies the hearing officer and the other party in writing within fifteen days of receipt that the receiving party believed the complaint did not meet the content requirements listed above. If the hearing officer finds the complaint to be sufficient, the hearing will proceed. If, however, the hearing officer determines the complaint is not sufficient, he or she must immediately notify both parties in writing within five days.

Amended Due Process Hearing Complaint

An insufficient complaint may be amended but only if

- The other party consents in writing to the amendment and is given the opportunity to resolve the issues raised in the due process complaint through a preliminary meeting/resolution session; or
- The hearing officer grants permission for the party to amend the due process hearing complaint.

However, the hearing officer must grant this permission not later than five days before a due process hearing occurs.

Preliminary Meetings/Prehearing Due Process Hearing Conference

Prehearing meetings held prior to the actual due process are important for clarifying timelines, scheduling sessions, discussing location, exchanging witness lists, making pre-hearing motions (if allowed by a state), identifying the issues that will be the explored in the hearing, addressing the hearing officer's preference for the introduction of exhibits, and other matters. Often in preliminary meetings both parties use alternative means of meeting participation, such as videoconferences and conference calls.

The person who coordinates the due process hearing will arrange the hearing date, the length of the hearing, and coordinate support services, such as the court reporter. Sometimes, the person who is appointed the due process hearing officer will perform these preliminary tasks.

Prehearing Subject Matter

The party requesting the due process hearing is not permitted to raise issues at the due process hearing that were not raised in the due process complaint or an amended due process complaint unless the other party agrees otherwise.

Disclosure of Exhibits, Witness List, and Introduction of Evidence

Not less than five business days prior to a due process hearing, each party must disclose all evaluations completed by that date, the witness list (e.g., name, title, occupation), exhibit list (e.g., written documents such as IEPs, reports, and records), and recommendations based on the offering party's evaluations that the party intends to use at the due process hearing. The purpose of this rule is to ensure that parties share the information that will be included in the hearing. Failure to disclose may result in a hearing officer prohibiting the introduction of the information at the hearing.

Stay-Put Rule

While the due process hearing is being held or an appeal in court is occurring, the student must remain in their present educational placement unless the parent and LEA agree otherwise. According to the U.S. Department of Education, the stay-put placement is the setting in which a student's IEP is currently being implemented (Federal Register, 2006). The stay-put rule often arises in due process hearings that involve the unilateral change of student placement because of disciplinary procedures.

Due Process Hearing Basics

The due process hearing for a student eligible for special education or thought to be an eligible must be conducted and held in the LEA or SEA at a place and time reasonably convenient to the parent and child involved. The hearing must be closed to the public unless the parent requests an open hearing. In an open hearing, the decision issued in the case, and only the decision, will be available to the public. In a closed hearing, the decision will be treated as a record of the child and may not be available to the public. Textbox 7.3 depicts the parties due process hearing rights.

Textbox 7.3.   Due Process Rights (IDEA Regulations, 34 C.F.R § 300.512 et seq.)

Either party has the right to:

- Be accompanied and advised by counsel and by individuals with special knowledge or training with respect to the problems of children with disabilities.
- Present evidence and confront, compel the attendance of witnesses.
- Prohibit the introduction of any evidence at the hearing that has not been disclosed to that party at least five business days before the hearing.

- Obtain a written, or, at the option of the parents, electronic, verbatim record of the hearing.
- Obtain a written, or, at the option of the parents, electronic findings of fact and decisions.

Parents have the right to:

- Have the child who is subject of the hearing present.
- Open the hearing to the public.
- Have the record of the hearing and the findings of facts and decisions provided at no cost to the parents.

The Conduct of the Due Process Hearing

A due process hearing is conducting in a way that is very similar to a state or federal court case. The hearing officer is much like a judge, usually positioned at the front and center of the room where the hearing is held. Typically, a court reporter (sometimes called a court stenographer) will be seated close to the hearing officer and takes verbatim notes during the hearing. The school district will be represented by an attorney who will be sometimes at a table to the front of the hearing officer. The parents and their attorney, if they have one, will often be at another table in front of the hearing officer. A student's parents may represent themselves in a hearing instead of using an attorney, which is referred to as pro se representation.

Usually both sides will make opening statements, which will be an explanation of the issues they will address, the law applicable to those issues, and what the evidence is expected to show (Lake, 2014). Both sides will call witnesses, who will give testimony in accordance with questioning by the attorney. The opposing attorney will then have an opportunity to cross-examine the witness. Witnesses will not come into the hearing until they are called to testify. When they do testify, they may be seated close to the hearing officer and court reporter. Exhibits will often be introduced and marked when witnesses testify.

Both sides will usually end by making closing statements. The purpose of the closing arguments is to summarize the case and to explain how the side presenting the statement proved their arguments regarding the dispute. The attorneys for each side often also submit written closing arguments. Textbox 7.4 depicts an example of how a due process hearing may be conducted.

The Burden of Proof in a Due Process Hearing

Neither the IDEA nor regulations address the burden of proof in due process hearings. In 2005, however, the U.S. Supreme Court ruled on this issue in *Schaffer v. Weast* (2005). According to Conroy and her colleagues (Conroy et al., 2008), the legal concept of burden of proof consists of two related concepts, the burden of production and the burden of persuasion. The party with the burden

---

Textbox 7.4. Example of the Flow of a Due Process Hearing

Starting the hearing

- Hearing officer greeting and name of the case.
- Statement of legal authority for the hearing.
- Explanation of the purpose of the hearing.
- Explanation of the hearing officer's role.
- Introduction of persons present at the hearing.
- Inform parents of the due process rights.
- Instructions on decorum at the hearing.

Conduct of the hearing

- Decisions made during prehearing activities and other preliminary matters.
- Opening statements by both sides.
- The school district presents their case, questioning of witnesses, introduction of documents into evidence.
  - Parents may cross-examine school district witnesses.
  - School district may reexamine their witnesses.
- The parents present their case, questioning of witnesses, introduction of documents into evidence.
  - School district may cross-examine parent's witnesses.
  - Parents may reexamine their witnesses.
- Closing statement from both sides (may be oral, written, or both oral and written).

Closing the hearing

- The hearing officer or ALJ explains what will happen next.
- The hearing officer or ALJ explains the appeal process.
- The hearing officer or ALJ thanks the participants and ends the hearing.

---

of production must produce sufficient evidence at the beginning of the action to be allowed to proceed. The burden of persuasion means that after both sides have presented their case, the party with the burden of persuasion must have convinced the trier of fact, in this case the hearing officer or ALJ, that they have the facts to prevail. Thus, the party with the burden of persuasion must convince the hearing officer or ALJ of their position. If they have not made their case, or even if the facts presented by both parties are closely balanced, the party with the burden of persuasion will lose. Justice Sandra Day O'Connor writing for the majority recognized that the term "burden of persuasion" is one of the slipperiest of legal terms, so she used the term "burden of proof" instead of burden of persuasion her ruling. In her opinion, Justice O'Connor wrote "the burden of proof in an administrative hearing challenging an IEP is properly placed on the party seeking relief" (*Schaffer v. Weast*, 2005, p. 537). Thus, when parents challenge a school district's special education program, the parents will bear the burden of proof.

Hearing Officers' Ruling

The ruling of the hearing officer must include findings of fact, discussion, and conclusions of law. Although a due process hearing is a formal presentation of the facts, technical rules of evidence may or may not be followed depending on the state in which the hearing is held. The hearing officer's decision must be based upon the substantial evidence presented at the hearing. A written, or at the option of the parent, electronic verbatim record of the hearing will be provided to the parent at no cost to the parent.

In FAPE cases, the written, summative decision made by a hearing officer must be made on substantive grounds, based upon a determination of whether a student received a FAPE. As we previously discussed (and was addressed in the *Rowley* and *Endrew F.* Supreme Court decisions), in disputes regarding procedural violations, the decision may find a student did not receive a FAPE only if the procedural inadequacies impeded the child's right to a free appropriate public education. Other procedural violations may include if the school district significantly impeded the parent's opportunity to participate in the decision-making process regarding the provision of a FAPE to the parent's child, or caused a deprivation of educational benefits. A hearing officer may order a school district to comply with procedural requirements even if the hearing officer determines the child received a FAPE.

Following the hearing, the hearing officer or ALJ has forty-five days to issue his or her ruling and mail the ruling to the parties. The SEA must remove personally identifiable information from the ruling and transmit the ruling to the state advisory panel and make the findings and decision available to the public (IDEA Regulations, 34 C.F.R. §300.513[d]).

Civil Action

Either the parent or LEA who disagrees with the findings and decision of the hearing officer has the right to file an appeal in state or federal court. According to the IDEA regulations, "Any party aggrieved by the findings and the decision . . . has the right to bring a civil action" (IDEA Regulations, 34 C.F.R. §300.516[a]). In a tier-one state, the appeal can be made directly to state or federal court. In a tier-two state, the appeal is made first to the SEA. Appealing a due process hearing decision will be addressed in chapter 14.

Conclusion

This chapter provided an overview of the basic components of a resolution meeting and a due process hearing. As was noted above, subsequent chapters and the appendixes go into greater detail on the specific components covered in this chapter. The basics of a due process hearing, the timeline, and the resulting actions are important components of the process used to ensure students with disabilities receive a free and appropriate public education.

References

Berney, D. J., & Gilsbach, T. (2017). Substantive vs. procedural violations under the IDEA. http://www.berneylaw.com/2017/11/12/substantive -vs-procedural-violations-idea/

Board of Education v. Rowley (1982). 458 U.S. 176 (1982).

Center for Appropriate Dispute Resolution in Special Education (CADRE; 2014). IDEA special education resolution meetings, Available at https://www.cadreworks.org/sites/default/files/resources/Resolution%20Meet ing%20Parent%20Guide%202014_0.pdf.

Conroy, T., Yell, M. L., & Katsiyannis, A. (2008). *Schaffer v. Weast*: The Supreme Court on the burden of persuasion when challenging IEPs. *Remedial and Special Education, 29*(2), 108–117. doi: 10.1177/0741932508317273.

Endrew F. v. Douglas County School District (2017). 137 S.Ct. 988 (2017).

Federal Register, Vol. 71, No. 156, 46,700 to 46,710 et seq., 2006.

IIDEA, 20 U.S.C. § 1401 et seq. 2004

IDEA Regulations, 34 C.F.R. § 300.01 et seq.

Katsiyannis, A., & Klare, K. (1991). State practices in due process hearings: Considerations for better practice: *Remedial and Special Education, 12,* 54–58, doi:10.1177/074193259101200210.

Lake, S. E. (2019). *What Do I Do When . . . The Answer Book on Special Education Practices and Procedures* (2nd ed.) LRP Publications.

Schaffer v. Weast, 546 U.S. 49 (2005).

CHAPTER 8

What to Expect in a Due Process Hearing

Advance Organizers

* What to expect before a hearing.
* What to expect at the actual hearing.
* What to expect as a part of the presentation of witnesses.
* What to expect after the hearing.
* What to expect if there is an appeal.

As we have stated multiple times throughout this book, we strongly encourage both sides to seek an amicable solution to the issue instead of litigating the issue(s) through a due process hearing. The reality of the situation is that sometimes there is such a difference between viewpoints that the only way to resolve the issue is through litigation. Many of us have seen courtroom dramas on television or in the movies, and while there are some similarities there are also big differences between the media's portrayals of litigation and what occurs in a due process hearing. This section will provide a rough overview of what to expect at a due process hearing. Your state may have somewhat different procedures or steps, but the main intent is basically the same. Understanding the process should help with the seriousness of preparation, both of documents that will be used as exhibits but also for just the psychological preparation of what to expect both before, during, and after the hearing.

The process starts with a dispute about the identification, evaluation, placement, or provision of FAPE of a student with disability, a student who may have a disability, or one that is thought to have a disability. The due process hearing is where both sides will get a chance to present their information to the hearing officer or administrative law judge and get a ruling on the issue.

Before the Hearing

Once a due process hearing is requested, a lot of work and maneuvering occurs prior to the actual sitting down in the room with the hearing officer. The IDEA is very specific that at least five days before the hearing the parents and the school district are to exchange copies of a list of all potential witnesses and all potential exhibits. If you do not disclose a witness or an exhibit, the hearing officer may not allow it to be a part of the hearing. There are to be no surprises. Additionally, this may help with settlement negotiations. We are strongly in favor of settlements as both parties have a say in what the final outcome will be, as opposed to having the hearing officer solely be the one dictating the outcome. Settlements may be reached at any time prior to the testimony, and may also occur after the hearing has begun. Be prepared to settle because you do not know how the hearing officer will rule.

One thing before we get into the specifics of the steps and procedures of a due process hearing is to highlight the big difference between litigation as portrayed in the media and the reality. It is exceedingly rare, if it ever happens, for a surprise document to be presented that will dramatically change everything. No one is going to stand up and say, "We have a new IEP that the district has not seen that is clearly defective because the student with a learning disability was not receiving ANY of the special education services that were to be provided. No one has noticed this before, and we need an immediate ruling that the school district is at fault, and the parents are to be immediately awarded many thousands of dollars." Both sides have to provide ALL documents that are to be used in the hearing at least five days ahead of the hearing, and they would typically have someone review all the documents once received to see what is covered. Do not expect a lot of drama.

Another difference is there is no jury. It is just the hearing officer or administrative law judge. There is no bailiff who brings in and swears in the witnesses. Depending on the state, the hearing officer or administrative law judge may or may not be wearing a judicial robe. Hearing officers typically do not wear robes. It is like a courtroom trial in that it is formal, with both the parents and the district having the ability to call witnesses, cross-examine witnesses, make legal arguments, and present the evidence they think is necessary to help the hearing officer make a ruling. More similarities are discussed below.

Location

Due process hearings can occur in one of two places, depending on the rules of your state. Many hearings occur in a conference room at the administration building of the school district. The hearing should be conducted in a fairly distraction-free room away from noise and crowds. The other location, depending on your state, may be for the hearing to occur in a state central administrative law building where both parties will travel to and present this evidence and testimony to an administrative law judge.

The room should be quiet. There should be tables set up for both parties to sit at comfortably, with the hearing officer in the front along with a court reporter.

The Actual Hearing

All hearings start with an introduction by the hearing officer. They will state the reason for the hearing, explain the process, and delineate the specific events that are to occur that day. The hearing officer may discuss the times for breaks, any stipulations, may remind all present that only one person at a time can speak as a court reporter is present, and general decorum at the hearing. An example of a hearing officer's opening statement is included in appendix D.

Stipulations

Often before there is an opening statement there is a chance to list everything that both parties agree on. This may reduce the need for testimony by others and may help streamline the hearing. The easy ones to stipulate to are that a student is a resident of the district, a student's birthdate, the disability label, the name of the school that a student attends, the date a student was found eligible for special education. If the hearing is related to discipline and there was a specific incident that triggered the manifestation determination review, both parties may stipulate that an incident occurred on a specific date. The reason for stipulations is that it reduces the time necessary for the hearing, allowing the hearing officer the chance to focus solely on the issue(s) for the hearing.

Opening Statements

After the hearing officer makes their introductory remarks, both parties will have an opportunity to make an opening statement. Even though opening statements are not evidence and a decision may not be based on the opening statements, they should still contain facts that help a hearing officer understand the different positions. For the party that filed the complaint, typically the parents, they should state why they asked for the hearing, the problems with what the school district has proposed or done, and why they believe their recommendations are necessary and what they feel the outcome of the case should be. The opening statement should be clear, jargon-free, and be framed so that a hearing officer will clearly understand what is being addressed and what remedy is sought.

The other party will then provide an opening statement in response to the other party's opening statement. They will explain why their proposal is appropriate, what they have done in the past, and state very specifically the manner in which they want the hearing officer to rule. In part, the opening statement of the respondents is a rebuttal to what was stated by the other side's opening statement. Again, it should be clear, jargon free, and provide the hearing officer with an understanding of what the ruling should be.

Presentation of Witnesses

After the opening statement comes the presentation of witnesses. Typically, the party that requested the hearing (again, typically the parents) calls their witnesses. Witnesses testify one at a time and are asked to swear or affirm that the testimony they will provide is the truth. Witnesses are to respond to the direct questions that are asked of them, and they may be asked to comment about documents or exhibits that are placed in front of them. It is very important that the witness understand the specifics of the questions that are asked of them, and may ask to have questions repeated if any clarification is needed. It is also important that witnesses do not speak when there is an objection. Let both parties state their reasons for the objection and have the hearing officer make a ruling before either answering the question or making a statement.

Hearings typically have a court reporter present who is making a transcript of the session for both parties to later review. These transcripts are also important in any appeal of the hearing. It is very important to work with the court reporter to make sure the transcript clearly reflects what was said during the hearing. Therefore, only one person at a time can talk, and it is very important to speak clearly and enunciate every word. If asked by the court reporter to repeat a phrase or word, work closely with them to assist the reporter to do their job to ensure the transcript reflects as accurately as possible what was said in the hearing.

After a witness has been called for direct testimony, the other side will have an opportunity for cross-examination. All witnesses should cooperate and work to answer all questions thoroughly. After cross-examination the first party who asked the initial questions can ask more questions based on statements made during cross-examination—this is called redirect. It is typically shorter than the first set of questions as it based on the questions and statements from cross-examinations. The second attorney will then get another chance to ask questions after the redirect. These questions are based on the redirect of the first attorney. Finally, the hearing officer may have a few questions for clarification. This typically ends a witnesses' testimony.

When the witness is finished testifying, another witness will be called and the process as described above will repeat itself. This is process through which the hearing officer learns the facts of the case to assist them in ruling. As witnesses testify it is also the manner by which exhibits are entered into the record and discussed. The witness list exchanged prior to the hearing is a list of all potential witnesses. If it becomes clear that a witnesses' testimony is not needed as someone has already covered that content, the content is irrelevant, or the hearing officer has ruled that is a topic area that will not be addressed, the witness will not need to testify. The important part is the witnesses are describing the facts of the case and the hearing officer needs to hear these facts in order to rule. Both parties have a chance to cross-examine the witnesses. It may seem like it takes a long time, but the point is to ensure the testimony is accurate and the facts of the case are presented.

When witnesses testify, they can only have the documents that are to be exhibits in front of them. They cannot have any notes or outlines. Any notes or outlines that are inadvertently brought to the witness area can be shared with opposing council and their parties to review. Do not assume that this will not happen.

Sequestration

So that witnesses may not be influenced by the testimony of other witnesses, sometimes attorneys request that the witnesses be sequestered, or prevented from hearing the others testimony, until they are called for direct testimony themselves. After a witness has completed their testimony, they may be able to sit and watch, but the point of sequestration is to prevent bias or other claims based on testimony of others.

Witness Offer

Not all witnesses requested to testify will be able to testify. The opposing council may ask for an offer of proof as to why this witness' testimony is necessary and second whether the testimony will be valid. If the witness is just going to repeat conversations others have already stated, or the witness is going to provide opinions without having either seen the child in action in school or reviewed the documents, the witness may be prevented from testifying. All witnesses have to be able to provide information to the hearing officer that will assist in understanding the issue, but also need to be able to clarify why it is important for this hearing. Finally, the witness may have good information but if it does to relate to the specifics of this case, then their testimony may not be necessary.

Expert Testimony

All of us may be an expert in some aspect of our life. However, in order for the testimony of the expert brought into testify, the credentials and experience of the expert need to be discussed and clarified as to what they will address as a part of the hearing. The individual may be a well-published special education expert with knowledge of the student and his or her special education program or placement. Attorneys will be certain that there is a clear link between the specific expertise the witness has and the issue(s) that are a part of the hearing. Just generally saying things are bad does little to assist the hearing officer in making a ruling.

Exhibits

As noted above, all of the exhibits need to be declared prior to the hearing. Just because an exhibit was declared prior to the hearing does not mean the exhibit will be entered into the record and reviewed by the hearing officer. All exhibits need to be formally entered and accepted by the hearing officer. It is good practice to make a list of all the exhibits, and when they are discussed or referred to make an offer to have them entered into the record. If a witness is going to testify to the contents of the exhibit it is important for the hearing officer to have the opportunity to see the exhibit. Just like all witnesses on the witness list may not testify, all exhibits may not be entered into the record as it becomes clear either the exhibit does not speak to the issues at hand, the exhibit is redundant, not clear, not necessary, or does not help the hearing officer in understanding the issues.

When entering exhibits, it is important to ensure they are labeled and marked so that when they are referred to in testimony they can be found later.

For example, if the exhibit is an exhibit that is to be entered by the parent, it may be labeled as parent exhibit 1, or P-1. Hence forth, all discussion to P-1 would address this exhibit. The pages of the exhibit would also be marked. So, if the witness is addressing an item on page 24 of P-1, it would be addressed in the record as P-1 page 24. This makes it easier for all to read and find later. Finally, do not highlight or mark up the exhibits that will be entered into the record. It is more than okay to mark up, highlight, attach sticky notes to your own exhibits to make it easier to find items or form questions. Additionally exhibits may be introduced by the plaintiffs or the respondent. Some exhibits are entered as evidence by both plaintiff and respondents.

Expedited Hearings

The IDEA allows for expedited hearings if the issue relates to the discipline of a student who is eligible or thought to be eligible. This means all the timelines discussed in your state's procedural safeguards notice are significantly shortened. You still have to provide a witness list ahead of time, an exhibit list ahead of time, but since the timelines are shorter it may be three days ahead of the hearing instead of five. Check with your state. Missing the timelines should not be a reason to not be able to call witnesses or enter exhibits, but if one does not follow the rules of the state, missing timelines could prevent both witnesses and exhibits.

Closing Statement

After all the witnesses have been called to testify, and after there has been discussion about which exhibits will be entered, both parties will have the opportunity to present closing statements. Like the opening statement, the hearing officer's decision is not based on the closing argument, and a closing argument IS NOT the time to present new evidence or testimony. A closing argument will summarize the information that has been presented through testimony and the exhibits that were entered into the record. It will often end with a statement about what they believe the ruling from the hearing officer should be in the matter. The party that requested the due process hearing often gives their closing statement last (like the other summarizing the issue) that have been presented and what they think the ruling should be.

Written Closing Statements

Sometimes the hearing officer may request a written closing statement instead of an oral closing statement at the end of the hearing. Sometimes both an oral and written statement will be given. A written closing statement, like the oral ones should summarize the presentation of facts and exhibits entered, ending with the recommendation for the ruling by the hearing officer. A very specific timeline will be provided by the hearing officer about when the written closing arguments need to be submitted.

Hearing Officer Ruling

Very few hearing officer rulings are issued that day at the end of the hearing. This is what makes hearings, in part, seem like they take a long time. There is so much work done behind the scenes to get ready for a hearing, and during the hearing there may be days spent in intense discussion, presentation of witnesses and evidence, and then the hearing officer will end the hearing and issue his or her ruling, which make take a few weeks to be written and provided to both parties. Expedited hearings have much shorter timelines. The receipt of the actual decision may be anti-climactic in that it may have been weeks since the hearing was over. A sample hearing officer's decision is included in appendix B.

Appeal

After the decision is released, one may make an appeal to the appropriate body. A few states have a second tier of hearing officers (e.g., South Carolina) who would then review and rule on the appeal. There is a thirty-day deadline for the second-tier hearing office to issue their ruling. The appeal is another reason why it is so very important to ensure the information from witnesses and exhibits is included in the official record. The reason for the first tier or hearing officer is to get all the information that is important related to the issue and have someone who is knowledgeable about special education and the law make a ruling before it moves up the systems of appeals where courts may not understand the difference between various aspects of special education programming that are at issue. In most states the appeal goes directly to state or federal court. Appeal to a court may take considerably longer than the original due process hearing.

Implementing the Decision

Once a ruling is final, it must be implemented as soon as possible. Typically state administrative agencies have compliance enforcement to ensure the ruling is being implemented. The whole process from filing for a due process hearing to the final ruling may take longer than one wants, but as noted above it is a very legalistic procedure with important steps along the way to ensure full participation by both parties.

Conclusion

In this chapter we have addressed what administrators, educators, and parents may expect at a due process hearing. A due process hearing is a complex and legalistic dispute resolution. Moreover, states may have slightly different ways on conducting hearings. Although we advise school districts to settle disputes using other means, there are times when a due process hearing is unavoidable. When this occurs, the best advice for parents and school district personnel is to understand how the hearing will proceed and to be prepared.

CHAPTER 9

Expert Testimony

Advance Organizers

* What are ethical considerations in expert witness testimony?
* What are the federal regulations related to expert testimony?
* What is an expert witness?
* What has the Supreme Court ruled about expert witnesses in special education matters?
* What are expert witness fees?
* What is the difference between an expert witness and a lay witness?
* What are tips for testifying as an expert witness?

A due process hearing is a forum in which the parents and school district have fair opportunity to present their facts, call witness, and submit evidence. Sometimes, to facilitate their case, either of the parties will bring in experts who have specific knowledge about the expected program and placement for the student. These experts may have previously worked with other students with similar disabilities, or they may have written or presented on topics being addressed during the hearing.

The role of the expert witness is to assist either party to convince the hearing officer of their understanding the complexities of the case and to offer their opinion about what an appropriate program for the student would look like. There are very specific rules about who can be an expert witness, the role they play, and the topics about which they may testify.

In some states an expert witness has to be accepted by the hearing officer as an expert in order to provide testimony. This means that the attorney presenting the expert must convince the hearing officer that the expert is qualified through training, knowledge, and experience to offer his or her expert opinion on the matter at hand. If the hearing officer accepts the exert witness, the attorney uses direct examination to elicit the expert's opinion. Of course, these opinions must be supported by the facts of the case. The expert will also be cross-examined by the opposing attorney to challenge the opinion of the expert, often by disputing the expert's qualifications or insufficient understanding of the evidence in the case.

As we have noted in other sections of this book, hearing officers who may hear multiple special education cases throughout the year may not always know about the specifics of a disability, nor may they understand the requirements for instruction and safety related to all the different disabilities. This is especially true for administrative law judges who may be hearing a case on insurance one day and a special education case the next day. Because of the breadth and depth of the requirements related to the education of students with disabilities it is not uncommon to rely on the use of expert witnesses or expert testimony as a part of the presentation of a due process hearing case. The clear and evenhanded explanations of all the necessary considerations involved in the provision of a free appropriate public education (FAPE) for students eligible for special education and related services can be of great assistance to all concerned in a special education due process hearing. It may appear that the side with the most proficient and authoritative testimony prevails. In this chapter, we address ethical considerations for expert witness testimony, the federal guidelines related to expert witnesses, relevant case, and conclude with specific recommendations related to the practical use of experts in a special education due process hearing.

Ethical Considerations

Most expert witnesses are only brought in to discuss a very narrow range of topics. They may not have the opportunity to see the "big picture." Given this, we need to make sure expert witnesses talk and address facts of which they are clear and have observed. Remember, a due process hearing is a presentation of facts for a hearing officer to decide the case.

Additionally, in not seeing the big picture, oftentimes expert witnesses are hired by attorneys to represent a specific legal opinion—one that need buttressing as a part of the presentation of their case. We realize this is easier said than done, however, an expert witness should only present and speak on topics of which they are trained and make conclusions of the program for a student where they have specific knowledge. Expert witnesses need to keep in perspective the fact that this dispute is about a child, and we need experts who represent the facts professionally, and are not trying to sell or expect to provide a service after the testimony. Therefore, we hope that experts do not talk about subjects for which they do not have training or work just because there a promise of a paycheck for the side that is asking you to present. These are questions that needs to be addressed for each individual case and sometimes multiple times within a case. For example, the expert may have great knowledge of the reading programs that would be effective for a child, but when asked about the students' progress on their speech and language goals has no specific training or background in this area. The expert should make sure the attorney with whom they are working understands what the expert can address, the knowledge they possess, and the specific components of a student's program that can be covered by their testimony.

These ethical questions should be addressed prior to testimony is provided. When an individual testifies, they will also be subject to cross-examination and as a result of that any credibility the expert has on one topic may be significantly reduced when they speak about topics of which they do not have training or background and this is discovered. All of their testimony will now come into question. The expert's testimony on the subject matter for which they are trained may have really helped both sides and the hearing officer to understand the issue. However, if their testimony is not in an area in which they have been trained, cross examination may reduce their value as a witness, waste time in the hearing, and may not influence the deliberations of the hearing officer. It also may make it unlikely that that expert will be called on to testify in another due process hearing because of the lack of creditability and the damage it has done to the case.

Expert Testimony and the Law

How does the federal law define experts for the sake of a hearing such as a due process hearing? According to the Federal Rules of Evidence, Rule 702:

> A witness who is qualified as an expert by knowledge, skill, experience, training, or education may testify in the form of an opinion or otherwise if:
>
> a. the expert's scientific, technical, or other specialized knowledge will help the trier of fact to understand the evidence or to determine a fact in issue;
> b. the testimony is based on sufficient facts or data;
> c. the testimony is the product of reliable principles and methods; and
> d. the expert has reliably applied the principles and methods to the facts of the case.

In a special education due process hearing (or any specialized hearing, for that matter), it is impossible for the hearing officer or administrative law judge to know about all the intricacies of the educational needs of the various disabilities served in special education.

What Is an Expert Witness?

An expert witness is someone who is viewed as a person qualified by knowledge, skill, experience, training, or education. There is not a strict test for whether someone is an expert or not and having three years' experience in an area does not make someone inferior to someone with four or more years of experience. It depends on the specific need(s) that are being addressed by the witness testimony. As due process hearings are the initial fact-finding process in a special education dispute, this is typically where an expert will testify, and therefore the hearing officer is the determiner of:

* Whether the expert is credible.
* The weight that should be provided to the expert's testimony.
* Whether one expert's opinion should be given more credence than another expert.
* Whether an expert is necessary for testimony.
* Whether the testimony by the expert is helpful.

Because the hearing officer or administrative law judge (ALJ) will determine the credibility of an expert witness, it is important that the attorney who has requested the specific expert ensure that the credentials are explained and clarified for the hearing. This is true both in states that require the hearing officer accepts the expert witness and allows them to testify and in states in which there are no such requirements.

The expert witness should also be prepared for providing direct testimony and being cross-examined by the opposing side's attorney in a due process hearing, and not just come prepared to lecture on his or her relevant knowledge about a particular subject matter. Expert witness, like lay witnesses, should be properly prepared by an attorney or consultant to testify in a due process hearing. Even though experts may be well versed in their information, they may not understand the specifics of a due process hearing. Most notably though the attorney is questioning them, the expert is presenting to the hearing officer or ALJ. The hearing officer or ALJ is the finder of facts, not the attorneys.

The following questions will help in determining whether the expert witness testimony is helpful. They are specific to special education due process hearings, but can be easily adapted for other administrative law hearings. The purpose of the following questions is not to denigrate an expert witness, but to ensure they are providing information that will be of assistance to the hearing officer in writing of their decision.

- Can the expert's testimony statements be tested? For example, if they say that a student has a certain disability and requires a specific form of education or a certain methodology, can this be tested?
- Is the expert open to educational techniques? Or is the expert only addressing a certain commercial reading program, or a specific commercial behavior program?
- Are the statements and theories stated by the expert ones that have been discussed and vetted as a part of a peer review process? Or are they novel theories that have not been tried or validated for the purpose that they are being discussed?
- Are the statement and theories as testified by the expert witness ones that are generally accepted by the profession? Or are they one's counter to what the professional establishment recommends for the services for a student with this type of disability?
- Are there problems with the recommendations made by the expert? Has this technique worked with other students with similar disabilities and needs and was that effective? Or is this technique or recommendation one that only worked once but has not worked since?
- Has the expert as a part of their testimony adequately accounted for obvious alternative explanations? When they state the child is frustrated, do they really know that the child is frustrated or are they speculating? When they say a child did this out of spite, do they know or are they speculating?

- Is the testimony provided by the expert witness directly related as an outgrowth of what they have researched or with their previous experiences, or are they testifying in an area that is not related or only tangentially related to their previous work? Did they develop their thoughts on this topic solely for the purpose of the testimony they are providing, or have they written or worked in this area before?
- For some students with extremely rare disabilities there may not be an individual with an expertise who has worked with this type of disability or previously addressed needs such as the student has. Do they make it clear that as an expert that they have not worked with students like this, or are they making definitive statements about the programming and educational expectations of the student? If they are making recommendations about the educational programming for the student, do they logically come from previous work and examples?
- Can the expert really provide information in the area where we require assistance? Could any person, or is the disability and needs of the student so unique that unless one has worked with the student for many hours there is no way to know the specifics of the needs in order to make valid recommendations.
- Is the expert just as open to cross-examination as they were to direct examination and as a result was the testimony helpful?
- Is the expert reliable? This means can the hearing officer and the side that called them to present rely on their testimony. Are they trustworthy, worthy of being relied upon for their testimony? We are not asking for them to be exactly correct, just whether we can rely upon them for what they said to be accurate.
- When an expert makes a statement that is so very different from what other experts state or one that is very different from what other experts in the field may be saying it calls into question the expert themselves, or the manner in which the expert reached their conclusion. Did the expert faithfully apply the generally accepted methodology used in the field to make this determination, or do they have a novel way of analyzing the information? If so, they need to be very clear about why they used this new method and how it deviates from the previous methods. If they do not make with of these points clear, these are reasons to call into question the reliability of their testimony. Any step that renders the expert testimony unreliable renders the expert's testimony inadmissible. This is true whether the step completely changes a reliable methodology or merely misapplies that methodology.
- All individuals need to be reviewed by the hearing officer to determine if they are credible, not just the expert witness. While the relevant factors for determining reliability will vary from expertise to expertise, we reject the premise that an expert's testimony should be treated more permissively simply because it comes from an expert. An opinion from an expert who is not

a special educator should receive the same degree of scrutiny for reliability as an opinion from an expert who purports to be a special educator. All individuals need to be reviewed for credibility—not just the experts.

- The hearing officer in all cases of proffered expert testimony must find that it is properly grounded, well reasoned, and not speculative before it can be admitted. The expert's testimony must be grounded in an accepted body of learning or experience in the expert's field, and the expert must explain how the conclusion is so grounded.

- Experience alone can make for the necessary qualifications for an expert witness. An expert may be qualified on the basis of experience alone. In certain fields, experience is the predominant, if not sole, basis for a great deal of reliable expert testimony. If the witness is relying solely or primarily on experience, then the witness must explain how that experience leads to the conclusion reached, why that experience is a sufficient basis for the opinion, and how that experience is reliably applied to the facts.

- The more subjective and controversial the expert's inquiry, the more likely the testimony should be excluded as unreliable. The testimony, as noted above, needs to be based on facts and observation, not just speculation.

- The hearing officer is the fact finder. When facts are in dispute, experts sometimes reach different conclusions based on competing versions of the facts. The emphasis in the amendment on "sufficient facts or data" is not intended to authorize a hearing officer to exclude an expert's testimony on the ground that they believe one version of the facts and not the other.

If the expert purports to apply principles and methods to the facts of the case, it is important that this application be conducted reliably. It also might be important in some cases for an expert to educate the hearing officer or ALJ about general principles of special education or specifics regarding the specifics of certain disabilities and the needs a student might have. These can be a part of the due process hearing without even attempting to apply these principles to the specific facts of the case. For example, experts might instruct the hearing officer on the process for extended school year determinations, or the specifics of the determination of least restrictive environment, or on how IEP teams can provide information about specialized transportation services for students with disabilities, without ever knowing about or trying to tie their testimony into the facts of the case. Expert testimony can educate the hearing officer on general principles of special education. For this kind of generalized testimony, it is expected that the expert meets these standards: (a) the expert be qualified; (b) the testimony addresses a subject matter on which the hearing officer can be assisted by an expert; (c) the testimony be reliable; and (d) the testimony "fit" the facts of the case.

Conflicting Experts

In many cases, both the parents and the school district will have expert witnesses to provide testimony in their cases. The parents may have an expert who testifies about an issue stating one thing is absolutely necessary, whereas the district may have an expert who testifies stating something very different is necessary. A hearing officer may determine that both experts are valid and reliable. This does not mean necessarily mean that contradictory expert testimony is unreliable. There can be differing opinions on the same topics. It is the hearing officer or ALJ who ultimately determine which side's expert provided the most convincing testimony.

Special Education Expert Witness and the Supreme Court

The U.S. Supreme Court in *Arlington v. Murphy* (2005) ruled even though parents may prevail in a special education due process hearing, they are not eligible for reimbursement of expert witness fees. In the *Arlington* case, the parents sought fees for services of an educational consultant used during all the legal proceedings related to the IDEA. The Supreme Court ruled the law does not authorize prevailing parents to recover expert fees. The parents had prevailed on their issues in the federal district court and the U.S. Court of Appeals for the Second Circuit affirmed the decision and as the prevailing party, the parents were also sought reimbursement for the $29,000 in fees paid to an educational consultant. There is no dispute this educational consultant assisted the parents throughout the proceedings, however, on an appeal, the U.S. Supreme Court ruled that the parents could not collect expert witness fees. The ruling relied on two factors: First the court noted Congress enacted IDEA and whereas the law provides an award of "reasonable attorneys' fees" for prevailing parties, the text of the law did not specifically authorize the award of additional expert fees, and the law failed to provide the clear notice that is required under the spending clause. Second, the court relied on two cases where witness fees and attorneys' fees were denied because they were not enumerated in the analogous statutes.

Position on Expert Witness Feed of the Council of Parent Attorneys and Advocates

The Council of Parent Attorneys and Advocates (COPAA) recently issued a statement about the inability of parents to recoup expert fees as a part of a prevailing IDEA claim. Textbox 9.1 includes the statement from COPPA. For more information on this from COPAA please see the following link: https://www.copaa.org/page/ExpertWitness.

Textbox 9.1. COPPA Statement on Expert Witnesses

Without the ability to recover their expert witness fees, few parents are able to afford to exercise constitutional, IDEA and 504 rights to challenge denial of Free Appropriate Public Education (FAPE).

This is because parents, who increasingly have the burden of proof after the Supreme Court decision in *Schaffer v. Weast*, must present admissible evidence about educational methodology, complex behavioral supports, medical issues, and other technical subjects. Only qualified expert witnesses can present this technical testimony and such testimony can easily cost many thousands of dollars, money that few parents have.

School districts, by way of contrast, employ and therefore are able to rely on psychologists, therapists, and other education experts on their staffs to serve as expert witnesses. There can be no equal opportunity and access to a public education that is both free and appropriate unless all families of children with disabilities—rich, poor, and those in the vast middle—can obtain an education on the same terms. Without the ability to recover expert costs, the due process playing field ceases to be level or fair.

Parents who bring IDEA cases act as private attorneys general, on whom IDEA's enforcement depends. When these parents successfully prosecute their cases and hearing officers or courts find that school districts have violated the law, then parents should recover their expert witness costs. (Of course, if the school district acted in accord with the law, and the parents lose, they recover no fees.)

COPAA is working hard to pass legislation entitled the IDEA Fairness Restoration Act that would reverse *Arlington Central School District v. Murphy* (2006) in which the Supreme Court decided that parents who win/prevail in their IDEA cases cannot get expert witness fees under the provision in the law that allows parents who win/prevail to get attorneys' fees. Although the legislative history to the IDEA fees provision clearly states that expert fees are covered, the Supreme Court refused to consider that history.

The passage of the IDEA Fairness Restoration Act was Congress' intent in 1986. When Congress passed the Handicapped Children's Protection Act, it recognized that school districts can use therapists, psychologists, and other expert witnesses on their own payroll, or hire outside experts with taxpayer dollars. Over twenty years later, few parents can afford the thousands of dollars needed to pay qualified experts. Almost two-thirds of children with disabilities live in families earning under $50,000 a year. When prevailing parents cannot recover expert costs, the playing field is neither level nor fair, and children are denied a free appropriate public education and other fundamental IDEA rights. Parents are left unable to enforce their children's rights unless they can pay for experts out of their pockets. Congress should allow prevailing parents to recover fees just like plaintiffs in ADA, Title VII, and other civil rights cases.

Expert Witness v. Lay Witness

As we have noted in discussing the role of the expert witness as a part of a due process hearing, it is important to draw a distinction between the different types of witnesses at a hearing. When a teacher or a school psychologist testifies at a due process hearing they are being asked to describe what they did, what they observed, and the results of any testing that were a part of regarding the student. Remember, the due process hearing is a fact-finding mission by the hearing officer and the hearing is largely a presentation of the facts. The difference between a teacher/administrator/school psychologist testifying and an expert witness is that the expert witness will be asked to state the facts as they have observed, but also to speak about their opinions regarding the program and placement for the student. The expert is someone, as noted above, who knows a lot about this specific area of the programming for a student, and therefore can provide the hearing officer with their interpretation of the facts and observations of others in order to assist the hearing officer with an understanding of what the facts mean and how they should be applied. In effect, they are experts (hence the term) and we should allow them the opportunity to use their unique or expert perspective to assist with the decision.

Given their unique status as an expert in the area of the programming for the student, it is important to strongly consider the ethical considerations as noted above. It is also very important to address and reflect on any biases or assumptions they have regarding services for students. This means the expert witness should ensure any program and placement recommendations for the student should reflect the specific needs of the student and not the specific needs of a private school that needs more students in order to stay financially solvent. Additionally, as noted above, the expert witness should ensure the hearing officer understands the expert's background, previous experience with students, previous cases, and any affiliations with private publishers/providers.

Testifying as an Expert Witness

Testifying as an expert witness in a due process hearing is often very different from other roles that the expert might have as a part of their professional responsibilities. For example, an expert who is a university professor is often not challenged as a part of any statement or generalization they make. In a due process hearing the expert witness will be asked to testify, and the attorney for the side that called them will ask them questions to verify that first, they are an expert in this subject matter, but then why and how they came to the conclusions they have related to the programming and placement for the student. When the attorney is done, the other attorney has the chance to ask extensive and detailed questions that may call into question the level of expertise that is brought to the hearing, and then the conclusions and recommendations made as a part of their direct testimony. For some, this is disconcerting, and there are also many who are not used to be asked about contradictory assumptions or recommendations.

Just to remind the reader that an expert witness is not called to testify because of prior involvement in previous activities with the student or with the school district related to this hearing. This is the case unless the parents have been using this individual for assessments over the years and for the district this person has provided consultation services on other special education–related topics. Specifically, an expert testifies because they have special knowledge, skill, experience, training, or education, and have expertise meaningful to either party as it is working to address the issues of the case and provide detail about why it believes it has the correct recommendation for the programming and placement of the student. Additionally, an expert witness testifies voluntarily and not by coercion or the need for a subpoena. A subpoena may be necessary for the individual to leave their other place of employment for a period of time, but not to coerce them to testify.

As noted above, the biggest difference between a principal, teacher, school psychologist, or special education administrator is that they are considered fact witnesses, talking about their role in the provision of services and what they saw, tested, or provided. An expert witness is a person who as a part of their testimony may provide an opinion on the facts and program for the student. Occasionally fact witnesses are queried for their opinion, but that is not why they are asked to testify—it is just an outgrowth of the process and the questions they address as a part of the hearing.

When an individual is called on to testify as an expert witness, the specific qualifications and relevant experience will be highlighted for the hearing officer. Typically, a recent copy of the individual's recent résumé or curriculum vitae will be entered into the record as an exhibit. It is important for the expert witness to have an up-to-date résumé that can readily be shared with both parties as a part of the hearing. This résumé should highlight relevant work experiences, degrees, teaching certifications (if any), publications, presentations, and other relevant work to the field.

An expert would likely meet with the attorney prior to the presentation of the case to first determine if the expert has specific knowledge of the facts and has experience in this matter. There will be extensive questions related to the qualifications of the witness and the experience they bring to the case.

After reviewing the information, if is determined the expert is necessary as a part of the presentation of the case, assuming that one has agreed to serve as an expert and the attorney have determined the testimony is necessary, the expert witness will often review educational records of the student relevant to the case. After the review, there will be meetings to discuss areas of questioning and what cross-examination might look like for this case and these files. There will also be questions about whether there needs to be observations of testing of the student in order to ensure the recommendations they are making are valid and supported by what is occurring with the student and not just based on a review of the records. The attorney may then consult with the expert witness to determine if there are records that are better suited as a part of the hearing, or are there additional records that are needed to help fully understand the implications of the educational program for the student. The expert witness may also have to spend time explaining the fine details of the special education program to the attorney to assist them not only with understanding their case but also understanding the opposing counsel's position and how they might be presenting their facts to the hearing officer. Finally, the positions of the opposing side will also be evaluated.

Second, the expert witness would likely be provided some documents to review and then to discuss with the attorney their thoughts and comments related to the program for the student. The attorney or their associate will likely then go through a series of questions related to the case, first to fully understand the content, but then to pick it apart as part of their preparation for cross-examination. This is also to prepare the expert for the rigors of a due process hearing. Finally, the attorney will meet with the expert witness to ensure the areas of testimony agree with the information the attorney feels is necessary as a part of their presentation of the case. There are times when it becomes clear the expert's testimony would be very different from what the attorney needs as a part of the presentation of their case, and if this occurs the expert obviously cannot honestly and effectively function continue to function in this case.

Third, just because an expert witness knows the information about the specifics related to the programming for the student, has credentials, has worked with students like this previously, does not necessarily make him or her an effective expert witness. An expert is also evaluated on the ability to present as a witness and to handle direct and often very difficult questions from attorneys. It can be a very stressful situation for even the most prepared individuals. Some may not have the necessary skill set to be able to articulate their thoughts under this pressure, and therefore would not necessarily be a good candidate for the role of an expert witness.

The first set of questions that are typically addressed to an expert witness relate to establishing the witness as an expert. Each case is different and the needs of the student and the issues for the hearing are all unique. Therefore, there is not one set of qualifications or standards that an expert is expected to hold or to have achieved. An individual who is an expert for one due process hearing may not be an expert for another based on the issues and their specific credential and experience. Typical questions that work to prove the individual is an expert would often relate to the evidence that is in place on the résumé.

Questions would likely be:

* Please state your name and spell your last name for the record.
* Please state your current job title and where you are employed.
* Please describe your educational background. Please list all of the degrees you have earned.
* Please describe any state certifications you may hold.
* Please describe additional trainings that you have related to this area.
* Please describe your experiences related to this area.
* Please describe your presentations (if any) to this area.
* Please describe your publications (if any) to this area.
* Please describe your work experiences related to this area.

- Please describe your expert witness experiences related to this area.
- Please describe any memberships in organizations related to this area.
- What other relevant information do you think the hearing officer needs to know about you as it relates to this area?

At the due process hearing, the expert witness will be asked by the attorney that has sought their expertise, to clarify their expertise with the questions that are listed above. After that, the expert will then testify related to their specific knowledge of the special education programming for the student. For example, the testimony may consist of the expert witness responding to questions providing facts or opinion or both. For example, if the expert is asked to describe the characteristics of specific disabilities, or the benefits of different forms of reading instruction, or methods or strategies for improving the behavior of a student who may frequently engage in inappropriate behavior, these are questions that request factual information. On the other hand, the expert witness might be asked if, in their opinion, a student was provided a certain reading program what might be the expected progress, or how a certain form of instruction for a student with autism might be better than another form. In addition to the expert witnesses' main role in providing testimony, expert witnesses frequently consult with attorneys as to various facts and background of a specific case and whether the facts assist with the development of their case and whether responding to these facts are part of the expert witness's area of expertise.

Depending on the issues for the hearing, the length of the testimony, and the expertise of the expert witness, an expert witness may be asked to sit in and observe the due process hearing to gain a better understanding of the case and its respective issues and to provide ongoing assistance to the attorneys. Additionally, in a given case, there may be more than one expert witness involved. For example, in a due process hearing involving a student with autism who is sixteen years old and who also engages in significant behavior problems on the bus and in the lunchroom, there may be three or more expert witnesses involved. There may be an expert witness who can address issues related to transition programming for students with autism. There may be another expert witness who can assist with issues related to transportation issues for students with autism. While there may still be a third expert witness who can address behavior problems in school and may speak to any sensory issues the student has while they are in the lunchroom. This is just the expert witnesses for one side's presentation of their case. The opposing side may have an equal number of expert witnesses who will be presenting as a part of their case. This is a lot of information for a hearing officer to decide about the expert's testimony and the facts as they are presented.

Unlike a fact witness, teachers, administrators, and school psychologists who are hired as a part the school district, and who will be testifying as a part of their job responsibilities, an expert is entitled to compensation for participation in the case.

Scheduling Issues

Scheduling a special education due process hearing is very difficult, and then scheduling of the dates of a specific testimony for a witness, fact, or expert is all but impossible. There are discussions between the hearing officer and the attorneys ahead of the testimony, possible settlement negotiations, other witnesses that may go ahead of the expert witness and problems in determining the effect of their testimony on the progress of the case, and the problems in identifying the length of their testimony. There are also off-the-record discussions, weather, or health issues that alter the trajectory of a due process hearing. All these factors may lead to difficulty in actual scheduling the specifics of the date and time for the testimony of an expert witness. During the hearing, there may be some shifting of the precise time during which the expert witness will testify. It is also fairly common to set dates for a hearing and to have those dates rescheduled because of conflicts.

Mutually Agreed Upon Experts

An important, but rare, component is the expert who is mutually agreed upon to issue a report on a part of the programming for the student. This may be an independent educational evaluation or an observation and consultation by the expert witness. In that case, the expert does not work with one side, and therefore will likely not be prepared for specifics of the testimony the attorney will be asking for. The same set of questions about the qualifications listed above would likely be asked, but there may also be statements indicated the individual who testifying as a joint witness. In either case, the expert witness would often be expected to generate a report ahead of time so that the attorneys can review the material and fully understand what the expert witness is likely to say under questioning in front of the hearing officer.

Conclusion

This chapter covers the points related to expert witness testimony in a due process hearing. Both sides may call an expert to assist the hearing officer in understanding the facts about the program and placement for the eligible student. The important part is to use an expert who truly understands special education and can articulately explain to the others their thoughts and ideas. As we as noted in the chapter, there are demands to assist parent counsels in obtaining reimbursement for their use of experts, but that may take time to occur.

References

Arlington Central School Dist. Bd. of Ed. v. Murphy, 548 U.S. 291 (2006)

Council of Parent Attorneys and Advocates (COPAA), (N.D.). Reinstate prevailing parents' right to expect prevailing witness fees. Available from https://www.copaa.org/page/ExpertWitness.

Federal Rules of Evidence. Available from the Cornell Legal Institute at https://www.law.cornell.edu/rules/fre

CHAPTER 10

Witness Preparation for a Due Process Hearing

Advance Organizers

* What are the steps to preparing a witness for a due process hearing?
* What is direct examination and cross-examination?
* What is the process of testifying?
* What are strategies for effective testimony?

The IDEA allows parents and school district personnel to present evidence and confront, cross-examine, and compel the attendance of witnesses during a due process hearing (IDEA, 34 C.F.R. § 300.512[a][2]). Attorneys will often plan a due process hearing around a central theme; for example, a school district failed to provide a free appropriate public education (FAPE) to a student. To structure their case around this theme, attorneys will (a) examine their witnesses; introduce evidence, which usually occurs during testimony; and (c) cross-examine the opposing side's witnesses. Thus, a majority of the time in a hearing will be witnesses being directly examined and cross-examined.

Our purpose in this chapter is to cover the basics of what is expected of witnesses, examine the process of testifying, and provide strategies that will help alleviate the anxiety inherent in providing testimony. Effective witnesses make the hearing process go more smoothly, generate a clearer record for the hearing officer to review afterward, and assist in providing accurate information about the program and placement of the eligible student. Moreover, careful preparation in these areas is the key to conducting a successful hearing. The strategies offered are broad, but should all be considered as measures to prepare witnesses and alleviate the stress that comes with having to be questioned and cross-examined. We begin by examining the basics of testifying.

The Basics of Testimony

Thorough witness preparation is a prerequisite to successful testimony. They are two types of testimony: Direct examination and cross-examination. We next describe direct examination and cross-examination and provide preparation strategies for each.

Direct Examination

During direct examination, an attorney will have preset questions for witnesses. The questions that will be asked of witnesses will be used by the attorney to present evidence that establishes the nature and extent of a student's disabilities, the student's educational needs, and what the district did in response to those needs (Shrybman, 1982). Principals, teachers, related service providers, and others who will testify will need to be ready to answer these questions regarding their experiences with a student. Usually, the attorney will use a person's testimony to introduce the exhibits or evidence that will be offered in the hearing (e.g., IEPs). Because direct examination usually consists of a preset list of questions, the witnesses will usually meet with the attorney or perhaps a consultant to prepare the witness for the examination. Before testifying, a witness should reread all notes, reports, and emails that may be referenced as a part of the testimony. Consistency adds to a witnesses' credibility. Textbox 10.1 includes information on testifying.

Textbox 10.1. Testifying

- Before testifying, review any notes or records you may have.
- Relax. Breathe.
- You will take an oath to tell the truth.
- Turn off your cell phone and do not bring it to the witness chair.
- Enunciate clearly. Do not use filler sounds or words when speaking (e.g., "uh-huh," "um," "ah").
- Listen carefully to the question being asked. Although you may know the answer to the question and you want to answer, wait until the entire question has been asked.
- Answer the question asked and don't volunteer additional information.
- If you don't understand the question, ask that it be repeated or explained.
- Be exact in your testimony.
- Pause and think before you answer questions.
- Brief, succinct answers are appropriate. Do not go beyond the scope of the question. Do not volunteer answers that were not asked for.
- Saying you do not know is an acceptable answer if you truly do not know.
- Maintain a consistent voice loudness throughout your testimony.
- Have a bottle of water with you because the more you talk, the likelihood is your mouth will get dry.

- Attempt to stop or significantly reduce distracting habits such as nail-biting, playing with your watch or jewelry, fidgeting with pens or pencils, or rocking back and forth in the witness seat.
- Dress professionally and appropriately for the hearing.
- Do not speak when others are talking. The court reporter will be taking verbatim notes and that task will be made considerably more difficult if people are talking over each other.
- Keep eye contact with the person conducting the questioning you unless you are being asked to examine or read from a document.
- Don't try to memorize what you are going to say. Doing so will make your testimony sound "pat" and unconvincing. Instead, be yourself, and prior to the hearing go over in your own mind the matter about which you will be questioned.
- Don't use jargon or acronyms. Use lay terms and explain all terms used to the hearing officer and attorney.
- Don't use excessive hand motions. Although it is fine to move your hands, the hearing involves a court reporter transcribing everything that is being said, and that those reading the transcripts later will be unable to see or understand the hand motions.
- Whenever a document is placed in front of you, make sure it is a document that you have seen before. If not, take time to read through the document and clarify its role in the education of the student.
- Stop speaking instantly when the hearing officer interrupts you, or when an attorney objects to a question. Wait for the hearing officer to tell you to continue before answering any further.

Cross-Examination

The cross-examination by the opposing attorney will likely be the most difficult part of testifying. Usually, the school's attorney or a consultant will assist witnesses to prepare for cross-examination, perhaps by role-playing, asked questions that he or she expects may be asked. One of the authors of this textbook, in preparing to be an expert witness in a hearing, was told by an attorney, "The opposing attorney will be friendly, but he is not your friend! He will try to diminish your credibility in the eyes of the hearing officer. He may question your expertise. He may try to upset you and will certainly try to discredit your testimony. Be candid and straightforward and do not get upset." In addition to the general information on testifying in textbox 10.1, textbox 10.2 includes more advice on testifying during cross-examination.

Following the cross-examination, the hearing officer will ask if there are further questions for the attorney. The attorney who conducted the direct examination may ask you a few questions, which is a process called redirect, if he or she believes some point needs to be clarified.

Then the hearing officer will dismiss you. Your part in the hearing is over!

Textbox 10.2. Testifying in Cross-Examination

- Answer only the question asked and don't volunteer information.
- If you don't understand the question, ask for it to be repeated or explained.
- If you do not know an answer, say so. Do not guess.
- Don't get angry or defensive. Stay cool, objective, and honest.
- Keep emotions in check. There may be questions about your qualifications or questions about why you did not do something that may have should have been done. Do not get defensive if you feel attacked by a line of questioning. Hopefully, if it is objectionable your attorney will take care of it. Remember why you are there and testify to what you know, based on your experience.
- Do not make flippant comments.
- Be careful about statements made (often in frustration) under your breath, thinking that only you can hear these comments. If the opposing party's attorney hears the comment, they may ask you to repeat the comment loudly enough for it to be recorded and transcribed.
- Do not take the questions personally. The attorney for the opposing other side is trying to prevail in the hearing and will try to question your credibility, clarify your knowledge, try to determine if you have any bias, and attempt to show you have difficulty with the facts.
- Behave in a way that is appropriate to the seriousness of a due process hearing. Do not roll your eyes with questions you think are poor or repeated. An arrogant or condescending attitude will be noticed by a hearing officer. Always behave professionally.
- Do not act in a superior manner or belittle the questions that are asked by giving answers such as, "Of course everyone should know that" or "I am an expert in the field and have explained that in enough terms that anyone can understand."
- If the opposing attorney asks you for a yes-or-no answer and you have a more extensive answer, ask the hearing office if you may provide an explanation.
- Take time to think about you answer before you reply. Do not let the opposing attorney rush you.
- If your answer was not correctly stated, correct it immediately. If your answer was not clear, clarify it immediately. It is better to correct a mistake yourself than to have the attorney discover an error in your testimony. If you realize you have answered incorrectly, say, "May I correct something I said earlier?" If this happens to you, don't get flustered. Just explain honestly why you were mistaken.

- Do not let the opposing attorney cut you off in the middle of a question. There may be times when you are testifying when you will be asked another question. Ask the attorney if you may finish your answer. It is important to go ahead and include any important portion of testimony even if it means answering the next question by stating that the previous question was not completely or accurately answered. Also, there may be additional questions about the issue after the other party's attorney finishes asking their question, and this will allow clarification.

Preparing Witnesses for Testifying

Testifying in a legal proceeding can be an anxiety-provoking experience. Witnesses may be worried about the examination and cross-examination. Additionally, they may be afraid of what they will say, afraid of what they won't say, and just worried about the procedure in general. We have advocated that school districts attempt to use alternative forms of dispute resolution so that a due process hearing is not necessary, but sometimes parents and school districts find themselves in a hearing, and testifying will be necessary. Additionally, witnesses will often be sequestered at a hearing, which may increase his or her anxiety. Most parents and educators have not participated in due process hearings, so the experience will be new to them.

The professional development activities and preservice training that special educators and administrators have received does not prepare them to provide testimony or for the back-and-forth necessary when sitting in the witness seat and testifying. Therefore, careful and thorough witness preparation before a hearing is essential.

Preparing for a due process hearing should not begin solely when one is requested by the parents or considered by a district, it should be a consideration in every action educators take in their involvement with a child and their parents. Read and share the section on steps districts should do when interacting with students and parents. We realize it is a lot of steps, but it is important to think about these steps and the responsibilities of educators before they are needed. As a witness use these strategies as a part of your preparation. Provide all individuals who will be testifying a copy of any evidence they will be asked to identify. Due process hearings are long, involved, and intense.

Every due process hearing is different. The issues may determine the process; additionally, every due process hearing officer has a different style. Some are more formal than others. There is not a "typical" due process hearing. The guidance below is to assist in preparation of the issues so that a hearing officer can decide about the program and placement for a student with a disability. This chapter will assist in the broad preparation of the case and hopefully demystify the process.

We have previously mentioned the due process training video that was developed in Pennsylvania. We highly recommend you spend forty-nine minutes and watch the mock due process hearing video.[1] This video developed by the Pennsylvania Office for Dispute Resolution and the hearing officers provides a great summary of what a hearing looks like, presenting facts, swearing in witnesses, and cross-examination. Again, your jurisdiction may be different but this will provide a visual context that will assist in forming questions for when the witnesses later meet with their respective attorneys.

The Importance of Thorough Preparation

Thorough preparation for testifying for a due process hearing involves making sure the witnesses read all the documents that might be referenced related to their testimony. This will involve providing the witnesses with the document prior to their testimony and then the attorney should meet with them to discuss the likely questions they should expect as a part of their testimony. We will discuss specifics for cross-examination below, but the witness should have a reasonable expectation of the questions they will receive. We are not preparing a witness to simply regurgitate facts but to help the hearing officer understand the facts of the case. There is a separate chapter on expert testimony.

The witness should develop their questions about the case, and their testimony so that when they meet with their attorney, they can get their questions answered and be ready to be a credible witness. This will also help the attorney as they prepare not only for their opening statements but also for questions for the witnesses.

The witness should read or reread any letters to parents, notices, forms sent to the other parents, or any documents that they should know about. The witness should be especially familiar with the documents they generated and provided to the parents. For teachers and related services personnel, they should be very familiar with the documents related to the progress monitoring of the student and should be able to explain those forms, the data on the forms, any problems with data, and all changes to the student's services as a result of lack of progress by the student.

The witness should also be very familiar with notes from other witnesses and the information provided by independent evaluators. Does the information from the independent evaluator indicate the student has problems in certain areas? If so, and what data does the school district have related to those areas. Is there information that the opposing witness might say that would be very different from the school district? If so, what background does the district have to comment related to that expert witness and what data does the district have related to this?

Generally, talk with the witness about the documents they will be asked to identify, their role in the development of the documents, and additional comments they have about the process. It is also important to help the witness to

---

[1] https://vimeo.com/279258179.

understand the types of questions they might get from the opposing party so they can be as prepared to testify as possible.

The Process of Testifying

The attorney should explain the process of a witness testimony in a due process hearing. Depending on the hearing officer and venue, witnesses may be observing the hearing while awaiting their chance to testify or they may be asked to wait outside until they are called to testify. They will be sworn in and asked to affirm they will tell the truth. The hearing officer may make a statement about the proceedings to them, and what to expect.

Typically, when witnesses are being prepared for testimony and cross-examination, they will be asked many questions and will have an opportunity to practice their answers. A critical step is to have your attorney or educational expert ask questions that will likely be addressed in the actual hearing. This will help the witness to relax because they will have had time to organize their thoughts and responses to questions. They can be coached about how to phrase their responses to point out key elements of the case. The pre-hearing questions should ensure witnesses know the responses to their questions and are capable of responding fluently. There will likely need to be instruction on how to respond to the questions without saying too much or making unnecessary or potentially damaging statements.

Typically, the direct examination by the district attorney is fairly easy because the attorney will ask questions and elicit testimony for which they have been prepared. The tough questions will often come from the opposing side's attorney during cross-examination. Opposing counsel may attempt to throw witnesses off by intimidating, confusing, or antagonizing them. The keys in responding to cross examination are (a) pausing before the response, (b) thinking through the response before speaking, and (c) answering yes or no when the questions warrant it without explaining or rationalizing the response. It is very important to treat the opposing counsel with respect, fully answering their questions, but ask to have them repeat questions when clarity is needed.

What to Take to the Witness Seat?

It is a good idea to bring a bottle of water that will help if the throat gets dry. Any and all notes that are brought to the witness seat must be shared with opposing attorney. Make sure you talk with your attorney about the notes. Show them what you have and clarify why you think it is important. The information on the notes should not have new information that has not been previously disclosed to the other party but should be there to help refresh the witness's memory of the relevant facts to the case.

A witness is first asked questions by the attorney who wants/needs their information to help make their case. The likely first set of questions that will be asked are listed below. This will likely be the attorney you have worked with as a part the preparation for the hearing, or an associate of theirs. When the attorney is finished asking questions, the opposing council will also then have a chance to ask questions. When they are done, your attorney will have a chance for redirect, a time to ask clarifying or extending questions based on the questions from the opposing party's attorney. This is not a time for new facts or issues. The important facts or issues should have been covered during the first set of questions. When they are done, the opposing council will have another opportunity for any questions related to what was just covered by the questioning by your attorney. When both attorneys have had two rounds of questioning, you are typically done. It is rare, but you may be called back later if there was testimony that strongly contradicted what you said. Also rare, the hearing officer may have a question or two about an item that was not covered or to clarify a statement you made.

It also a very good idea to understand the typical questions that will be a part of certifying the witness as either credible or valid to speak on the issue(s). Typical first questions include:

- What is your name?
- Please spell your last name for the court reporter.
- What is your current position with the school district?
- How long have you had that position?
- What other previous jobs or positions did you have relevant to your current position?
- What is your educational background?
- What certifications do you hold?
- What seminars or professional development have you had related to your position?
- How do you know the student?
- How long have you worked with the student?
- Have you observed the student in other classes or locations? If so, what did you observe?

These questions lay the foundation for the experience and understanding of the qualifications of the witness. This should always be done to help the hearing officer understand the information and background this witness brings to the hearing.

Making an Impression

As we have discussed, due process hearings are very much like courtroom trials without the jury. Both sides are usually represented by an attorney who makes an opening statement, introduces evidence, examine witnesses, and cross-examine witnesses. As a witness, you are the most important element of the attorney's case. It will be your testimony and the evidence presented that the attorney will use to convince the hearing officer of the correctness of his or her case.

When you find out that there is a due process hearing about a special education student in your school district, school, or classroom and you may be called to testify, you may feel a certain amount of anxiety. When you find out that you testify, you will be undoubtedly be anxious. When you actually testify during direct examination and cross-examination you will be very anxious! Do not worry, this is normal. The best way to combat anxiety is through thorough preparation. You will know in advance when you will be called to testify. Use the time before testimony to go over any notes from your preparation sessions. However, don't memorize your presentation.

When you are called to the witness stand and observe the attorneys, hearing officer, and others watching you, attempt to relax. Sit down, take a deep breath, and have a drink of water. Sit up straight and take the oath to tell the truth. Look directly at the attorney questioning you or at the hearing office if he or she asks you a question. Speak in a voice loudly enough to be heard, speak slowly, and enunciate clearly. Your answers should be direct, honest, and dignified. Be sincere and friendly. The attorney for your side will use their questions to develop your testimony. Answer the question that was asked directly, positively, and avoid elaboration or irrelevant facts. Always tell the truth.

When being cross-examined, listen to questions carefully, answer questions directly, and do not speculate. Do not volunteer information. Pause before answering and remain calm. If a question is unclear, ask that it be repeated or explained. If the attorney cuts you off in the middle of an answer, ask if you may finish your answer. Do not take cross-examination personally, all witness in hearings or trials are cross-examined. Answer questions with confidence but never be arrogant. It is extremely important that you never lose your temper or answer questions in a curt or demeaning manner. It is likely that the attorney may try to rush you; if you need time to consider your answer, say so. If there is an objection by an attorney or the hearing offer addresses you or the attorneys, stop talking immediately. If an attorney has objected, wait until the hearing officer sustains or overrules the objection. The hearing officer will most likely tell you to continue.

Create an impression! Dress professionally and speak warmly.

Conclusion

The purpose of this chapter was to address the extremely important role of testimony in a due process hearing. Most administrators and teachers do not have to testify frequently so they may feel unprepared and uncomfortable when they are called upon to testify in a hearing. The task of the witness is to provide testimony and refer to evidence that the attorney will use to convince the hearing officer of the correctness of his or her position. It is important that witnesses are carefully and thoroughly prepared for the testimony. The hearing officer does not know the case before holding the due process hearing but by the end of the hearing, the effective attorney will have helped the hearing officer to understand the case through the testimony of the witnesses. Additionally, after your testimony you can serve as a resource for others who are about to testify at a hearing. Remember—take it seriously and be prepared.

Reference

Shrybman, J. A. (1982). *Due Process in Special Education.* Aspen.

CHAPTER 11

School District Preparation for Due Process Hearings

Advance Organizers

* What questions should be asked prior to a due process hearing?
* What are some considerations to address prior to a due process hearing?
* How does one prepare for a due process hearing?
* What should one do after a hearing?

This chapter provides steps that school officials need to consider prior to going to a due process hearing. As we have mentioned, every other attempt to prevent or settle the conflict should have been exhausted; a due process hearing should be avoided whenever possible.

There are financial and emotional costs involved in due process hearings. For example, a due process hearing can be very expensive. Additionally, the amount of time spent on gathering and reviewing documents is usually considerable. Furthermore, the conflicts leading to and resulting in a due process hearing can irretrievably damage the parent–school relationship. Some of the parents who are a part of a due process hearing may live in the district for years afterward, and the IEP team will still have to work with them, and provide appropriate services for their child.

In most cases the school district will have an attorney who is either on staff or contracted to represent the district in the due process hearing. They will often direct the school district's preparation activities that must be accomplished prior to the hearing. In this chapter, we address (a) prehearing activities, (b) school district preparation, (b) situations that may lead a school district to request a hearing, and (d) post-hearing activities. Prior to this we briefly consider actions that school-based personnel should follow at all times to prevent the need for due process hearings.

Prevention

In chapter 2, we examined how school districts may avoid formal dispute resolution systems. Nonetheless, consideration and preparation for a due process

127

hearing should not occur just after a due process complaint is filed—it should occur with every interaction with a student and his or her parents. The most critical question that needs to be addressed during these sessions is the following: "Are we focused on the needs of the student to ensure that he or she makes progress in the special education program?" Of course, all school district personnel should understand that every interaction with a student and their parents should be respectful and professional. Moreover, personnel should always work diligently to develop and implement a special education program that enables a student to make progress appropriate in light of their circumstances (see U.S. Supreme Court ruling in *Endrew F. v. Douglas County School District*, 2017).

The field of special education is defined by the Individuals with Disabilities Education Act (IDEA) and as a result of the dispute resolution procedures in the law, it is a litigious area. Therefore, every interaction with a student, every email exchange with a parent, and every IEP needs to be viewed as possibly an item that may come up in a future due process hearing. This may seem overly alarming; however, one never knows what might lead to conflict.

Going to a due process hearing is similar to going to a bench trial in court. Each side has witnesses and introduces evidence (e.g., IEPs, assessments). Witnesses, typically teachers, principals, IEP team members, parents, and often expert witnesses, will be examined by their party's attorney and then cross-examined by the opposing party's attorney. This likely will include having to answer questions about their background, their professionalism, and whether they performed the job exactly as they are supposed to be performing it. Shortly after the hearing ends, the hearing officer or administrative law judge will issue a ruling.

In chapters 4 and 5, we examined alternative dispute resolution systems and the use of mediation to settle disputes, and resolution meetings. The object of these mechanisms is to settle disputes without have to go to a due process hearing. At any of these stages parents and school districts officials may choose to settle the dispute. A conflict can even be settled during a due process hearing. Settling a dispute is preferred over going to a due process hearing because there is less stress and expense involved. Additionally, the parent–school relationship can often be salvaged during if an agreement can be reached.

After means to resolve the dispute are exhausted and district officials determine that there is no other alternative course of action but to go to a due process hearing, the district personnel need to meticulously prepare their case.

The Due Process Hearing Complaint

Although a student's parents are most likely to file a due process complaint against a school district, either parents or a school district may file the due process hearing complaint over any matter related to the identification, evaluation, placement, or provision of a free appropriate public education (FAPE) to a student (IDEA Regulations, 34 C.F.R. § 300.507 [a][2]). The party that files a due process complaint must do so with the state educational agency (SEA) and must also copy the other party. When the parent files the complaint, school district should begin prehearing activities to prepare for due process hearing.

Preparing for a Due Process Hearing

Preparing for a hearing will require considerable preparation in a short period of time. The following actions should be based on issue(s) raised in the parents request for a due process hearing. These actions could also be incorporated into a district's procedures manual, which may beneficial for future due process hearing complaints.

Notifying and Interviewing Personnel Who May Be Involved in the Hearing

Because a due process hearing complaint is filed with the SEA and copied to the school district, the district's special education director will likely be the first person to be notified. The special education director should inform the following persons who may be involved in the due process hearing.

Superintendent of the School District

The special education director should first inform the superintendent of the school district that a due process hearing has been requested. Additionally, the superintendent should be apprised of the issues that may be brought out during the hearing, the district's case, settlement discussions, and the status of the hearing.

Attorney for the School District

If the school district employs an attorney or if the school district has an attorney or group of attorneys on retainer, they should be notified as soon as a parent files a due process hearing request. The attorney may provide advice to school district personnel on conducting the resolution meeting even though they will not attend unless the parent brings an attorney. The attorney will also help to clarify the issues and ensure that all personnel who might be involved in the hearing understand the issues involved. They will assist in determining what documents need to be reviewed prior to the hearing. Additionally, the attorney may take responsibility for prehearing activities such as preparing witnesses for the hearing (see chapter 10).

Insurance Carrier for the School District

Most school districts have insurance policies that may cover some of the costs of a special education due process hearing. Often there is a deductible paid for by the school district and the insurance carrier will pay the costs above this amount. It is important to notify the insurance carrier as soon as the district decides to go to a hearing or learns that a parent or guardian has filed a due process complaint. Occasionally, an insurance carrier will assign its own attorney to represent the school district. If the district fails to notify the insurance carrier in a timely manner, that may jeopardize the carrier's coverage of the expenses for the case.

Principals, Teachers, and Others Who May Be Involved

All school district personnel who may be involved in the hearing should be informed of the possibility. Moreover, after the issues have been clarified everyone who has worked with the student, had interactions with the parent(s), or evaluated the student should be interviewed. The purpose of the interviews is to develop the facts about what happened, what should have happened, and their perspectives about the education and needs of the student. The school district's attorney may want to participate in or conduct these interviews.

A student's special education teacher will usually be called upon as a witness in a due process hearing. Because most due process hearings are about whether a student has received a FAPE, the special education teacher will often be providing testimony about the student's IEP, including the present levels of academic achievement and functional statements (e.g., Do the statements reflect all the areas of student need?), measurable annual goals (e.g., Are the goals measurable? Were the goals measured?), student progress (e.g., Did you collect data on student progress? Was the data reported to the student's parents on a regular basis? Was the IEP modified if the data indicated the student did not make progress?), special education services (e.g., Were special education services provided that met the student's needs? Were the special education services provided based on peer-reviewed research?). The special education teacher should be told they may expect these questions during a hearing.

School personnel including the principal and a student's general education teacher may be involved and possibly called to testify during a hearing. The time necessary for the actual preparation for testimony before the due process hearing is long and involved. The attorney and likely the special education director will meet to discuss the case, who will need to testify, who will need to be ready to possibly testify, what documents are necessary, and may be necessary. There should be a concerted effort to prepare the witnesses for testimony. This includes how to answer questions, when to rephrase, and what to expect as a part of the procedure. There may be interviews with some of the witnesses seeking to clarify what they will be asking, and how valid they sound when they are describing the efforts in the provision of services for the student.

These interviews will usually include the school psychologist who evaluated and worked with the student. School psychologists are frequently called on as witnesses at due process hearings because they have often completed many of the assessments that were used to determine the student's eligibility for special education and related services. Often the school psychologist has also served on the student's IEP team in interpreting the instructional implications of the evaluation results (see IDEA Regulations, 34 C.F.R. § 300.321[5]). Moreover, because the information collected by the school psychologist often serves as the baseline for the program that is offered by the district, he or she may be called on to provide information about the student's progress.

The special education director and/or attorney should interview all individuals who provide educational services to the student. This includes all general and special teachers, paraprofessionals and aides, related services providers, bus drivers if necessary, and anyone else who works with or oversees the student. Ask them detailed questions about the issues that have been raised by the parents, but also spend time with them seeking information about other components of the student's education program. The goal here is to get as accurate and as full picture as possible about everything that relates to this student's education.

School district administrators, including the special education director, should be prepared to provide an answer to the U.S. Supreme Court's admonition that hearing officers and court "may fairly expect those authorities to be able to offer a cogent and responsive explanation for their decisions that shows the IEP is reasonably calculated to enable the child to make progress appropriate in light of his circumstances" (*Endrew F. v. Douglas County School* District, 2017, p. 993).

Time spent at the hearing itself is also a factor districts should consider. How will the work the administrators need to do be covered while they are in the hearing—or awaiting to testify? If a district expects to call two or three teachers, an administrator, a related services provider, a school psychologist, to testify, and the hearing lasts several days, that is a lot of instructional or assessment time that is spent preparing for the hearing but also in attending the hearing itself. If the hearing lasts several days, that just multiplies the amount of time involved.

Districts need to be prepared to have witnesses ready for these kinds of questions (see chapter 10 on witness preparation). When a person is in the witness chair, everything the person says will be analyzed very closely, dissected, and then asked about in a different way. Every email the employees have sent to the parents will also be available for analysis. Teachers are often not ready for a due process hearing. They are prepared to provide instruction, not to be cross-examined by an attorney on the program they offer for a student. Thus, witness preparation is extremely important.

The attorney or person who prepares the witnesses will assess how good a witness these individuals will be. This is based on their ability to function calmly while being questioned during cross-examination. Their ability to articulate facts must be in a manner that answers questions but does not volunteer information beyond that which is being requested will be assessed. Witnesses must project themselves as credible and truthful.

Gathering Relevant Documents

Someone in the district, typically the special education director or someone they appoint to the task, will gather all the relevant documents related to the conflict (e.g., assessments, IEPs, prior written notices [PWNs], email exchanges, data collection sheets, progress reports). Make sure the documents that are mandated by federal and/or state laws and regulations are included, such as evaluation reports, IEPs, and any notices provided to the parent about where the program will be located.

All the documents should be put into a sequential order and catalogued with a brief description about their importance. The documents should be organized by date and an index of the documents that are being reviewed should be created. A summary should be developed for each document that lets the school district attorney understand the importance of the document and how it relates to the issues. The annotation for some of the documents will just list their title, such as Notice to Parent about Transportation, while others would require a few sentences to help a reader understand the major documents, such as a recent IEP. Three-ring binders are useful for collecting this information. The binder should begin with a table of contents and include tabs with descriptions of the content under each tab (e.g., "IEP from [date]").

As the documents are being annotated make sure they are legally compliant, and reflect the individual needs of the student, the services provided, and if the student made progress. This should be done for all documents as they are being reviewed, as the opposing counsel will be reviewing the same documents and asking those questions. It is better for the team to decide about the legally compliant forms before others see them, as finding a document that is not appropriate may hasten settlement discussions.

Ensure the documents are internally consistent based on the needs of the student. Check that the data from the evaluation documentation is linked to the present education levels within the IEP. Next, make sure the IEP goals and benchmarks are linked to the present education levels. There needs to be a logical flow from the evaluation data to the description of goals and objectives, and the data used for progress monitoring. If you do not have this flow then this is a major problem with the program that is offered to the student.

When indexing documents, review them for timeline violations. Check that the dates on the documents are congruent with federal or state timeline requirements. This is a key area to substantiate that not only were the necessary steps taken, but also, the steps were completed in a timely fashion, which are part of the procedural requirements from the *Rowley/Endrew* two-part standard (see chapter 1). The two-part standard of a case analysis in special education is procedural and substantive. If procedural deficiencies do exist, district officials should determine if these errors have resulted in substantive harm to a student's education or appropriateness of his or her program. This is referred to as the "harmless error" argument (Zirkle & Hetrick, 2017). Though not providing the requisite testing or services in a timely fashion may lay the foundation for a compensatory education claim.

The documents collected and indexed should also include all emails sent from representatives of the district regarding this student. Review these emails and determine if there are any statements made indicating the need for more or different services and the resulting action. For example, if there are emails that the student was possibly bullied on the bus and no longer wanted to come to school, clarify what was done as a result of that email. Was there a meeting? Were there any changes made to the student's program or transportation? If so, what was the result? If not, why? If not then there may be a reason to settle if there are unaddressed problems.

The following sections review additional types of documents that should be collected and indexed.

Anecdotal Notes

Gather any anecdotal notes all personnel have kept who work with the student. Check with everyone who provides services or supervises the program, including the general and special education teachers; speech, occupational, or physical therapists; nurses; and personal care aides. Many related service providers maintain a log of when, how long, and what services were provided. Also, billing information may provide valuable documentation substantiating the services that were delivered.

Emails and Correspondence

Collect and review emails and correspondence to and from the parents. Highlight any concerns from the parents and note how they were addressed by the district. Did the parents raise the issue regarding the bullying on the bus, and what was the email response from the parents? All emails sent should be reviewed regarding the education of the student. Many districts learn as the result of a due process hearing that when there is a concern raised by a parent, there should be a policy of alerting others about the problems. There should at least be an informal meeting, with notes kept about the results of the informal meeting. All too often a parent raises a concern about their child, alerts a teacher, and then nothing is done to address the concern/problem/issue. Again, this could be a possible reason to settle or at least potentially award compensatory education when there is an unaddressed problem.

When reviewing documents (and interviewing school personnel), look for holes or gaps in services. Read every file and complete every interview with an eye toward a worst-case scenario highlighting the problems with the documents or services provided. Was there a delay in completing the initial assessment? Were all the services listed in the IEP provided, and provided in a timely fashion? Are all the individuals providing the services to the student certified for the role? Were the parents kept abreast of the progress of their child? And importantly, when there was a problem, was a meeting held to determine if changes to the IEP were necessary?

All of this needs to be done within a few days of the receipt of the due process hearing request because the files and their contents need to be available for the school district's attorney to review. It is unlikely that the person responsible for gathering all of this information will be able to get other parts to their job done during this frenzied period. The school district attorney will most likely review the documents and clarify the issues.

After a Hearing

Regardless of the decision in the due process hearing, school district personnel can certainly learn things from the hearing that may help them prevent future hearings. Additionally, many issues may arise during a hearing that school district personnel may need to address, including staff morale, staff development, sharing lessons learned, and rebuilding relationships with parents or guardians. From these experiences, perhaps the most important lessons come from the issues that caused the due process hearing, and if the school district loses the hearing, then strategies or procedures need to be changed so that future hearings and losses in hearings may be avoided.

We next describe strategies and procedures that should follow the due process hearing.

Reviewing the Hearing Officer's Order

Steps that should immediately occur after a due process hearing include:

* Review the hearing officer's Order.
* Determine the individuals responsible for the implementation of the Order.
* Meet with the necessary staff. Review the Order with them.
* Determine what needs to occur to implement the Order.
* Ensure district staff are implementing the hearing officer's order.

Implementing the letter and the spirit of the Order demonstrate the district has taken the first step toward reconciling with the family.

Addressing Staff Morale

After a due process hearing in which the staff's professionalism may have been questioned, the hearing officer ruled that the school district did not provide appropriate services to a student, school personnel may have a lower morale about themselves or their job. All members of the school district need to monitor the others to determine whether this is occurring. There may be a palpable sense of frustration, or there may be downright anger at either the parent's attorney for how they questioned witnesses or with the hearing officer for their interpretation of what was presented.

As a result of this, administrators and fellow teachers need to be supportive. Administrators especially need to reassure teachers and other staff that they have done all that they could, given the resources at hand. What is important is this message needs to be conveyed to not only the staff who were involved in the due process hearing, but the rest of the staff as well. If there were problems made in providing services or the student did not make progress, acknowledge the problems and work to determine a solution. If the problems were caused by teachers and staff not having the necessary resources or there were errors or flaws in the system as designed by the administrators, then administrators need to own up to those flaws and work to rectify the deficiencies. It should be the role of the administrator to support the first line of providing services, teachers, staff and related services personnel.

Addressing Inappropriate Actions by School Personnel

If a teacher, administrator, or staff member ignored policies and procedures, then disciplinary actions may be warranted. Certainly extensive training should be conducted to ensure that school personnel are aware of the school district systems and policies and their responsibilities under the IDEA. Many of the egregious violations by school personnel will be found during the preparation for the hearing. When a district finds a problem with school personnel not doing their job properly, or an evaluation is found to be seriously lacking, the school district officials must engage in professional development activities to prevent future occurrences of the problem. For example, if is determined that a student's goals were not measurable and data on student progress was not collected, professional development activities should target these deficiencies.

We have previously addressed the *Rowley/Endrew* two-part test for determining whether a student has received FAPE, procedural and substantive. If procedural problems are found in the preparation for the hearing, school district personnel should determine if the errors prevented the students from receiving FAPE. If they did not, the defense in this situation is the "no harm, no foul" defense. This defense is one where the procedural errors are admitted to, but attorney attempts to convince the hearing officer that these procedural errors did not deny the student a FAPE. The goal of admitting procedural problems and then clarifying the student made progress is to work to reduce an award of compensatory education. After the hearing, school district officials should ensure that training is provided on meeting the requirements of state and federal special education law.

Providing Staff Development

The issues surrounding a due process can have many implications and the experience gained can be significant. It is beneficial for other educators to gain the insights into the issues and how they were applied to the law and what can be learned from the case. A meeting might be worthwhile to present a summary of a case to staff and explain the outcome. Even if the district prevailed on every issue, in the preparation and aftermath of the due process hearing important lessons may be learned. Share with others so they can also improve services for students with disabilities.

In chapter 1 we examined the language in the IDEA that requires that a hearing officer is to make his or her decision "on substantive grounds based on a determination of whether a child received a free appropriate public education" (20 U.S.C. § 1415[f][3][i]). Furthermore, the law required that, "In matters alleging a procedural violation, a hearing officer may only find that a child did not receive a free appropriate public education if the procedural violations resulted in substantive harm" (20 U.S.C. § 1415[f][3][ii]). Moreover, the only procedural violations that could lead to substantive harm are violations that (a) impede a student's right to a FAPE, (b) impede the parents' opportunity to participate in the decision-making process regarding their child's FAPE, or (c) cause a deprivation of educational benefit. Procedural violations that are "merely technical violation of the IDEA" may not result in substantive hard, thus not violating the IDEA (Berney & Gilsbach, 2012, p. 7).

School district officials, therefore, should provide meaningful and evidence-based professional development for administrators, principals, and teachers on both the procedural and substantive requirements of state and federal special education law. The procedural requirements of the law, which include completing PWN when required, having required members on the IEP team, completing the evaluation within the specific timelines (missing by a few days, not a few months), or failing to implement the IEP as agreed on, are specifically addressed in state and federal law. Although the IDEA is less clear on what exactly constitutes a substantive violation, it is generally believed that substantive violations concern the content of the IEP. For example, do the present levels of academic achievement and functional performance statements address all of a student's needs? Are a student's annual goals written in ways that are measurable and are they actually measured? If data shows that a student will not achieve their goals, are changes made to the student's program? Professional development activities in substantive actives may be in developing educational meaningful and legal correct IEPS, writing measurable goals, and collecting and reacting to student data.

Rebuilding Relationships with Parents

If either a parent or school district filed a due process complaint, clearly there was an issue that the parties could not agree on. In most cases the district and the parents still have to work together during and after the due process hearing. There may have been accusations of lack of professionalism, or the parents as a result of the hearing heard testimony that the teachers were not always doing their jobs. One party may have clearly lost the due process hearing after spending an enormous amount of time in preparing and participating in the hearing, and they may be upset with the outcome. Regardless which party prevails in a special education due process hearing, the district needs to work to rebuild the relationship with parents or guardians. Even though district staff may be upset with the decision, they need to be reminded that the goal of special education is to meet the needs of students with disabilities. As noted in other parts of this book, these students have disabilities at no fault of their own and need assistance to make it through school. Continued animosity between parents and school district personnel is not compatible with this goal.

A common result of a due process hearing is a new IEP or program for a student. This will necessitate an IEP meeting. The temperaments of the district staff and the parents may be highly charged with anger, resentment, and/or humiliation. It is important to use this opportunity to reestablish positive communication with the parents if they are willing to allow the district to do so.

District staff should prepare very thoroughly for this meeting, and staff need to remain calm, respectful, and work to reduce emotions.

Adjusting Policies and Procedures

Following the receipt of the hearing officer's ruling, districts should meet to determine what policies and procedures need to be changed. The policies and procedures may be compliant with the intent of federal and state regulations but the issues in the special education due processing hearing were about proper implementation of existing policies and procedures. In other cases, school district personnel may need to address a systemic problem. Is there another student with a similar disability whose program should be analyzed to see if there are similar problems? Is the problem with a paraprofessional, teacher, principal, school psychologist, or a related services provider? Is there a problem with the school district's special education administration? School district officials should determine the problem areas and what needs to be changed to address the problem.

Conclusion

Special education due process hearings can be a very intense experience for all parties. School district staff need to keep in mind that a special education due process is about resolving disputes. Most special education disputes relate to what is appropriate programming for a student. Parents want what is best for their child but school districts only have to provide appropriate services. This is where dispute resolution often begins. A special education due process hearing provides an objective third-party perspective. After the hearing is over, it is important that school districts implement the order (or settlement), learn from the experience, and conduct the necessary follow-up activities. Remind staff of the need to rebuild the relationship with families in order to provide the appropriate programs for students.

References

Berney, D. J., & Gilsbach, T. (2017). Substantive vs. procedural violations under the IDEA. http://www.berneylaw.com/2017/11/12/substantive-vs-procedural-violations-idea/.

Granelli, L. J., & Sims, B. L (2018). Special education disputes litigate or settle: That is the question. Annual pre-convention school law seminar. Available at https://www.nyssba.org/clientuploads/nyssba_pdf/Events/precon-law-2018/06-special-ed-disputes-outline.pdf.

Johnson v. District of Columbia, 190 F.Supp.2d 34 (D.D.C. 2002).

Lake, S. E. (2014). *What Do I Do When . . . The Answer Book on Special Education Practice and Procedure* (2nd ed.). LRP.

U. S. Department of Education, Office of Special Education (2007). Letter to Shaw. Available at https://sites.ed.gov/idea/files/idea/policy/speced/guid/idea/letters/2007-4/shaw121207dph4q2007.pdf.

Zirkel, P. A. & Hetrick, A. (2017). Which procedural parts of the IEP are most judicially vulnerable? *Exceptional Children, 83*(2), 219–235. DOI: 10.1177/0011665l849.

CHAPTER 12

Parent Preparation for a Due Process Hearing

Advance Organizers

* Why may parents request a due process hearing?
* What is the process of requesting a hearing?
* What strategies should parents use in preparing for a hearing?
* What are some important pre-hearing complaint steps?
* How to choose an attorney.
* What is pro se representation?

Parents[1] may request a due process hearing over any dispute related to the identification, evaluation, educational placement, or the provision of a free appropriate public education (FAPE) to their child (IDEA Regulations, 34 C.F.R.§ 300.507[a]). The due process hearing provisions of the Individuals with Disabilities Education Act (IDEA) created a formal mechanism that parents could use for resolving disputes with a school district. A due hearing process begins with a decision to file a due process complaint and ends with a settlement agreement or a decision by a due process hearing office or administrative law judge (ALJ).

The process of deciding to request a due process hearing is a long but important one. It is also one that that should not be taken lightly. Due process hearings are complex legal proceedings that may require an attorney and be very expensive.

For parents, there are many decisions that need to be made throughout the process. Some are easy; some will require careful consideration. An important part of the process is to not make it personal about a specific individual who may be providing services, but to make certain your child receives a FAPE. Additionally, as we have mentioned throughout this book, strongly consider a settlement. It is quicker, one has more say in the final process, and it may save a lot of time and money.

---

[1] As in other chapters, we will use to the term "parent" to refer to both parents and guardians throughout this chapter.

Why Parents File Due Process Complaints

Parents may request a due process hearing for a variety of reasons. Examples include that a student's parents believe (a) the school is not implementing the specially designed instruction in their child's individualized education program (IEP); (b) their child needs different special education services than those they are receiving; (c) their child needs a greater amount of special education services; (d) the amount of progress a student is expected to make in the special education program is not meaningful; (e) their child should be eligible for special education services; or (f) the outcome of a manifestation determination review was in error. There are also many situations in which a due process hearing is not the appropriate forum for a dispute, such as the assignment of a student to a particular teacher; the assignment of a particular aide to the student; the hiring (or firing) of school staff, a teacher insulted their family, the parents demand a specific commercial curriculum for a student, the parents reject the specific school to which the student is assigned unless it relates directly to an LRE issue. Additionally, due process is use for resolving special education disputes. There is no similar mechanism for general education.

Parents of students with disabilities should view special education due process hearings in a similar light as any legal proceeding. If the parents choose to request a hearing, then appropriate preparation is paramount.

Prior to discussing how to prepare for a hearing we will cover strategies on how to approach school district personnel to build a better working relationship that will likely more quickly facilitate the student with a disability receiving an appropriate education. We addressed these issues in chapter 2, but will provide the following tips, which are beneficial regardless of the decision to go or not go to a due process hearing. Special education is a team effort and in order for progress to be made there needs to be communication about working together, not animosity or bickering.

Strategies for Improving Collaboration

Strategy #1: Stay Child-Centered

The main purpose of special education is for the student to make progress. Keep that as the focus. You may not have liked how a teacher addressed you, or a teacher ignored you when you were out in public—both may indicate problems but keep the focus on the progress of the child, not on personality differences you might have with the school staff. It is okay to keep asking, "Is my child making appropriate progress?," as that should be the focus of all conversations relating to the child.

Strategy #2: Treat Others Respectfully

Be careful about what you text or email to teachers or administrators. Do not put staff on the defensive or make the dispute personal. When a parent believes they are not getting enough information regarding progress reports they need to approach school staff in a respectful and nonthreatening manner. An example of a nonthreatening email is the following: "Would you please let me know how my son is doing in your reading class? Specifically, how is doing on his IEP goal related to reading?" An example of an email that is not respectful and may be interpreted as threatening is the following: "Would you please let me know how my son is doing in your reading class? I never get updates, and think you are not meeting my son's needs." Be positive in your email correspondences. The nonthreatening example asks for clarity. The threatening example asks for the same information but then provides an opinion that would likely put a teacher on the defensive.

Additionally, be careful how many times you email the staff/administrators. If you believe your questions are not being addressed, arrange a face-to-face meeting with them to go into greater detail on the issue(s). You need to allow them time to provide instruction to the students–not just to respond to emails. Also, don't just send emails to everyone. Choose the correct person and copy others, but do not just email everyone.

Listen to the perspective of others and attempt to understand where they are coming from. Ask questions without putting teachers or administrators on the defensive. Use active listening to show that you are attentive to what a teacher or administrator is saying. For example, a common method in active listening is to restate what was stated with phrases such as, "I hear you saying . . ." or " Do I understand you correctly that . . ." If you do not understand what is being stated, say, "I'm not sure I understand what is being said, can you explain it a differently?" Again, keep asking questions until there is clarity about what is being said.

Strategy #3: Meet Face-to-Face

It is also very important to clarify procedures for talking with staff face-to-face. Some parents get nervous when they are meeting face-to-face, so it is important to practice what you are going to say before you sit down with the staff. Take notes about what you want to cover or address in the meeting so you do not get distracted or sidetracked. The following areas are suggestions to follow during the meeting:

- Remember to keep the child the focus of the meeting, being certain to address the progress the student is making.
- If possible, let the teacher or administrator know ahead of time what will be discussed so the teacher or administrator can have the right people in the meeting and the documents available to answer your questions.
- Begin with and focus on the positives. No matter the education a child is receiving there is likely room for improvement but focus on what is working first.
- Really listen to what is being said. Take notes. It can often be overwhelming with all the information that is being presented, or all the acronyms we use in special education.

* Consider taking a friend who can help with taking notes. This will assist with recall later.
* In face-to-face communication realize that much of what people perceive is nonverbal. Make eye contact and be careful the tone of voice that is used. Do not act dismissively to the teacher or administrators when ideas are discussed. Write the ideas down and consider them.

Strategy #4: Contact the Correct School District Personnel

When contacting school district personnel, make sure you contact the person who has responsibility for the issues of concern. If you are unsure about whom to address, clarify in emails that if the person addressed is not the correct person for this issue, could you have them respond with the name and contact information or the correct person. Given this, often the best person to address all questions with is the one who works directly with your child, likely a teacher or a related services provider.

Strategy #5: Identify the Primary Issue

What is the priority? Emphasize the primary issue that you believe is causing problems. Attempt to get that issue clarified or resolved. How to you determine the priority issues? What should be addressed now and what can wait until later? When the priority issue is addressed, then move on to the next priority. Keep a list of the items that need to be addressed.

Strategy #6: Do Your Research

Learn about your child's disabilities and appropriate methods of providing services to address his or her needs. Go to websites and organizations that are not trying to profit from your contacts nor trying to sell you services. There are many legitimate organizations that provide free information for parents and professionals related to special education. Be careful and be very skeptical of others. Use this research to help learn more about what you will be talking about with the staff. Miscommunication and misunderstanding of what can occur will cause additional problems.

When addressing the staff ask questions that begin with how and what. For example, "Who can help my son get safely off the bus every day?" "What is a skill that needs to be addressed related to bus riding?" Asking questions that begin this way provide more opportunities for the team to think and not put anyone on the defensive. It also provides a goal and direction for the team about what needs to be addressed.

When asking questions that begin with who and why can lead to defensiveness. It targets one individual who may have the responsibility for the problem or seeks to clarify the motive of the actions that were done.

Strategy #7: Have Follow-Up Meetings

Be willing to have another meeting while the school district develops strategies to address your issue. They may need to meet to see if there is a transportation issue, or a timing issue, or if the related services professional will be in the building at that time. This also allows for teachers and staff to develop other possible alternatives to assist with the issue.

We believe that many due process hearings can be avoided if both parties simply take more time talking about the problems and try to come to a solution instead of resorting to a due process hearing. You should try to avoid a situation where both sides are antagonistic, reject compromise, and then have to live with a solution imposed upon. As will be noted later, a good relationship must be maintained between parents and schools to provide an appropriate education for the child.

Deciding to Request a Due Process Hearing

There are many important steps parents need to take before filing a due process complaint. This book is filled with steps and strategies and we recommend paying attention to all of them, as the next set of steps will help in deciding first whether to go to a hearing, and second if you decide to request a hearing, how to help you prepare. Hopefully, it has been made abundantly clear throughout this book that we advocate not going to hearing and working through less adversarial means of solving the issues. But sometimes it is necessary.

Of course, parents want what is best for their child, and they may often get very emotional about making sure their children get what they believe is appropriate. However, school districts do not have to offer the best education, but one that is appropriate. Also, sometimes when parents are emotionally involved it is difficult to make informed decisions when evidence is presented to them. Therefore, the steps below are provided to assist in preparation and asking questions about the program and offer by the district.

Pre-Hearing Request Steps

Before filing a due process hearing request, realize that due process hearings take time. Examples include (a) time while the issue is developing, (b) time for preparation, (c) time for preparing and participating in the resolution meeting, (d) time for the hearing itself, (e) time waiting for the decision, and then (f) time for the implementation of the hearing officer's order. It does not happen immediately. Be prepared for this.

Read through the procedural safeguards notice that has been regularly provided. It will include information related to (a) where to file a due process complaint, (b) the differences between a hearing and a state complaint, and (c) what the requirements are for filing a due process complaint. Parents who read this form often learn other valuable information about how services will be provided and the responsibilities of the school district personnel related to those services. Many districts have the procedural safeguards notice available on their website or one can be obtained from the state education agency (SEA).

The following steps should occur before thinking about hiring an attorney. We recommend completing the steps in order because the information for each step build upon the previous steps.

Step One: Identify the Issue

Identify the issue(s) and concern(s) that lead you to consider filing a due process complaint. This step will drive the rest of the process. We cover the identification of issues(s) in other parts of this book. Keep the focus on the issue.

Step Two: Consider the Outcome

Once the issue is identified, think about the outcome you seek from the due process hearing. Is what you are seeking something that can be realistically obtained from a due process hearing? As noted in other parts of this book, a due process hearing cannot force a district to change teachers/aides/bus drivers, and a school district is under no obligation to maximize your child's potential. They must, however, provide an appropriate education.

Step Three: Gather and Organize All of the Files

Gather all written correspondence regarding your child. Get copies of all requests for you to attend meetings, requests for testing, IEPs, notes home that your child is doing well/poorly, evaluation reports, recommendations for placement, and so on. Save every document the school district sends home. Sign, date, copy, and return documents the school needs in its possession. When gathering documents, this may involve a records request of the school district. Parents have the right to see and obtain copies of all the files a school keeps in your child's cumulative file. It may take a few days to obtain the copies after there is a record request, so plan this into a timeline. There also may be a copying fee if the school district has previously provided you with copies of your child's files.

Step Four: Review the Files

With every file, piece of correspondence, report, or IEP you review keep in mind the central question from Step One and continually ask does this paper/file/ report relate to the issues or concerns? If it does relate, then it may be a part of the presentation of the case. If it does not relate, keep the file but place in a different pile. This is a difficult and time-consuming task because it requires reviewing the documents objectively, looking at what is there, not what you are hoping to find. Do not throw anything away.

Step Five: Organize

Step three was about determining whether you were missing specific documents. This is the step where you organize the files so that there may be quick retrieval. Take all the necessary paperwork as a part of your case and organize it by date. This will help with four important components of preparation for a due process hearing. First, it will hopefully help you see changes in your child's education over time. Second, it will help you determine if there are documents missing that you should have in your possession. Third, it will also help later when you are discussing a date for a hearing and if there are problems with that date. Fourth, once organized you will be able to quickly pull out the necessary document.

Step Six: Table of Contents

Once you have organized the file chronologically, develop a table of contents of all the files. This will take time but develop a one-line description of each document regarding your child that you have collected, and place this on the top of the documents. It will be helpful to use a thick binder and a three-hole punch to put the documents in order. Place numbered tabs between each file, and make sure the numbered tabs correspond to your table of contents numbers. It may take multiple binders. Your goal is to be able to have any document you need accessible and available quickly. The table of contents is for you, but it is also for others who will be reviewing the documents, a school district attorney, or your own attorney if you choose to hire one. Therefore, it is important to keep your organizational structure simple, easy to understand, and consistent. You are building this for others.

Step Seven: Review Your Documents

Review each document to ensure you have the full copy of each file. Some IEPs are long, but do not cull out parts that you might think are important. Provide the whole and complete copy of the IEP. Also, be certain that the original copies do not have notes or comments on them. If the document has notes you have written or highlighted on them, work to obtain clean copies in their place. You can use your notes or highlights later when presenting the case or asking questions of witnesses, but the ones provided to the school district as a part of your case or placed in front of a witness who is testifying need to be clean.

Deciding on Hiring an Attorney

The decision about whether to hire an attorney may rest on the potential costs. If you decide to file a due process complaint, the district will almost certainly be represented by an attorney who most likely specializes in matters related to special education. Not having an attorney will put the parents at a great disadvantage. Nonetheless, the cost of hiring an attorney may be fairly substantial.

We have advocated for less adversarial means of resolving disputes throughout this book. This is done not because we do not want to involve attorneys, or we believe due process hearing system should be abolished. There are clear times when a due process hearing is absolutely necessary. We have advocated for less adversarial means of resolving disputes because the cost of hiring an attorney may be prohibitive for many families, making the whole due process exercise one for just wealthy parents because the school district will likely have an attorney present regardless of whether the parent has an attorney. For many parents this feels like the deck is stacked against them.

How much will an attorney cost? This depends on the prevailing rate for attorney representation in the area in which you live. In major metropolitan areas it is not uncommon for the attorney to require a large retainer up front as they review your files and determine if there is a case, and what can be reasonably expected based on their experience. There are some law firms that take cases on contingency—meaning they think there is a reasonable chance of prevailing and they will receive their fees at that time from the school district.

There may be law firms that will take certain cases pro bono, which means there will be no charge for the parents. Additionally, some clinics do pro bono work. Such clinics will be organized by a law school professor and are often staffed by advanced law school students.

Choosing an Attorney

Special education is a highly specialized area. You do not want an attorney who does not understand the intricacies of special education. The same attorney who was great about helping with your taxes or who handled the recent car accident and helped obtain the necessary insurance may not understand special education.

How does a parent choose an attorney? This person will be representing you in a very personal matter involving your child and may also be fairly expensive. You will need to be very comfortable with this person, and believe they have your best interests in mind as they work to advance your case. You also need to realize that the moment you let the school district know you have an attorney that all settlement discussions will go directly through your attorney—not you. You want an attorney you can trust and one who will not make claims about your child or will not compromise without discussing this with you.

Questions you need to consider include the following:

Is the possible attorney local? Can you visit easily when you or the attorney have questions? Or is the attorney located in a separate part of the state—or even from out of state?

Can the attorney practice law in your state? If the attorney is from out of state, do they have the necessary credentials to practice law in your state? Parents often do not factor in the time and child care responsibilities for meeting with an attorney who works two to three hours away. Increasingly meetings can be conducted virtually, but parents may want to meet the attorney and see or assess their level of comfort with him or her.

Does the attorney have special education experience? As noted above, special education law is very nuanced. Have they been a part of a hearing or settlement discussions? What is their experience in working with families of children with disabilities? Do they have an educational specialist who works with them who reviews the IEPs and evaluations?

Talk with other parents about these issues. There are parent advocacy groups in most states and on the internet, where parents that can be accessed to talk with other parents about their experiences with different attorneys. Would they use their attorney again? What advice do they have about specific attorneys? Do they have positive things to say about their attorney? As noted elsewhere, most hearing requests end with a settlement. Did they believe the attorney represented them appropriately or did they feel they were forced to take a settlement? Did they believe they were a part of the discussion for the settlement or where they left out of the process? Did the attorney have problems getting back to them when they had questions? Overall, what were their impressions? This is probably one of the most important steps in the consideration about whether to hire an attorney or not.

Often local special education advocacy groups may have recommendations for good attorneys who have experience in due process hearings. Contacting law schools may be useful because someone at the law school may be able to refer attorneys.

When you do meet with the attorney, determine if you feel comfortable with him or her. You will be working very closely with this person for a few very intense weeks.

Finally, the law of special education can be very overwhelming. See the glossary of terms in appendix E for the many different terms that are related to a due process hearing. If you decide to request a due process hearing without an attorney, then you need to be prepared to respond to motions from the school's attorney, keep track and respond to their letters, be able to see the big picture when a potential settlement offer is made, and then be able to cross-examine witnesses to get your point across.

Pro Se Representation

"Pro Se" is a Latin term meaning in one's own behalf. Usually in due process hearings or litigation both parties will be resented by attorneys who will argue the parents or school district's case. However, occasionally parents will proceed to a due process hearing or court case without being represented by an attorney. The parents will be said to be proceeding pro se.

Positive Aspects of Proceeding Pro Se

If a parent decides to move forward to a hearing without an attorney, they may do so because they will know the child better than everyone else and will remember how the child acted when he came home when he performed poorly on a test. Additionally, there is no financial outlay to get to the hearing. For some parents this is the overriding reason why they do not use an attorney. There is also potentially a time savings in that the parents do not have to get the attorney informed about the issues. Finally, all settlement negotiations can go directly through the parent, not filtered through an attorney.

Negative Aspects of Proceeding Pro Se

The school district will have an attorney. The language and structure of a due process hearing is unlike any other education meetings parents have previously attended. It is a legal proceeding, that is conducted in accordance with acceptable legal practices. There are terms, deadlines, requirements, and evidentiary rules to follow. Additionally, questioning a witness to get the facts about what they did related to a student so that a hearing officer can decide the case may be difficult for parents who are not trained in questioning a witness. Such questioning may be difficult for a parent because they are emotionally invested in the child. Parents who represent themselves in a hearing sometimes do not focus on the issues relating to the education of the child, and instead take the time to cross-examine witnesses about personal attacks or why phone calls were not returned immediately. Keep the focus the education on the child and leave the personal attacks and questions out of the hearing.

Furthermore, if during the filing a due process complaint an issue is not raised that could have been important in the due process hearing, that issue probably cannot be raised in an appeal or civil action (Lake, 2019). It may be more likely that parents who represent themselves will miss important issues, whereas attorneys' well-versed in special education law would not have failed to address these issues.

The federal regulations to the IDEA describe the due process procedures that are to be available to parents and school districts, however, many states have slightly different procedures for filing complaints and conducting due process hearings. The methods of conducting due process hearings in your state may alter the decision about whether legal representation is necessary. Some states have hearing officers who travel the state holding due process hearings in a local school district building. Some states have a panel of three hearing officers, an attorney, a parent, and a special educator who hear the case and then make the decision. Finally, there are some states that have panels of administrative judges who may be hearing an insurance dispute in the morning and then in the afternoon will be hearing a special education matter. Finally, some states have due process hearings that are extremely formal, while others are more casual. The assigned hearing officer may also be more formal or informal than others.

Additional Advice for Parents

There are parent groups at the local, state, and national level that parents should consider joining. These groups are useful forums getting support and gathering information. It will help parents to meet other parents who have been through similar experiences with the IDEA's dispute resolution procedures and get their advice. Every state has a parent training institute (PTI) and many have a parent training and resource center (PTRC) that focuses on working with parents who have questions about special education procedures and methods of resolving disputes. Often, such groups can also provide information about using legitimate educational advocates to assist with preparation for dispute resolution. Textbox 12.1 is a list of resources that parents may access for useful information.

Textbox 12.1. Resources for Parents

Resource: IDEAs that work
Website: https://osepideasthatwork.org/
Description: This IDEAs that work website is designed to provide easy access to information from research to practice initiatives funded by the Office of Special Education Programs (OSEP) that address the provisions of the Individuals with Disabilities Education Act (IDEA) and ESSA. This website includes resources, links, and other important information relevant to OSEP's research to practice efforts.

Resource: Training and Information for Parents of Children with Disabilities
Website: https://osepideasthatwork.org/resources-grantees/program-areas/training-and-information-parents-children-disabilities#:~:text=The%20OSEP%20Parent%20Training%20and,Disabilities%20Education%20Act%20(IDEA)
Description: The OSEP Parent Training and Information Center (Parent) program is a source of support for families of children with disabilities and youth with disabilities of the IDEA.

Resource: Find Your Parent Center
Website: https://www.parentcenterhub.org/find-your-center/
Description: This website contains links to the Parent and Training Information Center in each state.

Resource: Understood
Website: Understood.org
Description: A website of resources for parents of students with disabilities. Understood now consists of fifteen nonprofit organizations that came together to provide families with a comprehensive resource that no single organization could provide.

Resource: Center for Parent Information and Resources
Website: https://www.parentcenterhub.org/
Description: The center is the federal hub for the materials that have been created and archived for Parent Centers around the country to help

them provide support and services to the families they serve. The center is funded by the Office of Special Education Program in the U.S. Department of Education.

Resource: Progress Center
Website: https://promotingprogress.org
Description: This OSEP funded Center provides educations and special education leaders information, resources, and supports to ensure access to a free appropriate public education (FAPE) to all students with disabilities. It contains excellent resources on IEP development.

Resource: Council for Exceptional Children
Website: https://exceptionalchildren.org
Description: The Council for Exceptional Children is the largest international professional organization devoted to improving the success of students with disabilities

Resource: Wrightslaw Special Education Law and Advocacy
Website: https://wrightslaw.com
Description: Free access to articles, legal information, training, and resources about special education law and advocacy.

Resource: Your Special Education Rights
Website: Subscribe at https://www.youtube.com/c/YourSpedRights
Description: Your special education rights is a series on You Tube. Provides brief overviews of the rights of students with disabilities.

Resource: The Center for Appropriate Dispute Resolution in Special Education (CADRE)
Website: cadreworks.org
Description: The OSEP-funded website contains a wealth of information on dispute resolution in special education.

Resource: The official IDEA Website
Website: sites.ed.gov/ideal
Description: The U.S. Department of Educations on IDEA brings together resources from the department and their grantees.

The IDEA also requires that the public agency must provide parents with information on free or low-cost attorneys and other relevant services available in the area if either the parent or school district files a due process complaint (IDEA Regulations, 34 C.F.R. § 300.507[b]).

Parents may also want to seek a temporary solution to the problems. There may be a trial solution to your problem. Be willing to try a new placement for a marking period, or even a new curriculum if a student is having reading problems. Let the district take data and observe what happens while they are implementing the new effort. A parent can always request this information.

Parents should ensure they have all their child's educational records before proceeding to dispute resolution. These education records are available to parents under a federal law titled the Family Educational Rights and Privacy Act (FERPA). For example, school district personnel will place all of the information obtained as a part of the assessment process to determine whether a student has a disability in the student's file, if a parent does not have access to these records, they have a right to request them under FERPA. Additionally, a student's educational file should include evaluation reports, IEPs, and summaries of attainments toward the IEP goals and objectives.

In addition to the federal regulations regarding the implementation of the IDEA, each state education agency issues regulations relating to how they will ensure students with disabilities will receive a FAPE. Some states just adopt the federal regulations or cite to them, whereas other states may add to the federal regulation, such as requiring transition programming for students be provided at an earlier age (e.g., fourteen years of age), timeline differences, different terms for the levels of services, the procedures for filing due process hearings, or the conduct of a due process hearing. Because states have different formats for conducting due process hearings it is important that parents understand their state's process. These regulations can be obtained from the state department of education's website or by calling the state department of educations.

Filing a Due Process Complaint

The IDEA and regulations require that parents who seek a due process hearing must first file a due process hearing complaint (IDEA Regulations, 34 C.F.R. § 300.507). The due process complaint must allege that the incident occurred not more than two years before the date that the parent or school district knew or should have known before the action that forms the basis of the due process complaint (IDEA Regulations, 34 C.F.R. § 300.507[a][2]). Textbox 12.2 depicts the contents that must be included in the complaint.

Attorneys for school districts will often challenge the sufficiency of a complaint. It is, therefore, very important that the compliant is filled out accurately and with specificity. In completing the complaint, ensure that you are very specific about the problems that you perceive to be occurring and what you are seeking as a result of this action. This includes describing the specific actions (or inactions) you feel are causing the problem(s). Examples include: the general education classroom teacher is not making the modifications to my child's tests according to the IEP, or the IEP says my child is to receive services from a teacher of students with learning disabilities for ninety minutes a day, and they are only getting services twice a week for sixty minutes per session.

Textbox 12.2.   Contents of the Complaint (IDEA Regulation, 34 C.F.R. § 300.508[b])

- The name of the child.
- The address of the residence of the child.
- The name of the school the child is attending.
- In the case of a homeless child or youth, available contact information and the name of the school the child is attending.
- A description of the nature of the problem of the child related to the proposed or refused initiation or change, including the facts related to the problem.
- A proposed resolution of the problem to the extent known and available to the party at the time.

Pay attention to the procedural safeguards notice to understand the specific steps your state has for filing a due process complaint. In some states the request needs to go to the school district. District officials will then forward the request to the state agency that coordinates due process hearings. In other states the request needs to come directly to the state from the parents, with a copy being provided to the school district at the same time.

It may be advisable to ask someone else read your complaint. This could be an advocate or friend, but this person should provide you with honest feedback about whether they understand what you are requesting. Try to get individuals who are not special education knowledgeable to read and see if they can understand what you are seeking, and why. Do not make accusation in the complaint. Keep the focus on the special education services for the child. Revise the complaint if necessary. Be very specific about what you expect and by whom. Again, the school district does not have to provide the best services for your child, just an appropriate education. Keep this in mind so that what you are seeking is reasonable. A reasonable request is more likely to get a settlement than one that is so very different from the school district position. Again, keep the focus on the student and their needs.

After you file a complaint, you will be contacted by school district officials to arrange a resolution meeting. This meeting represents an opportunity to settle the dispute without involving attorneys, a due process hearing office, or an ALJ. It is important that the meeting be approached with the utmost seriousness and willingness to participate in a meaningful manner. The resolution meeting is required by the IDEA. When parents have chosen not to participate in the meeting, due process hearing officers and ALJs have dismissed their due process complaints and these rulings have been upheld by the courts. In chapter 5 we provided detailed information on resolution meetings.

Consider Settling the Dispute

Settling the issues with the school district is a way to end a dispute and may result in getting appropriate services for a student more quickly. Additionally, a settlement has the advantage of avoiding the costs and time spent on a due process hearing and the potential animosity that will likely occur if a parent were to file a due process complaint. See chapter 7 on settlement disputes for elaboration.

You may lose. If you have spent the time preparing for the hearing as noted above, with reading, revising, and developing a table of contents for the information. You have sought out and met with other parents. Considered hiring an attorney, or even hired an attorney and provided a retainer. This is a massive time, and possibly financial commitment. It is also an emotional investment. In the end you may have the exact same level of service and amount of education for your child as when you started this process. This is why it is important to talk with others and make sure what you are seeking is within the law, and there are clear needs for your child to have these services.

Participating in a Due Process Hearing

The actual hearing will go better for a parent if they have spent time in preparation. The state of Pennsylvania has a video of what a typical hearing looks like, we recommend watching the entire video and you can see the level of detailed and how formal the process is of a hearing where a due process officer would come to the district hear testimony. The video is only fifty minutes long—many due process hearings are much longer, but it is worth the watch.[2]

Each hearing is individualized, focusing on the specific needs and questions presented to the hearing office. Your hearing may be very different based on the personality and leadership style of the hearing officer, your attorney, or the school district's attorney. Also, the issues may alter the dynamics of the hearing. We have seen some hearings that are completed in a few hours, while others may take multiple eight-hour sessions.

Depending on the hearing officers' style and availability, they may meet with representatives of both parties prior to the hearing, often a few days before the hearing starts. If you have an attorney the hearing officer will meet with your attorney and the school district attorney in a phone call or Zoom session. If the parents are not represented, then it is the parent and the attorney for the district. The purpose of this session is to clarify the issues for the hearing, the process, who will be testifying, and any issues relating to scheduling of session dates and witnesses. Most likely there will also be an attempt to settle all or most of the issues prior to the commencement of testimony.

The time right before a hearing is often a very good time to try to settle as both parties are now very focused on the issues and have been preparing and hopefully really understand the positives and negative of their case. For some parents it is the time where even if they do not achieve all they were seeking

---

[2] Pennsylvania due process hearing video: https://vimeo.com/279258179.

from the district, they have the districts undivided attention and feel like their child's education will be more closely monitored from this point forward.

If the attorneys did not conference with the hearing officer a few days prior to the hearing there will be a face-to-face conference with the hearing officer just prior to the start of the hearing. Again, if you are represented by an attorney then you will likely not be a part of this meeting as it is the time for the two attorneys to meet with the hearing officer and talk about the issue(s) and the format for the proceedings. This is typically done in a separate room and the length of time can vary from a few minutes to much longer as they are working out the details behind the scenes. If you do not have an attorney you will meet with the hearing officer and the attorney for the school district. Again, like above, there may be a discussion of a possible settlement. For specific information in the due process hearing, see chapter 6.

Conclusion

Due process hearings are a time and emotionally intensive process for parents. However, they also may be very important to ensure your child with a disability receives the FAPE to which they are eligible. We have extensively advocated not going to a hearing and pursuing every other available way to settle the issue first. The seriousness of the process cannot be overstated—it is important for all parties to remember this. There are many reasons not to go to a hearing. There are also many steps that parents should take before requesting a due process hearing. If you are going to go, make sure you are prepared. This might be your only chance for someone from the outside of your district to hear your side of the story. Take it seriously.

References

IDEA, 20 U.S.C. § 1401 et seq.
IDEA Regulations, 34 C.F.R. § 300 et seq.

CHAPTER 13

How to Read a
Due Process Hearing Decision

Advance Organizers

- What is a due process hearing decision?
- How does one read a due process hearing decision?
- What are the various parts of a due process hearing decision?
- What is the discussion and conclusion of law?
- What is the Order? Where is this found?
- What happens after the decision?

At the conclusion of the hearing, the hearing officer has the very important and difficult task of writing his or her decision. During the decision writing phase, the hearing officer weighs the issues raised during the hearing, the evidence submitted, and the testimony provided. These considerations are weighed against the statutes, regulations, and relevant interpretations by the courts. The most important court interpretations the hearing officer will weigh will be rulings from the U.S. Court of Appeals in the circuit in which the due process hearing occurred, which are controlling in that circuit, and rulings of the U.S. Supreme Court, which are controlling throughout the United States and territories.

The decision must be released within forty-five calendar days after the expiration of the thirty-day resolution meeting (IDEA Regulations, 34 C.F.R. § 300.515). At the time, a copy of the decision must be made available to all parties. The decision will contain all of the information from the hearing, summarize the important parts of the law(s), and make conclusions from their perspective about the program and placement for the student. This decision is binding on both parties unless it is appealed. When one receives a decision from a hearing officer, it is very important to read the entire document and digest the decision before making any determinations about whether there will be an appeal. The following chapter describes how to read a due process hearing decision[1] and offers tips and strategies for reviewing the document.

---

[1] Although due process decisions will contain similar information, hearing officers have their own individual styles of writing so the format may vary from decision to decision.

The culminating event of a due process hearing is the hearing officer issuing a written ruling on the facts of the case. They will have heard the testimony, reviewed the files and reports, and then are sent the transcript to read again. They are working to get the decision out in a timely fashion. The period between when the hearing ends and the receipt of the decision often seems like a long time to wait, but there really is a lot that has to occur in order for this to happen. During the waiting period, there is nothing that can be done to change the contents of the decision, but this is also a waiting period where the student is still needing to be receiving an education. Therefore, meetings about the child's day-to-day education and needs still need to be addressed. However, the waiting for the decision seems like a long time.

The decision will address only those issues where relevant testimony and evidence was presented throughout the due process hearing sessions. The identified issues that were agreed to at the pre-hearing conference prior to the due process hearing will be addressed in the final decision. If there was agreement on issues during the hearing then the hearing officer will state there was agreement and write a decision on the issues. The decision is the determination of the hearing officer of the issues in dispute that was the basis for the hearing. The decision is reached only after both sides of the dispute are heard and all issues are examined.

In general, the ruling by a due process hearing officer contain the following parts, but not all hearing officers include every section listed below. The final ruling written by the hearing officer does not begin until the section located at the very end of the document, which is often titled opinion or order. We will reference the hearing officer decision that is included in appendix B as we go through this chapter. The order of the hearing officer in that case, like many others, is the last page of the decision. We will discuss the components of the hearing officer's decision and provide commentary about what is important about those parts, and why they are included.

What Is a Decision?

In some jurisdictions this is called an Opinion. When a hearing officer hears a case and arrives at a judgment, an explanation or analysis of the reasoning behind the decision is written. The analysis, called a Decision or Opinion, is then forwarded to the parties involved in the hearing. Frequently, the reader will have to determine the relevant facts, issues, and holding from the body of the decision or opinion. The bulk of the decision or opinion of a hearing officer will usually consist of an analysis of the case, which includes the school districts arguments and supporting evidence, and the parent's argument and supporting evidence, and then their review of the cases, statutes, and facts applicable to the hearing. The hearing officer will set forth the cases, statutes, and facts upon which the decision or order is based. A decision usually contains the following general categories of information: title, facts, issue, decision, and order.

The decision will be in written form and will be provided to both parties involved in the due process hearing after all testimony and evidence have been presented. The testimony and evidence need to be reviewed by the hearing officer to help them in making and writing their decision. This section will present information on the components of the due process hearing decision, how the decision is written, what the decision means to both parties involved, and what may occur as a result of the decision. This section should be read in conjunction with the decision that is included in appendix B. Understanding keys aspects of the decision helps participants prepare for the due process hearing.

The hearing officer's decision must be supported by testimony given by witnesses and evidence presented at the hearing. Hearing officers have the responsibility of making determinations regarding the relevancy of the evidence and testimony. There may be some testimony that was presented that the hearing officer decides was not germane to the issues, and the hearing officer will give more weight to testimony based on the witness's qualifications and credibility and to evidence related to the issues needed to be decided upon. Finally, in addition to testimony and evidence, the due process hearing officer will rely on federal and state laws and prior litigation related to the IDEA in making their decision. If the decision is appealed, the reviewing officer or judge will rely on the hearing officer's ruling.

How to Read a Decision

First, start at the beginning. It is tempting to just go to the last page and read the final order, but it is very important to understand the issues, facts, and legal cases cited that lead to the order, and that can only be done by reading from the beginning. The case really should build upon itself, and be logical to follow, especially if it contains all the parts as we discuss below. Use the first few pages of a decision to orient yourself and get a good idea of what the case is about and what the ultimate decision was.

Part One: Cover Page

This is typically page one of the decision. The purpose of the cover page is to identify the particular case and the parties involved in the hearing. Although states may have rules regarding what should appear on the cover page, it will typically identify the student's name (often just the initials), a file number for the SEA responsible for overseeing due process hearings, the date(s) of the due process hearing session(s), the parent(s) names and address and the name and address of the parent's representative, the name and address of the school/school district and the name and address of their representative, the date that the final due process hearing transcript was received by the hearing officer, the date the decision was rendered by the hearing officer and the name of the due process hearing officer. Often, the only personally identifiable information on the student and the participants in the hearing will appear on the cover page and nowhere else in the hearing officer's decision. For example, in the decision the student is often referred to a "student" or "child" and not by name. Sometimes the parties will by referred to as "petitioner" and "respondent." Information that may be included on the over page is listed in textbox 13.1.

> ## Textbox 13.1. A list of items that may be included on the cover page
>
> - The name of the case
> - The name of the hearing officer
> - The student's name (often redacted)
> - The name of the attorneys for the parents and the school district
> - The name of the school district
> - The date of the hearing
> - The date of the hearing officer's decision

Many due process hearing decisions also include whether the decision was an open or closed hearing. In an open hearing, anyone from the public may attend and the decision, with the student's name but not the transcript and other materials from the hearing may be released and made available to interested persons. In a closed hearing, only the parents, the student, the parents' representative, others designated by the parents, school officials, witnesses to be called upon to testify, the hearing officer, and the recorder may attend. The decision will be released in an identifiable form only to the parties to the hearing and those persons who must implement the decision. The decision, when released, is often redacted and in a form where parties outside of the hearing would not be able to determine who the hearing was about, as hearing, and the facts around the matter, involve a minor.

Part Two: Executive Summary

Some hearing officer decisions provide a short executive summary of the case. This summary may include very brief information about the issues brought up in the hearing. Often it will include information about the hearing such as how many sessions the hearing lasted, if the sessions were delayed by illness, or the current status of the student.

Part Three: The Issues in the Case

Because a due process hearing is a legal proceeding, the issues of conflict between the parents and school district that are the grist of the hearing will be presented. The issue is the disputed point or question of law related to the appropriateness of the special education services for a student. The issues were agreed to in the preferring conference and stated on the record by the hearing officer, often asking if both parties agree that these are the issues. Both parties to the due process hearing have narrowed their claims or allegations, and the hearing is necessary to obtain a decision on the remaining issue. The issues in a due process hearing can involve the identification, programming, or the appropriateness of the educational or related services provided to the student. The issues serve as the basis for the due process hearing. This will potentially reduce the issues for the hearing and also reduce the days necessary to present the case and will move the education forward more quickly for a student.

The following are examples of statements of issues:

* Did the district deny the student FAPE for the period February 2021 through June 2022? 2. If this question is in the affirmative, is the student entitled to a remedy?
* The only issue presented in this matter is: Are the parents entitled to an IEE at the district's expense.
* Whether the parents have proven that the student's placement in general education classes rather than in special education classes violated the IDEA. Whether the parents have proven that the student's IEPs denied the student a free and appropriate public education.
* Has the district provided the student with FAPE over the period of the student's enrollment at the district, from April 2021 through January 2022? Has the district treated the student with deliberate indifference, amounting to discrimination against the student on the basis of disability? If either/both of the questions is/are answered in the affirmative what, if any, remedy is owed to the student?
* Should the district have identified the student as a student with an intellectual disability prior to November 2020? If so, did this mis-identification deny the student FAPE? Regardless of the answers to the foregoing questions, did the District provide FAPE to the student through its programming over the period from late August 2020–November 2022? Is the student owed compensatory education for certain days of absence due to district transportation issues?

Part Four: The Facts of the Case

Typically, this is where the facts the hiring officer based their decision on are located. Facts include that the student is a resident of the district, the student's birthdate, whether they are eligible for special education, dates of meetings, locations of services, and test scores. Facts are circumstances, events, or occurrences as they actually took place and can also be physical objects as they actually exist or existed. A fact is an event. It is also a reality as distinguished from fiction or error. There may have been disputes about the facts as well as the law. If a fact is agreed to it may have been referred to as a stipulation.

A common way of presenting the facts is as a chronological listing of information obtained from the notes of testimony and evidence/exhibits placed into the record. The due process hearing officer will cite only those facts that were relied upon in making the decision as well as facts that were agreed upon by both parties if they are relevant in the hearing officer's decision.

To make it easier for both parties and for appeals, the hearing officer may use a uniform numbering and lettering system relating to the exhibits there were entered into the record, and the specific pages of testimony from the transcript.

Let's use the following as an example, it is from the decision that is included in appendix B. The abbreviation P-8 means it is located in the Parent exhibit that was the eighth one entered into the hearing. P-1 would be the first one, P-2 the second, and so on. The abbreviation S-1 means the first exhibit entered into the hearing by the school district. NT means note to transcript. NT 14 means the information can be found on page 14 of the transcript. The due process hearing officer will often cite every *finding of fact* that is relevant to their decision.

1. A. was born on April 22, 2009. He is currently thirteen years of age (P-8, p. 1)
2. A. is a resident of the district (P-6, p. 14, NT 14).
3. A. is eligible for special education and related services as a student with a learning disability (P-4, NT 14).
4. There have been two previous due process hearings involving A. (S-1, S-2, S-3, S-4; NT 18, 24, 31).
5. In December 2019, the student was reevaluated by the neighboring school district. (Joint Exhibit ["J"]-2).
6. The December 2019 reevaluation report showed that the student was "well below expectations" in word reading, reading comprehension, spelling, and math computation. The student received direct instruction/academic support in reading and mathematics. (J-2).
7. The December 2019 reevaluation report recommended the student continue to be identified as a student with a learning disability and a health impairment and that the student continue to receive academic support. (J-2).
8. The student attended the neighboring school district until mid-April 2020, when the student enrolled at the district in fourth grade. (J-2, J-6; Notes of Testimony ["NT"] at 26–54, 74–123).
9. Upon enrolling, the district notified the parents that the district would implement the student's individualized education program ("IEP") (S-13).
10. In December 2019, the student had only just enrolled in the neighboring school district, transferring there from a different school district, where the student had been identified as a student with a learning disability and a health impairment. (J-2 at pages 2–3). Four months later, in April 2020, the student enrolled in the district, against whom the complaint in this matter was filed. On May 1, 2020, two weeks after the student enrolled in the District, the District held an IEP meeting to discuss the student's programming at the District. Parents did not attend the IEP meeting. (J-3, J-6; NT at 26–54, 58–71, 74–123).
11. The May 2020 IEP included curriculum-based assessments for the present-levels of functional and academic performance, which showed adequate achievement at the 3rd grade level and lower levels of achievement at the 4th grade level. (J-3; NT at 74–123).
12. The May 2020 IEP contained five goals (reading fluency, reading comprehension, written expression, math computation, and math concepts/applications). (J-3).
13. The student's special education teacher testified that the goals in the May 2020 IEP were written at the fourth grade level to show one year's progress over the instructional year. (NT at 74–123).

14. Over the six weeks remaining in the 2020–2021 school year, the student showed progress across all five IEP goals. (J-3 at pages 18–22).
15. The student lacked focus and needed significant redirection. Specially designed instruction and program modifications in the May 2020 IEP addressed this need. (J-3; NT at 74–123).

Part Five: Discussion and Conclusion of Law

Hearing officer decisions may use legalistic language in the decision. Because the IDEA requires that a hearing officer's decision be based solely on the evidence presented at the hearing, often hearing officers will refer directly to the evidence and to the specific provisions of statutes, regulations, and applicable case law at throughout the decision. Read through the decision and pay attention to the statements of law. This section, which is often the bulk of the ruling, is where the hearing officer discusses the issues along with the evidence and testimony from the hearing that the hearing officer has used to make his or her decision. Hearing officers will often cite back to the testimony, the exhibits, the findings of fact, and link their discussion with relevant laws, regulations, and applicable cases. The main responsibility of a due process hearing officer is to sort out the facts presented at the due process hearing (either testimony or exhibits) and apply the law to these facts.

The discussion and conclusions of law lead the hearing officer to the order. This is why it is important to read a hearing officer's decision from start to finish as the document builds upon itself, and it is often very difficult to understand an order without reading and understanding the previous sections.

Part Six: The Hearing Officer's Order

This is the final statement on the due process hearing. This is the culmination of all the preparation, discussions, witnesses, and exhibits. The order should address the specific issues that were agreed to by both parties and should be clear and concise. The order should very specifically state the obligations of the district related to the education of the student and what is now enforceable by law. This is the new programming for the student unless it is appealed (see below). This is also the last page of the decision.

The following are examples of different orders from hearing officers.

* In accord with the findings of fact and conclusions of law as set forth above, the #### School District did not deny the student a free appropriate public education. Any claim not specifically addressed in this decision and order is denied and dismissed.
* Based upon the foregoing, it is HEREBY ORDERED that all relief requested in the due process complaint is hereby denied. The complaint is dismissed. IT IS SO ORDERED.
* It is hereby ORDERED as follows: 1. The District's Evaluation, dated ###, is appropriate. 2. The Parents are not entitled to an IEE at public expense. 3. Nothing herein alters the Parents right to obtain an IEE at their own

expense or the District's obligation to consider any such IEE if the Parents obtain one. It is FURTHER ORDERED that any claim not specifically addressed in this order is DENIED and DISMISSED.

* In accord with the findings of fact and conclusions of law as set forth above, the #### School District met its obligations to propose and to implement appropriate special education programming for the student. The school district did not treat the student with deliberate indifference as a student with a disability. Any claim not specifically addressed in this decision and order is denied and dismissed.

* In accord with the findings of fact and conclusions of law as set forth above, the student is awarded 115 hours of compensatory education. Any claim not specifically addressed in this decision and order is denied and dismissed.

* The Parents are entitled to reimbursement for actual tuition and related expenses that they incurred for the Private School for the 2020–2021 and 2021–2022 school years, less a reduction of 10 percent of those total costs. Within fifteen calendar days of the date of this decision, the Parents shall provide new documentation to the District of all current invoices and receipts for tuition and related expenses for Student for the 2020–2021 and 2021–2022 school years. Within fifteen calendar days of the date of this decision, the District shall reimburse the Parents for 90 percent of the full amount of invoices and receipts provided pursuant to this decision.

The final statement in an order will usually include the guidelines and dates for filing an appeal.

What Happens After the Decision?

The decision is the culmination of the due process hearing procedures. As we have noted repeatedly throughout this text, both parties will have to work together to provide the education for the student after the hearing is complete. As you can see from the Orders above, they are directing both parties one way or another, and hopefully this will have resolved the issues that led to the due process hearing. The next set of steps depend on whether the decision of the hearing officer is appealed. If the decision of the hearing officer is not appealed, the order is the final statement on this issue and both parties will have to then implement that order. In some states if the order is not implemented then a complaint can be filed to ensure implementation.

If the order is appealed by either party then the case goes to the next level for the appeal. If the state is a one-tier state then the appeal goes to either state or federal court. If the state is a two-tier state (hearing officer and appeals panel of hearing officers) then the appeal goes to the panel. The decision, transcript, exhibits, and the reason(s) for the appeal are forwarded to the next level. A due process hearing and the decision of the hearing officer is to occur within the prescribed amount of time unless there are extenuating circumstances and there is a need for a continuance. The timelines that hearing officers have do not apply to state or federal court so there may be a lengthy delay in obtaining a hearing and decision from the court. Additionally, because the due process hearing is the fact-finding part of the process, it is a necessity as a part of seeking adjudication on an issue. This means a parent or school district cannot go directly into state or federal court without first having a due process hearing on the issue(s).

If there is an appeal of the decision of the due process hearing officer and a judicial action is pending, the last agreed upon, or pendent placement holds. The school district may not change the student's placement without parental consent or a court order.

Conclusion

When one commits to being a party in a due process hearing, one also commits to the fact there may be an adversarial ruling on the issues. This chapter covers the parts of a decision and provides steps for how to review the document. This ruling is binding on both parties until is appealed. Appeals in the majority of states that have one tier often take longer than the initial due process hearing.

CHAPTER 14

After a Due Process Hearing

Advance Organizers

* What should be done after a due process hearing?
* What should be one of the first steps after a hearing?
* What changes should be made after a hearing?
* What are the costs of a hearing?
* What are legal recourses following a hearing?
* What are the steps in appealing a decision?

Following a due process hearing three very important events will occur. First, if the hearing officer's decision is against the school district, there may be an award of relief or remedies for the parents. Second, either party may appeal the decision. Third, school district personnel have an opportunity to make proactive changes to ensure that the problems that led to the hearing do not recur. In this chapter we address these three areas.

The Relief that a Hearing Officer May Order

The IDEA authorizes courts to provide relief to the prevailing party. According to the language of the IDEA,

> (i) the court shall receive the records of the administrative proceedings, (ii) shall hear additional evidence at the request of a party, and (iii) basing its decision on the preponderance of the evidence, shall grant such relief as the court determines is appropriate. (IDEA, 20 U.S.C. § 14151415[i][2][C][iii])

However, neither the IDEA nor the regulations implementing the IDEA clarify what constitutes appropriate relief that courts may award and, therefore, types of relief that a hearing office may order is not addressed in the law.

Court rulings, including decision by the U.S. Supreme Court, have clarified the type of relief that may be awarded to prevailing plaintiffs in a special education dispute. Table 14.1 includes the various forms of relief that courts may order, a description of these types of relief, and relevant court decisions or citations in the law or regulations that address the particular type of relief.

Table 14.1.   Relief that Courts May Order

Relief	Description	Statute and/or Court Ruling
Tuition reimbursement	Tuition reimbursement is available if (a) the school district's special education failed to provide a FAPE, and (b) the private school provide an appropriate education	• *Burlington v. Department of Education of Massachusetts* (1982) • *Florence School District Four v. Carter* (1993) • *Forest Grove v. T.A.* (2009) • IDEA, 20 U.S.C. § 1412(a)(10)(C)(ii)
Compensatory education	The purpose of compensatory education is to place students with disabilities in the same position they would have been in if a school district's violations had provided the student with a FAPE.	• *Meiner v. Missouri* (1986) • *G.L. v. Ligonier Valley School District* (2015). • *Doe v. East Lyme Board of Education* (2015)
Attorneys' fees	Prevailing parties may be awarded reimbursement for reasonable attorneys' fees in a lawsuit brought under the IDEA. A court may also award attorney's fees to a school district against the parents' attorney who files a complaint or a subsequent cause of action that is frivolous, unreasonable, or without foundation, or if the parents' attorney continued to litigate after the litigation became unreasonable or without foundation.	• *A.R. v. New York City Department of Education* (2005). • *Neosho R-V School District v. Clark* (2003) • *Schaffer v. Weast* (2005) • IDEA, 20 U.S.C. § 1415l(i)(3(B)
Injunctive Relief	An injunctive remedy is awarded to require a party to refrain from or discontinue a certain action. It is a preventive measure.	• *Light v. Parkway School District* (1994).

It is less clear, however, about what types of relief that hearing officers may order. The IDEA does provide hearing officers with the authority to award tuition reimbursement:

> If the parents of a child with a disability, who previously received special education and related services under the authority of a public agency, enroll the child in a private elementary school or secondary school without the consent of or referral by the public agency, a court or a hearing officer may require the agency to reimburse the parents for the cost of that enrollment if the court or hearing officer finds that the agency had not made a free appropriate public education available to the child in a timely manner prior to that enrollment. (IDEA, 20 U.S.C. § 1412[a][10][C][ii])

Additionally, hearing officers may award compensatory education. Compensatory education awards may include educational services such as extended school year, private tutoring, speech services, and psychological services. Hearing officers can also provide reimbursement for an independent educational evaluation purchased by prevailing parents.

Hearing officers may also order prospective relief, which means a hearing officer may order a school district to take certain actions such as developing a new IEP, providing for an independent educational evaluation, or arranging for personnel development training for school personnel.

A reading of the IDEA and regulations indicate that only courts, not hearing officers, have the authority under the law to award attorney's fees. According to a section in the IDEA on the jurisdiction of district courts, "(T)he district courts of the United States shall have jurisdiction . . . in (B) (A)ward of attorneys' fees—(i) the court, in its discretion may award reasonable attorneys' fees" (IDEA, 20 U.S.C. § 1415[i][3]B][i]). Additionally, courts have ruled that courts are specifically authorized to award attorneys' fees in actions under the IDEA but that this authorization does not extend to hearing officers (Lake, 2019). However, officials at the Office of Special Education Programs (OSEP) in the U.S. Department of Education have concluded that the IDEA neither authorizes nor prohibits states from allowing hearing officers to award attorneys fees (*Letter to Anonymous*, 1992).

Appealing a Due Process Hearing Decision

According to the IDEA's regulations, "A decision made in a hearing . . . is final, except that either party involved in the hearing may appeal the decision" (IDEA Regulations, 34 C.F.R. § 300.514[a]). Once a decision is rendered, therefore, the parties must comply with the decision, unless an appeal is filed. The appealing party must first decide if they will file an appeal.

Should There Be an Appeal?

The decision to appeal a due process hearing decision rests on a variety of factors. One of the most important factors in the decision process to consider is the extended length of time the case will consume and the emotional strain you will experience if you appeal. The opportunities for that student to receive an appropriate education get shorter with each passing day. As noted above, the timelines for a due process hearing are fairly straightforward. An appeal in a two tier state will take thirty days, however, appeals to courts will typically take another full year and one still might not receive the desired ruling.

If the hearing officer overseeing your case made some serious mistakes or they disregarded the current law, then an appeal should be considered. Mistakes that hearing officers make that are considered appealable include refusing vital pieces of evidence, refusing to admit expert testimony, showing an obvious bias, or clearly misunderstanding the law. These are factors that should strongly be considered for an appeal.

There is not a case where we would absolutely recommend that there needs to be an appeal. Remember the child, and remember that sometimes, we need to just move on and work together. It may have become obvious to during the due process hearing that your side was lacking evidence, the other side clearly had the data to demonstrate what they are doing was effective, or the other side had the right argument. Learning that should help you realize it is time to stop.

Typically, an appeals brief must be submitted to a federal courthouse within thirty days of the hearing officer's judgment in order to be valid. If the appeal is at all late, it will not be heard. If you are considering appealing, it is usually best to seek out an attorney experienced with appellate matters as soon as you have reached the conclusion that an appeal is best. Otherwise, you may miss your chance.

Whether or not you should go through the appeals process is thus going to vary depending upon both whether it is likely you can prevail on an argument there was a problem with the original decision, as well as on whether it is worth the cost and time to fight the original court decision.

When you appeal the decision, you will be prolonging the outcome of the case, but you also need to realize there is a chance you may not prevail at the appeal. You have already received a negative outcome from the hearing officer and you need to realize that this may happen again. There is no guarantee of success or outcome with an appeal. There may be a considerable time and money put into the appeal to receive the same outcome as what the hearing officer determined. Keep this in mind.

Appealing a Hearing Officer's Decision

If there is an appeal in a one-tier state, either party "has the right to bring a civil action" in state or federal court (IDEA Regulations, 34 C.F.R. § 300.516[a]). An appeal to a court must be made within ninety days unless a state of a timeline for submitting an appeal (IDEA Regulations, 34 C.F.R. § 300.516[B]).

In a two-tier state, an appeal is made to a review officer or state appeals panel. A decision must be made and transmitted to both parties within thirty days. Regulations to the IDEA require that the review officer or hearing panel (a) review the record of the hearing, (b) ensure that the procedures at the hearing were conducting consistent with the requirements of due process, (c) afford the parties an opportunity for oral or written or both at the review officer's discretion, and (d) seek additional evidence if needed (IDEA Regulations, 34 C.F.R. § 300.514[b][[2][11-1v]). Moreover, although the decision made by the review officer must be an independent decision, the reviewing officer must give deference to the local hearing officer's findings (Clark County School District, 2013). In other words, the review officer must conduct an independent review of the hearing officer's decision while also deciding how much deference is due the decision. Following the decision of the tier two hearing officer or panel, an appeal may be filed with a state or federal court.

Either the court, review officer, or appeals panel will receive the record of the due process hearing, hear additional evidence at the request of a party, and base its decision on the preponderance of evidence (IDEA Regulations, 34 C.F.R § 300.516). In all cases, the review is limited to issues appealed by the appealing party (IDEA Regulations, 34 C.F.R. § 300.514). Moreover, if an issue was not raised in the due process hearing it will most likely be prohibited to be considered on appeal (Lake, 2019). The appeals body would review what transpired in the due process hearing proceedings for any errors of law. In an appeal, a hearing officer's ruling may be upheld, reversed, or upheld in part and reversed in part, which means that some of the hearing officer's decision is affirmed but other parts are reversed.

Often people incorrectly believe in an appeal that they get a "do over." However, the party that appeals a due process may only challenge decisions that may have resulted from errors, such as a misinterpretation of legal precedent or reliance on evidence that should have been excluded. The purpose of this section is to discuss the determination that needs to be made about whether to appeal an unfavorable decision from a hearing officer. In order to offer guidance on this topic, we need to clarify the process and basics of an appeal.

It is strongly recommended that if either party decides to appeal a case, they have competent legal counsel to assist with that process. Hopefully the parties do not appeal a hearing decision because they want to prolong the litigation relating to the education of a student with a disability. In fact, if either party files a due process hearing complaint or civil action that is "frivolous, unreasonable, or without foundation" or for any "improper purpose, such as to harass, to cause unnecessary delay, or to needlessly increase the cost of litigation," that party could find attorney's fees being assessed against them (IDEA Regulations, 34 C.F.R. § 300.517[a][ii–iii]).

The hope of an appeal is to overturn the adverse ruling that was received in the due process hearing. This will only occur if the appeals court finds an error of law or fact finding that contributed to the due process hearing officer's decision. If that happens, the appeals court could reverse all or part of the hearing officer's decision.

The Appeals Process

In the appeals process, the parties to the due process hearing, typically attorneys, submit briefs to the court, review officer, or appeals panel. The reviewing body then conducts an independent review based on the entire record. A due process hearing and an appeal have a few similarities, but also many important differences. Understanding the differences can help aggrieved parties decide about whether to appeal the hearing officer's decision.

Information in an Appeal of a Hearing

At a due process hearing, the parties present their cases, calling witnesses for testimony and presenting other pieces of evidence, such as documents, student reports, evaluations, observations, teacher notes, behavioral records, etc. The due process hearing officer controls the activities in the hearing and makes all the legal decisions, such as ruling on motions and on objections raised by the attorneys. The due process hearing officer weighs this evidence and determines the facts of the case, that is, what they believe actually happened. A due process hearing officer is therefore referred to as the "finder of fact."

An appeal is a review of the due process hearing officer's application of the law. There is no jury in an appeal, nor do the lawyers present witnesses or, typically, other forms of evidence. The court will accept the facts as they were revealed in the due process hearing unless a factual finding is clearly against the weight of the evidence.

Appellate Briefs

The primary source of information provided to the appeals court, review officer, or hearing panel, in addition to the hearing transcripts and evidence, is the written appellate brief, filed by attorney for each party. With this brief, the party that received the adverse determination by the hearing officer in the due process hearing will argue the hearing officer incorrectly applied the law. The party that had a more positive decision from the hearing officer will argue the hearing officer's decision and determination was correct. Both parties will need to support their positions with reference to applicable case law and statutes.

The big difference between a due process hearing and an appeal is that an appeal is a more scholarly proceeding than a trial. Whereas the attorney must be an active presence in the due process hearing, calling witnesses, cross-examining, and making motions or objections, the appellate lawyer builds their case in the brief before the appeal is heard. Appeals often include a short period for oral argument, but the judges often consume this period with questions for the attorney, prompted by the briefs.

The Transcript of the Due Process Hearing

In an appeal, the transcript of the due process hearing is a very important part of the process. This is the official transcript and exhibits that were used as a part of the due process hearing. All exhibits entered into the record during the hearing, all testimony, including comments made by the hearing office constitute the record of the hearing. Appeals decisions rely on this record and exhibits from the due process hearing. The record contains the pleadings, plaintiff's complaint and defendant's answer, pre-trial motions, a transcript of what occurred during trial, the exhibits put into evidence, post-trial motions, and any discussion with the due process hearing officer that did not take place "off the record." The decision in an appeal depends on what occurred during the hearing. If an attorney or parent failed to raise important issues, introduce to get critical, available evidence into the record, or to object to something prejudicial, the opportunity to do so is lost.

After Appealing a Court Decision

The party that loses in a state or federal appeals court may appeal to the state Supreme Court or continue in the federal court system. This does not guarantee a hearing, as these courts receive many more requests for review than they can handle. They typically grant review only to cases involving unsettled questions of law. Finally, the U.S. Supreme Court only reviews cases that raise some federal or constitutional issue. For example, cases that concern state law exclusively are beyond its jurisdiction. By the time a case has been appealed to the Supreme Court, the parties have already had the case reviewed multiple times, reducing their tendency to see the decisions as biased or contrary to law.

Learning from a Due Process Hearing or State Complaint

After a hearing officer's decision is issued, the district will still have to provide educational services for the student. The teachers will still have to work with the family, and the staff who have been implementing the IEP are likely to be still employed by the district. Just because the hearing is over does not mean that everything will return to how it was before the hearing. Obviously, there was a need to bring in someone from the outside to adjudicate a dispute. That should be a sign that something is amiss in how services are provided. It is imperative for the district to learn from what happened as a part of the dispute and to take that information to make changes so that there is less likelihood for additional disputes or problems to occur.

A district in Pennsylvania of about 1,200 students recently went through a protracted due process hearing, which eventually ended in an award of $65,000 in compensatory education plus attorney's fees. The district had about 155 students eligible for special education and related services, which was a percentage a little below the state average. Over the past few years, the district had been averaging about five to six special education due process hearing requests a year or complaints to the state department of education. The district dutifully pays its insurance every year and makes certain it has attorney coverage for these cases. The teachers in the district are getting used to producing documents and testifying. The school psychologist spends many hours getting ready for her testimony, and the district has changed special education directors four times in the past eight years. The district spends a lot of time and money on special education concerns and litigation.

It is easy to write off this district's story as a litigation nightmare, a rare convergence of events that have stuck a small district that has had a lot of turnover in staff and administration. However, federal data has shown that what has happened to this district has happened to many districts across the nation, and more is expected as a direct result of the recent Supreme Court decision in *Endrew F. v. Douglas County School District* (2017). There are numerous hearings, complaints, and lawsuits filed relating to special education every year. Special education is easily the most litigious field in education.

It would be normal to expect a few dozen complaints each year, and depending on the size of your district some may turn into a due process hearing. There are sometimes, no matter what you do, personalities that will cause a dispute. And there are some people who, no matter what you do, cannot be pleased. But the fact remains that there are many of these special education cases and the trend is toward more. This points to a much bigger problem in how we provide services to students with disabilities.

The fact that there are thousands of these lawsuits and complaints to state departments of education is often considered the price of doing business in the area of special education. It is often stated that special education is a field defined by a law, that came about as a result of lawsuits, and that litigation to hold districts' accountable through the ability to file a due process hearing is an unavoidable side effect of having to provide services to students with disabilities, often with not enough resources and appropriately trained staff.

However, there are some districts that have decided this should not be the case, and have decided to do something about this.

Plane v. Car Crash Analogy

VOX.com[1] used an analogy in the past that describes the way to look at tragedies as either a car crash or a plane crash. When there is a plane crash, there is often a very thorough investigation into the timeline of the accident, the specifics of the people who were involved, the processes that were followed and the procedures that happened up to the moment of the crash. As a result of the investigation, there is often a change in either procedures, training, or policies that hopefully will decrease the likelihood of a plane crashing as a result of the actions that are taken.

When there is a car crash, however, very rarely is there an investigation into the training, the procedures, the timeline up to the event, nor are there policies or anything often changed. Occasionally, if there are enough deaths in a certain intersection or stretch of road, they may change the signage, but that is a rare change. Car crashes are often viewed as the price of doing business.

When school districts are sued relating to special education, that is sometimes treated the same manner as if it is a car crash—as something that is inevitable and the price of doing business. However, there are some districts that have treated every due process hearing and complaint filed with the state department of education as a plane crash. These districts have responded by convening a team to do a critical analysis to determine what changes are necessary, implement the changes, and evaluate if that works or whether efforts are necessary.

---

[1] https://www.advisory.com/en/daily-briefing/2015/07/13/how-to-stop-infections-vox.

Opportunities to Learn from Due Process Hearings and State Complaints

We believe that it is important to study due process hearings and state complaints so that mistakes are not repeated. By learning from previous mistakes and problems, we will not only improve the services for students with disabilities, but will also improve morale among staff, because they will feel more comfortable with what they are doing and better understand the specifics of their job. Additionally, they will understand and be a part of corrective actions that make programs better for everyone—not in a punishing way—but in a manner that brings everyone on board to facilitate the education of students with disabilities.

This is not to say that making changes and preventing reoccurrences of special education disputes is easy. There may need to be staffing changes, additional people hired, or fairly dramatic changes to the previous policies of the school district that some employees may be uncomfortable with. Change is not easy. However, it is important to use the precipitating event of a lawsuit or complaint to initiate the changes necessary. The goal after a due process hearing is complete is to implement changes to prevent the same issues or problems that resulted in a hearing or complaint from occurring again. Doing the same, just because that has been the way we did it in the past, should not be the response to any lawsuit or complaint or crisis. Yes, we can learn from the past, but clearly there was a problem in the past and hence the need for change.

The process outlined in this book will help to provide a better understanding of why litigation in special education not only exists, but also to clarify the need to learn from what has occurred. This does not mean just in your own district; rather, it is important to learn what has happened in other districts and not make the same mistakes. Special education leaders should become students of special education law and keep abreast of recent changes as a result of litigation and regulations.

There are a number of action special education leaders can take to learn from due process hearings and state complaints. First, find changes that can be made that will be highly effective. A highly effective way of checking on the education of students in the district is ensure that all special education teachers are implementing the IEPs as written. Require teachers to review the amount and level of services that students are expected to receive in their IEPs and have them check that those services are being implemented. It is better for the teachers to find this out and not external sources such as compliance monitors or parent attorneys.

Second, implement a change that will be low-risk. An example of a low-risk change is sending notes to staff. For example, "the individuals who are listed on the IEP as participants must actually attend the IEP meeting. It is not acceptable to sign the IEP after the fact and list an individual as a participant if the person did not actually attend the IEP meeting. The list of participants on the IEP form documents attendance at the IEP meeting."

Third, special education leaders should consider the possibility of writing an intra-district blog to address possible issues that may need to be addressed regarding due process hearings and state complaints. One of the authors of this textbook knows a special education director in one of the larger school district in the state who regularly writes a blog of this nature. Moreover, meetings of special education teachers are regularly held, and frequently these blogs will be discussed.

We advocate the use of alternatives to due process hearings, which are less adversarial approaches to solving special education problems. We are aware there may be times when a due process hearing is necessary, however, special education leaders should strive to reduce these incidences that may lead to hearings. For many special education administrators and principals who may be involved with a due process hearing, there are important strategies and tips that should be used with staff.

Special education leaders should continually ask the question, "Is my district less likely this year to have litigation or state complaints than last year?" This is a question that many school board members rightfully have as they are concerned about the excessive costs districts incur when they are involved in litigation. Decisions over the next year about staffing, checking progress monitoring data, ensuring compliance with timelines and what is written into the IEPs is important. Additional questions that special education leaders should ask themselves are as follows:

- Are all decisions about service provided to students made based on the individual needs of the child? This may seem basic, but sometimes decisions are inappropriately based on the student's disability label, assuming all students with that disability label require a certain service or location of service.
- Are students' IEPs reasonably calculated to enable a student to make progress appropriate in light of the student's circumstances? This is the test from the U.S. Supreme Court's ruling in *Endrew F. v. Douglas County School District* (2017) that every hearing officer will use to determine if a student's IEP provided FAPE. Have we provided and implemented a program for the student that has clear expectations and the determinations are based on their potential?
- Do the present levels of academic achievement and functional performance address all of a student's needs and do these statements lead to measurable annual goals, services based on peer-reviewed research, or both measurable goals and services of challenging, ambitious goals for every student?
- Are the goals ambitious, measurable, and regularly measured and reported to parents? All goals for the student needs be quantified. If you cannot quantify the goal, it is probably not a good goal. Review all IEPs to ensure the goals are measurable and that staff are regularly measuring the goals, and not just once or twice a marking period. Goals need to be measured multiple times so that trends and determinations can be made about whether the student is making progress. Without regular measurement, it is impossible to make this determination.

- If a student is not making progress on their IEP goals and objectives, do special education teachers make changes to the student' program and continue to collect data? It may take more than one change to the program, but the only way this can occur is if there is regular data being kept on the student's goals. District may be accountable for a student's failure to make progress.
- If the student is identified as having a behavioral problem, make sure there are strategies within the IEP addressing those problems, or there are supports necessary to help the student make progress. For every need identified in a student's IEP, there has to be a corresponding support, or services for the student that addresses that need. When a student of academic and functional needs, a measurable annual goal and a way to measure progress toward that need will usually be required.

All due process hearings and state complaints are unique and individualized to the specific child, but special education leaders can learn from hearing complaints and state complaints. When a school district has a due process or state investigation filed, the special education leader should examine the complaint very carefully. Often when a complaint is filed there are multiple issues that are to be addressed. Take every one of the issues seriously and gather as much information about each issue as possible. Determine if the issues in the complaint could apply to other students in the district. Ensure that the necessary changes are made to students' IEPs, their level of services, the level of supports, and the implementation of the IEP so that further complaints can be avoided. Often when there is a problem with one child because of what is being provided (or not provided) there are issues with another child. Move quickly to implement the new program for the students.

Determine why the issues in the due process hearing or state complaint occurred. Was it because of one teacher writing a poor IEP? Was it due to lack of progress monitoring data by the district? Did the student need an aide and one was not provided? Did the aide do something they should not have been done as a part of the implementation of the IEP? Was something said to the parents that could easily be misinterpreted? Identify the issues and work to determine what is responsible for this occurring. Look at hiring practices, internal training, and internal monitoring of the program. Do not ignore any aspect of the program when looking at what happened. The important part is to identify the root cause of the problems.

After deciding about the issues or reasons for the problems, the special education leader should determine if additional training is necessary. Is additional training necessary for the paraprofessionals or aides? Do the bus drivers need training? Is there a problem with HR that needs to be addressed related to hiring? Do the teachers need training on progress monitoring data? The training necessary is dependent upon the issues that caused or were a part of the due process hearing. After the training and corrective actions are put into place, is there monitoring to ensure changes have occurred and the changes are being implemented as they should? There may need to be follow-up training to ensure there really is a change to the programs. Textbox 14.1 depicts additional changes that should be considered.

> ### Textbox 14.1. Additional Questions Regarding Changes to Consider
>
> - Does there need to be a policy change of any sort?
> - How are the students identified?
> - Is there a plan for making transportation decisions?
> - How do students transfer between classes?
> - What questions are asked of parents when they enroll their children in the district?
> - Are there other changes to the overall policies of the school (or district) that need to be made so as to help reduce the likelihood of another due process hearing?
> - Is there a need for professional development? Hirings? Removal of staff? Changes to policies? Or all of the above?

The purpose of all of this is to learn what was wrong, to work on improvement, and prevent additional problems. Throughout this book we have provided suggestions for working with parents, and for parents to work with district staff to reduce the likelihood of having a hearing. The monetary, emotional, and time costs of a due process hearing are enormous. Consider everything that can be done to reduce the chances of it happening again.

Expenses to Be Weighed

One of the biggest costs in a due process hearing is the payment of attorney's fees. School districts and parents may use an attorney to represent the district. The attorney's fees for a due process hearing will likely be considerable. Additionally, the district or parent may use an expert witness to assist with the case. These are costs that both parties are to pay regardless of who prevails in the due process hearing. The costs for adequate representation in a due process hearing should be considered early in the process as it may facilitate discussions related to a settlement. Why is this so? If the costs to defend the district in a due process hearing is going to be $10,000 to $15,000 and the service that is being requested by the parents will only cost $8,000, it is important to compare both and take this into consideration when deciding whether to settle or go to hearing. Additionally, school districts may spend $12,000 on representation and not prevail at the due process hearing and then also have to pay for the costs of the services, and the parents' attorney's fees (see below).

A court, in its discretion, may award reasonable attorneys' fees as part of the costs to a prevailing party who is the parent of a child with a disability. As long as there are not frivolous expenditures and unnecessary delays as a part of the litigation, fees awarded will be based on rates prevailing in the community in which the action or proceeding arose for the kind and quantity of attorney services furnished. The fee for the parent attorney may be more than the service or award for the child. However, due process hearing officers may not award attorney's fees so to recuperate these fees will require additional litigation, and expense, in the courts.

Federal law, and subsequent case law, imposes certain requirements upon the parent and in some circumstances may limit attorney fee awards. Parents should consult with their attorney regarding these matters. Parent attorneys' fees may not be awarded and related costs may not be reimbursed in any action or proceeding for services performed subsequent to the time of a written offer of settlement to the parent if the offer is made within the time prescribed by Rule 68 of the Federal Rules of Civil Procedures, or, in the case of an administrative hearing, at any time more than ten days before the proceeding begins; the offer is not accepted within ten days; and the court finds that the relief finally obtained by the parent is not more favorable to the parent than the offer of settlement.

An award of attorneys' fees and related costs may be made to the parent who is the prevailing party and who was substantially justified in rejecting the settlement offer. As noted above, a court may reduce the amount of any attorneys' fee award when (a) the parent, or the parent's attorney, during the course of the action or proceeding, unreasonably protracted the final resolution of the controversy; (b) the amount of the attorneys' fees otherwise authorized to be awarded unreasonably exceeds the hourly rate prevailing in the community for similar services by attorneys of reasonably comparable skill, reputation, and experience; (c) the time spent and legal services furnished were excessive considering the nature of the action or proceeding; or (d) the attorney representing the parent did not provide to the local educational agency the appropriate information in the due process hearing request.

Conclusions

To many families with a member with a disability, the special education due process experience is a very emotional experience—they are working to assist a family member who has a disability as much as possible. For educators, they leave a due process hearing with their professionalism questioned and unsure of whether they are doing what they are supposed to be doing. The due process hearing may not bring the closure to the issue that both parties are seeking. The problem with appeals is that they prolong the issue and take time, energy, and money. The goal of the due process hearing is to work to ensure that a student with a disability receives an appropriate education. Keep that as the focus.

References

A.R. v. New York City Department of Education, 407 F.3d 65 (2nd Cir. 2005).

Clark County School District, 113 LRP 52613 (SEA NV 2013).

Endrew F. v. Douglas County School District Re-1, 580 U.S. __ (2017).

Florence County School District Four v. Carter, 510 U.S. 7 (1993).

Forest Grove School District v. T.A., 557 U.S. 230 (2009).

G.L. v. Ligonier Valley Sch. Dist. Authority, 802 F.3d 601 (3rd Cir. 2015)

Individuals with Disabilities Education Act (IDEA), 20 U.S.C. § 1400 *et seq.*

Individuals with Disabilities Education Act Regulations, 34 C.F.R. § 300 et seq.

Lake, S. E. (2019). What Do I Do When . . . The Answer Book on Special Education Practice and Procedure (2nd ed.). LRP Publications.

Letter to Anonymous, 19 IDELR 277 (OSEP 1992).

Light v. Parkway School District, 41 F .3d 1223 (8th Cir. 1994).

Meiner v. Missouri, 673 F.2d 969 (8th Cir. 1986).

Neosho R-V School District v. Clark, 315 F.3d 1022 (8th Cir. 2003)

Schaeffer v. Weast, 546 U.S. 49 (2005).

School Committee of the Town of Burlington v. Department of Education of Massachusetts, 471 U.S. 359 (1985).

Appendix A

SETTLEMENT AND RELEASE AGREEMENT

This Agreement is entered into by and between **SCHOOL DISTRICT NAME** and other released parties (referred to as the "District" and/or "Released Parties"); **MICHAEL BLACK,** student (referred to as the "Student") by and through his parents and legal guardians **OWEN BLACK** (referred to as Parent/Father) and **LEAH BLACK** (referred to as the Parent/Mother) of Michael Black, of 123 Busytown Street, CITY, STATE.

Whereas, the Student was identified as a student receiving special education services in the District; and

Whereas, the parties including legal counsel participated in an IEP meeting on March 14, 2021; and

Whereas, the parents, through their counsel, on May 2, 2021, filed a Due Process Complaint with the STATE OFFICE FOR DUE PROCESS HEARINGS; and

Whereas, the parties and their legal counsel participated in a Resolution meeting on May 18, 2021; and

WHEREAS, as an outgrowth of discussions on May 18, 2021, the parties have come to terms on a resolution of the issues; and

WHEREAS, as a result of discussions and communications between the District and Parent, the parties have agreed to the terms of this Agreement as the terms as hereinafter set forth, and they believe the terms are fair, reasonable, and appropriate; and

WHEREAS, the Parents avers that they understand the nature and scope of the Agreement and willingly, voluntarily and knowingly enter into this Agreement.

NOW THEREFORE, intending to be legally bound and to resolve any and all claims between them as it relates to the two above-identified issues, known and unknown, the parties hereby agree as follows:

- **Placement at the PRIVATE School for 2021–2022 and 2022–2023.** The District shall pay the tuition for the Student to attend the PRIVATE School for the 2021–2022 and 2022–2023 school years. The Parents have researched the information and had an opportunity to visit the School and speak to the Director(s) regarding the program that is available to their son. After making an investigation and weighing the pros and cons of attending the PRIVATE School, it is the desire of the Parents to have their son attend the PRIVATE School at SCHOOL ADDRESS.
  - It is the understanding of the parties that the current tuition rate is $39,100. Should the tuition fee increase for 2022–2023, the District agrees to pay the increase in tuition.

- ◦ The District shall also pay the activity fee of $2,200 for 2021–2022 and 2022–2023. If the activity fee would increase for the 2022–2023 school term, the District agrees to pay the increase in fee.
- ◦ It is understood and agreed between the parties that the District's obligation to pay this tuition and activity fees shall immediately cease in the event the parents are no longer residents within the NAME HERE School District.
- **Speech and language services.** The District and Parent is awaiting the report of the Independent Evaluator (NAME HERE). It is the understanding of the parties that NAME HERE is recommending forty-five-minute speech and language therapy sessions two times per week for the Student.
  - ◦ The parties agree that NAME HERE shall complete her report and provide the parties with a copy of same. The District shall have an opportunity to respond and comment on the NAME HERE report.
  - ◦ The parties agree that the PRIVATE School shall have the benefit of the District's most recent speech and language evaluation and that of NAME HERE as well as the benefit of the District's speech and language pathologist's rebuttal of NAME HERE's report and make a decision going into the 2021–2022 school year whether the student needs speech and language services and whether that would be up to a maximum of two forty-five-minute sessions per week or something short thereof based on the assessment of the records that were being supplied by the Independent Evaluator and the District's evaluators and School District records.
  - ◦ It is agreed that at the end of the 2021–2022 school year, PRIVATE School will look at the speech and language services that were provided and make a recommendation for the 2022–2023 school year. The District shall not unreasonably deny the request if the speech and language recommendation is to once again forty-five-minute sessions two times per week.
- **Portability.** In the event the parents would make a determination that they would want to change the placement and/or delivery of services of the Student, it is understood and agreed that the District's obligation for payment toward tuition to attend the change in placement shall not exceed the amounts it would have paid on the Students' behalf to attend the PRIVATE School (or other private placement) for 2021–2022 and 2022–2023.
- **Extended School Year.** The District agrees to pay a total not to exceed Eight Thousand Dollars ($8,000.00) toward Extended School year tuition/fees for the Student's ESY programming in the summer of 2021, 2022, and 2023. In the summer of 2021, the District agrees to reimburse the parents for expenses for their private tutor to continue private tutoring. The Tutor shall bill the District directly for these services. Payment to the tutor shall be made within ten to fifteen days of receipt of said invoices. It is further agreed that any invoices for ESY services in the summer of 2022 and 2023 shall be billed directly to the NAME HERE School District by the private school at which the extended school year services are being provided. Payment shall be made within ten to fifteen days of receipt of said invoice up to

an amount not to exceed the amount of Eight Thousand ($8,000.00) over a three (3) year period.

- **Transportation**. It is understood and agreed that the parents shall responsible for all transportation as it relates to transporting the student from his home within the SCHOOL DISTRICT to the PRIVATE SCHOOL. The District agrees to reimburse the family to transport the Student to and from the PRIVATE SCHOOL in (approximately sixty miles per day). The parent agrees to notify the District in the event that this transportation arrangement will be altered in any way that could impact reimbursement under the Agreement. The District shall be invoiced on a monthly basis by the family for the transportation to and from the PRIVATE School from their residence. The reimbursement will be at the then-current IRS mileage rate at the time the transportation is undertaken/provided. Transportation will be for those days school is in session and for which the student attends. The District shall be entitled to attendance records to confirm the Student's attendance at the PRIVATE School. In the event a different school is selected, this arrangement shall be void.

- **Tutor costs**. In addition to paying for tutoring during the summer of 2021 as outlined in Item 4 above, the District shall reimburse the parent Two Thousand Five Hundred Dollars ($2,500.00) for the parents' expenditures for previous payments to a tutor subject to verification by receipt, invoice, or some other method/manner acceptable to the District and/or its Auditors.

- **Attorneys' fees**. The District shall reimburse the parents' attorney for attorneys' fees incurred by the parents in the amount of Twenty Eight Thousand Dollars ($28,000.00) for representation of the parents in this matter. Parents' counsel agrees to provide a completed W-9 form and itemized invoice of professional services. Parents and parents' counsel agree that the fees shall not exceed Twenty Eight Thousand Dollars ($28,000.00) and include the time spent in the Resolution meeting and the time required to review and finalize this settlement agreement. The check for attorneys fees shall be made payable to "LAW FIRM NAME HERE."

- **Placement in Lieu of FAPE**. It is understood and agreed to between the parties that placement at the PRIVATE School or a subsequent private school is a placement in lieu of FAPE. In other words, the District is not responsible for the educational programming of the student during the Student's stay at the private school.

  1. It is understood and agreed that the District shall not be issuing a PWN for this placement.

  2. Both Parents further acknowledge and understand the placement of their son in the PRIVATE School (or other private placement) is and will be considered a placement in lieu of FAPE (Free and Appropriate Public Education). To that end, the Parents are providing a full and complete release of any and all claims against NAME HERE School District for any and all claims, or potential claims, for denial of FAPE or educational services while the Student attends the PRIVATE School (or other private placement).

- **Transition back to NAME HERE School District.** This Agreement encompasses the District paying tuition and other costs identified in the preceding paragraphs for the 2021–2022 and 2022–2023 school years to include ESY, transportation, and related services in speech.
  - It is understood and agreed that pendency for the 2022–2023 school year is not at PRIVATE School or other private school. The parties agree that in preparing for the student's programming for the 2023–2024 school year, the District shall undertake and complete a Reevaluation of the student by April 1, 2023.
  - The reevaluation shall encompass those test assessments and other evaluations as determined to be applicable by the School District.
  - By executing the Agreement, the parents consent to such a Permission to Reevaluate but also agree for compliance purposes to complete, execute and return a PTRE form within seven (7) business days of receipt from the School District authorizing the District to proceed with the evaluation.
- In addition to the above and in exchange for the consideration set forth above, the Student and Parents, individually and on behalf of their child/Student knowingly, willingly, and voluntarily releases and forever discharges the District, and the District's past and present Directors, elected or otherwise, administrators, employees, agents, attorneys representatives, insurers, successors, and assigns (collectively the "Released Parties") of and from any and all claims or demands, known and unknown, including but not limited to any claims for educational expenses, expert witness or consultant fees, compensatory education, compensatory damages, special education relief of any kind, punitive damages or attorneys fees that have been or could be incurred by the Parents and/or Student (their heirs, executors, administrators, successors, representatives and assigns or anyone claiming through, by or on behalf of the Parents and Student) against the District from the time of the Student's initial enrollment in the NAME HERE School District through the date of execution of this Agreement and as otherwise noted, arising out of, by reason of, in connection with or as a result of any aspect of the Parents'/Student's request through their counsel to include, but not limited to, all issues raised in any correspondences or discussions from the Parents or Parents' attorney, including the Request for Due Process filed on May 2, 2021, as well as any other corresponding emails as it relates to the issues of compensatory education or claims, as well as any and all issues raised in meetings or discussions held between the parties, regarding those same issues. It is understood and agreed as a result of this settlement, the Student's and Parents' claims based on their contention that the Student was not receiving appropriate education are hereby resolved by execution of this Agreement. It is understood and agreed that this release of claims and other requested relief as outlined in the Due Process Complaint filed on May 2, 2021, includes, but is not limited to, costs, administrative and equitable relief of any kind, any alleged violation of: 42 U.S.C. sections 1981, 1983, 1985, 1986, and 1988; the Americans with Disabilities Act of

1990, its implementing regulations (as well as the ADA Amendments Act of 2008 and its implementing regulations); the Individuals with Disabilities Education Act and any implementing regulations; Section 504 of the Rehabilitation Act of 1973 and any implementing regulations; 22 Pa. Code 14.1, et seq., 15.1 et seq., and any other applicable federal, state, local civil, or human rights, disability or educational law, and any attorneys fees (except as referenced herein at Paragraph 7), as well as any rights under *Winkelman ex rel. Winkelman v. Parma City Sch. Dist.*, 550 US 516, 127 S.Ct. 1994, 2001, 167 Led.2d 904 2007, and/or any claims that were or could have been asserted in a special education action. In addition to the above, the Parents/Guardians and Student (their heirs, executors, administrators, successors, representatives and assigns or anyone claiming through, by, or on behalf of the Parents/Guardians and Student), also release and discharge the District and heretofore "Released Parties" from any and all claims regarding the Student's educational program and placement for the period of time of the in lieu of FAPE placement. This waiver shall remain in place so long as the Student is enrolled in the PRIVATE School, or other similar placement wherein the District is responsible for the cost of the tuition of the Student as outlined in Paragraph 1 above.

* Nothing in this Settlement and Release Agreement or the furnishing of the consideration for this Settlement and Release Agreement shall be deemed or construed at any time for any purposes as an acknowledgment of fault, liability, wrongdoing, or any admission of unlawful conduct by the District. The Parties further agree that this Agreement is made in compromise of disputed claims and to avoid the expense and inconvenience of further litigation and defending same.

* **Approval at Board meeting.** The agreement shall be presented to both the District and its Board of School Directors for consideration at its June 9, 2021, Board meeting.

* **Compensatory Education.** Other than what has been listed above, there shall be no other compensatory education paid beyond what is outlined within the body of the Agreement.

* **Student Records.** The School District shall receive from the PRIVATE School or other private school the Student attends, the functional equivalent of an IEP or educational plan as otherwise developed for the education of the student while attending the PRIVATE School or other private school. The District shall also be entitled to receive progress reports, report cards, and any other samples of student work that would help demonstrate mile markers, progress or otherwise indicate how the student is performing in the school. This information shall be provided to the District in December and June. The private school shall also provide any other information that would be generated as a result of participation in Extended School Year. Records shall include, but not be limited to, educational progress reports, diagnostic assessments, behavioral checklists, functional behavioral assessments, positive support behavior plans, attendance records and report

cards, etc. The Parents agree to complete and execute any necessary releases to permit release of information to the District by the private placement.

- The intent of the parties to this Agreement and Release is to extinguish and end any and all possible liability of the Released Parties arising out of or in connection with the claims or possible claims surrounding the educational program and placement of the Student from the time of his initial enrollment in the NAME HERE School District through the signing of this Agreement and during the time that the Student is at the PRIVATE School or other private placement.

- **The Parents agrees that (a) they has received notification of their and the Student's rights under state and federal law (b) they are fully aware of these rights and of the extent to which they are waiving them in this Release and Agreement, (c) they have been apprised that they have the ability to consult with counsel prior to execution of this Release and Agreement; (d) they are fully aware that they are waiving rights on behalf of themselves and the Student; (e) they have had the opportunity, if they so choose, to consult with counsel concerning their rights as well as the Student's rights and this Release and Agreement; (f) they understand the terms of the Release and Agreement; and (g) they are signing this Release and Agreement, including this waiver of important rights willingly, voluntarily, and knowingly.**

- The Parents waive their rights to file any charge or complaint on their own behalf and/or to participate in any charge or complaint that may be made by any other person or organization on their behalf, before any federal, state, or local court or administrative agency against the Released Parties, except as such waiver is prohibited by law. Should any such charge or complaint be filed, Parents agree that they will not accept any relief or recovery therefrom. The Parents confirm that no charge, complaint, or action exists in any forum or form that they have filed against the NAME HERE School District. Except as prohibited by law, in the event that any such claim is filed, it shall be dismissed with prejudice upon presentation of this Agreement and General Release.

- This Agreement and Release sets forth the entire agreement between the parties hereof regarding the issues addressed herein, and fully supersedes any prior agreements or understandings between the parties.

- This Agreement shall be interpreted with the laws of the Commonwealth of Pennsylvania, as well as federal law covering the jurisdiction in which the United States District Court for the Middle District of Pennsylvania has venue and jurisdiction.

- The above recitals are incorporated by reference as if set forth more fully herein.

- Should any provision of this Agreement and Release be held to be illegal or invalid, the validity of the remaining parts, terms, or provisions, shall not be affected thereby and this illegal or invalid part shall be deemed not to be a part of this Agreement and Release.

- The individual(s) signing on behalf of the District and state that they have been duly authorized in accordance with law to enter into and execute this

Agreement on behalf of and with permanent binding effect upon release of either in their individual or official capacity. Likewise, the Parents and Student warrant they can execute this Agreement with permanent binding effect.

- This Agreement is deemed to have been prepared jointly by the parties hereto and any uncertainty or ambiguity existing herein, if any, shall not be interpreted against any party, but shall be interpreted according to the application of the rules and interpretation for arms-length agreements.

IN WITNESS WHEREFORE, and intending to be legally bound, the parties set their hands and seals on the days outlined below. If required, the Parents agree to execute any supplementary documents necessary to affect the intent of this and Release Agreement.

_____

Witness

_____

Owen Black, individually and as Father and legal guardian of Michael Black

Date: _____

_____

Witness

_____

Leah Black, individually and as Mother and legal guardian of Michael Black

Date: _____

NAME HERE SCHOOL DISTRICT

_____   _____
Board Secretary   Board President

                                     Date: _____

Seal:

Appendix B

Due Process Hearing Decision

Due Process Hearing for A. H.
Date of Birth: April 22, 2004
File Number: ##

Dates of Hearings:
January 11, 2021; February 6, 2021; March 17, 2021

CLOSED HEARING

Parties: Representatives:

Date Transcript Received: March 24, 2021
Date Closing Arguments Received: April 25, 2021
Date of Decision: May 10, 2021
Hearing Officer: ####

Background

A. is a fifteen-year-old eligible resident of the #### School District (District) with a learning disability, whose Parents requested this Hearing seeking reimbursement for the 2019–2020 school year at the PRIVATE SCHOOL and related transportation costs. The District alleges their program is appropriate, is the least restrictive environment, and that since it would provide an appropriate program the various reimbursements sought are unwarranted.

There have been several previous due process hearings for A. He currently attends the PRIVATE SCHOOL.

Issue Presented

Is A. eligible for tuition reimbursement (and transportation) for the 2019–2020 school year to the PRIVATE SCHOOL?

Findings of Fact[1]

A. Background

1. A. was born on April 22, 2005. He is currently fifteen years of age (P-8, p. 1).
    *   A. is a resident of the District (P-6, p. 14, NT 14).
    *   A. is eligible for special education and related services as a student with a learning disability (P-4, p. 12; NT 14).
    *   There have been two previous due process hearings involving A. (S-1, S-2, S-3, S-4; NT 18, 24, 31).
    *   The District completed an evaluation on October 4, 2017 (P-4). This report found his continuing eligibility for special education and related services (P-4, p. 10).
    *   On June 18, 2019, the District sent a letter to the Parents regarding IEP development and the need for information from the PRIVATE SCHOOL (S-23).
    *   The District sent a letter on June 27, 2019, to the PRIVATE SCHOOL requesting information regarding A.'s progress (S-5).
2. On June 27, 2019, the District sent a letter to the PRIVATE SCHOOL seeking a release of records (S-25).
3. On July 18, 2019, the District sent a letter to the Parents requesting information from the PRIVATE SCHOOL for IEP development (S-24).
4. On July 24, 2019, the Parents sent a letter to the District regarding the summer assessments (P-5, p. 28).
    *   The District completed a baseline writing prompt on July 31, 2019 (P-3, p. 14). The report found a below basic level.
5. Achievement test results on July 31, 2019, indicate percentile ranks ranging from 9th to 43rd percentile (S-8, p. 4; S-21).
    *   A. currently attends the PRIVATE SCHOOL (NT 30-31).
    *   The District sent a letter to the Parents on August 13, 2019, about reviewing the IEP prior to the meeting (S-7).
6. The District held an IEP meeting on August 14, 2019 (P-3, p. 5). This is the IEP in dispute for this due process hearing. The IEP contains information from the PRIVATE SCHOOL in the present levels of performance
7. The District sent a letter to the Parents on August 15, 2019, stating it would like to review the information from the PRIVATE SCHOOL to incorporate into the IEP (S-8).
8. A PWN was issued on August 15, 2019, that was revised with updated information (S-26).
    *   The Parents rejected the IEP on August 29, 2019. It was received at the District on September 4, 2007. The Parents in their letter stated A. would

---

[1] References to notes of testimony will be designated "NT" followed by the relevant page number. References to District evidentiary exhibits will be designated "S" followed by the relevant exhibit number. References to Parents' evidentiary exhibits will be designated "P" followed by the relevant exhibit number. Findings of Fact will be designated by "FF" followed by the relevant fact number.

be attending the PRIVATE SCHOOL and are seeking tuition reimbursement from the District (S-9). The reasons the Parents rejected the IEP were: The IEP does not address organizational and attention issues and does not adequately address language arts and math (S-9, p. 3).

- On September 6, 2019, the District sent a letter to the Parents requesting permission to evaluate (S-10). The Parents did not provide permission.
- On September 28, 2019, the Parents sent a letter to the District stating they did not understand the reason for the reevaluation (S-13).
- The District sent a letter to the Parents on October 15, 2019, indicating the reasons for the reevaluation request (S-27).
- A resolution meeting was held on October 19, 2019 (S-14). There was no resolution.
- The Parents sent a letter to the District on November 3, 2019, indicating they are still unclear of the reasons for the reevaluation request (P-5, p. 27).
- A.'s eighth grade state scores indicate proficiency in reading and below basic in math (NT 211).

Discussion and Conclusion of the Law

This Hearing was delayed numerous times due to scheduling difficulties of witnesses, witness illness, and numerous other factors. All parties to this Hearing made a good faith effort to move this along in a timely fashion but outside factors kept getting in the way.

A.'s Educational Placement

The legal standard to which the District is held in educational matters such as this is clearly established by statute and the courts. The IDEA, as interpreted by the Supreme Court, does not require states to develop IEP's that maximize the potential of students eligible for special education but merely requires that students make progress. (See *Endrew F. v. Douglas County School District RE–1*, 580 U.S. ___ [2017]). The IDEA requires that the public school program provides access to specialized instruction and related services, which are "reasonably calculated" to have the student make progress based on their individual circumstances. What the statute guarantees is an "appropriate" education, "not one that provides everything that might be thought desirable by 'loving parents.'" *Tucker v. Bayshore Union Free School District*, 873 F.2d 563, 567 (2d Cir. 1989). The Third Circuit had previously adopted this minimal standard for educational benefit and has refined it to mean that more than "trivial" or "de minimus" benefit is required. *See Polk v. Central Susquehanna Intermediate Unit 16*, 853 F.2d 171, 1179 (3d Cir. 1998), *cert. denied* 488 U.S. 1030 (1989). *See also Carlisle Area School v. Scott P.*, 62 F.3d 520, 533–34 (3d Cir. 1995), quoting *Rowley*, 458 U.S. at 201; (School districts "need not provide the optimal level of services, or even a level that would confirm additional benefits, since the IEP required by IDEA represents only a "basic floor of opportunity"). Previously school districts were held to the *Rowley* standard, but are now held to the progress standard elucidated by the *Endrew* decision.

Moreover, the Third Circuit has determined that a student's demonstrated progress in an educational program is sufficient to show that a school district's IEP allows for significant learning and provides meaningful benefit as necessary to satisfy the IDEA's FAPE standard. *See Ridgewood Board of Education v. N.E.*, 172 F.3d 238, 242 (3d Cir. 1999). Given that progress is relevant to the determination of whether a student with a disability received an educational benefit, it is therefore also relevant to determining whether a reimbursement award is due.

Parents Request for Reimbursement to the PRIVATE SCHOOL

Under the two-part test for private school reimbursement established by the Supreme Court, the school district must establish the appropriateness of the education it provided to the student.[2] If the school district is unable to establish

---

[2] This Hearing occurred after *Schaffer v. Weast*, 126 S.Ct. 528, and the Parents had the burden of demonstrating the District's program was inappropriate.

the appropriateness of its own educational program, the burden then shifts to the parents to prove that the private school selected for their child did provide an appropriate education. See *Burlington School Committee v. Massachusetts Department of Education*, 471 U.S. 379 (1985).[3]

As the *Endrew/Rowley* principles have been applied in the context of private placements, a disabled child is "not . . . entitled to placement in a residential school merely because the latter would more nearly enable the child to reach his or her full potential." *Abrahamson v. Hirschman*, 701 F.2d 223, 227 (1st Cir. 1983). In making a determination regarding a school district's obligation to pay for private placement, a court must make the following inquiries:

First, the court must ask whether the district's IEP was reasonably calculated to confer an educational benefit on the student. If the court determines that the IEP was not so calculated, the court must then ask whether the parents' unilateral choice to place a student in a residential setting is the appropriate educational choice for the student. If the answer to the second inquiry is yes, then the parents would be entitled to reimbursement from the school district for the cost of the placement.

Importantly, in gauging the appropriateness of the District's actions toward A., the IEP must be judged as to its appropriateness at the time that it is written, and not with respect to subsequently obtained information about the student. The ideas that "an IEP is a snapshot, not a retrospective," and that the IEP must take into account what was objectively reasonable at the time that the IEP was drafted were recognized by the First Circuit in *Roland M.*, supra, and have been adopted in the Third Circuit. See, e.g., *Carlisle Area Sch. v. Scott P.*, 62 F.3d 520, 534 (3d Cir. 1995); *Fuhrmann v. East Hanover Board of Educ.*, 993 F.2d 1031, 1040 (3rd Cir. 1993). See also *Philadelphia School District*, 22 IDELR 825, 826 (SEA PA 1995).

It is true that school districts have been required to pay for the educational components of private placements even in cases where the students require those placements solely for medical reasons when the school district's own educational programming for the student is deemed deficient. See *Board of Education of Oak Park and River Forest High School v. Illinois State Board of Education*, 29 IDELR 52 (N.D. Ill 1998), (Where student's need for private placement was primarily for non-educational reasons, district court limited parents' claim for reimbursement to the educational component of the private placement given that the school district's educational provisions for the student were inappropriate, and the academic program the student received at the school was appropriate).

A review of the IEP at issue in this case reveals that it is reasonably calculated to provide meaningful educational progress. Specific reasons for the conclusion follow. It should be pointed out the IEP was developed without records

---

[3] Later, in *Florence County Sch. Dist. v. Carter*, 114 S.Ct. 361 (1993), the Supreme Court reaffirmed the test for private school tuition reimbursement established in *Burlington* and added that private school placements selected by parents need not be at facilities, which are approved by state departments of education for the provision of education to students with disabilities.

from the PRIVATE SCHOOL, despite numerous requests (NT 214, 218-219, 253, 254–255, 291).

A.'s disability is stated very clearly right away in the first paragraph (P-3). In addition, the discrepancy is explained. The second and third paragraphs go on to explain his more recent educational history. The fourth paragraph contains measurable and observable CBA data with, "A. was able to read passages on a sixth grade level at a rate of 125 words per minute."

In the fifth paragraph the math teacher reported to the IEP drafter that A. did "fairly well" on his exam and at another part reported that he "did a good job."

Overall on the first page (S-8, page 11 of 34) there were some curriculum-based assessments. The teachers mostly reported based on their own anecdotal observations and opinions.

On the third page (S-8, page 13 of 34); the assessment results from the Woodcock-Johnson III were included, which is very measurable and observable. Additionally, on the fourth page is the explanation of the State Writing Prompt that is based on the State writing rubric.

One question about the IEP is what is "Fund of knowledge"? How is it measured?

It is clear as a part of the statewide assessment how A. will participate. The accommodations are spelled out on this page for the different State tests.

The objectives for the IEP, on the whole, are clearly stated, providing a direction and guidance for individuals who would be implementing the IEP. There are some basic minor details that need to be addressed, but it is clear the team that developed the IEP spent a lot of time working to craft one for a student where there have been multiple due process hearings.

The first goal, the reading fluency goal, should have an expected level of achievement of one year's growth. The goal states to an eighth grade equivalent however the WJ-III baseline is a 6.7 grade equivalent. This goal also needs to be more measurable and observable.

The decoding/word identification skills goal is not very observable and measurable. What is meant by three consecutive weekly probes? Does that mean three times per week, or does that mean one every week for three weeks in a row?

The next goal, the reading comprehension skills and understanding of word meaning and language structure was listed as a strength but is not a strength according to the WJ-III. A.'s WJ-III grade equivalent for passage comprehension was a 5.2. His English teacher indicated in Present Educational Levels that he comprehends text well especially when taking the opportunity to listen to someone read aloud or to recorded texts. This is an accommodation. Reading comprehension is a need of A.'s therefore it is appropriate to have as an Annual Goal but should be removed as a strength.

The spelling goal could also be more measurable and observable.

For the math fluency goal, the WJ-III indicates a need in math with a grade equivalent of 5.3 but according to the first paragraph of the Present Ed. Levels A. was diagnosed with a language-based Learning Disability, specifically in the areas of reading and written expression. Therefore, it doesn't seem like he has a math Learning Disability. If this is the case, it then brings into question the need for a math Annual Goal.

For the math multi-step word problems goal, it's an appropriate goal to keep because it deals with multi-step word problems and he has a language-based Learning Disability. Interestingly enough, A. did better in this area on the WJ-III test (7.7), which deals with his area of disability. Overall, he did well with math according to the WJ-III but is still functioning below grade level.

Other than being unsure of the purpose of the first specially designed instruction, the SDI seems appropriate for A. (see also NT 170–171, 178–179). The related services component also provides appropriate detail.

Above is listed some details that might need to be changed, but the IEP, taken as a whole, is reasonably calculated to provide meaningful educational benefit.

"Perfection is not required" in an IEP.[4] "[T]he law is clear that technical perfection is not the objective of the statute."[5] Accordingly, "not every procedural error will render an IEP 'legally inadequate.'"[6] The question in the face of a procedural failing is whether the failing interfered with access to FAPE or resulted in an educational loss.[7] "Vagueness and measurability problems" with goals are mere technical non-compliance.[8] "The types of IEP procedural defects that have been held to violate a child's right to a FAPE are those that 'result in the loss of educational opportunity,' 'seriously infringe upon the Parents' opportunity to participate in the IEP formulation process,' or 'cause[ ] a deprivation of educational benefits.'"[9]

In this case there were testimony and comments about the requested private school placement that need be addressed even though the IEP and program offered by the District has been ruled to be appropriate. In that connection, the second part of the Burlington-Carter test is the appropriateness of the private school placement. See *Burlington School Committee v. Massachusetts*

---

[4] *Loren F. v. Atlanta Ind. Sch. Sys.*, 349 F.3d 1309, 1312 (11th Cir. 2003).

[5] *Escambia County Bd. of Educ. v. Benton*, 406 F. Supp. 2d 1248, 1273 (S. D. Ala. 2005).

[6] *Viola v. Arlington Cent. Sch. Dist.*, 414 F. Supp. 2d 366, 378 (S.D. N.Y.) (citing *Grim v. Rhinebeck Cent. Sch. Dist.*, 346 F.3d 377, 381 [2d Cir. 2003]). *See also School Bd. of Collier County v. K.C.*, 285 F.3d 977, 982 (11th Cir. 2002) ("A procedurally defective IEP does not automatically entitle a party to relief."). *See also* 20 U.S.C. § 1415(f)(3)(E); 34 CFR § 300.513.

[7] See, among many others, *Wagner v. Board of Educ. of Montgomery County*, 340 F. Supp. 2d 603, 616 (D. Md. 2004) (citing cases); *Adam J.*, 328 F.3d at 811-12 (citing cases).

[8] *Escambia County Bd. of Educ.*, 406 F. Supp. 2d at 1273. See also *Nack v. Orange City Sch. Dist.*, 454 F.3d 604, 611-12 (6th Cir. 2006) (applying "procedural harm" analysis to claims of insufficient present levels and measurable goals); *Adam J.*, 328 F.3d at 811 (stating procedural issues relate to development of IEPs, including, e.g., measurable goals and objectives, and present levels of education).

[9] Escambia County Bd. of Educ., 406 F. Supp. 2d at 1273 (citing A.I. v. District of Columbia, 402 F. Supp. 2d 152 (D. D.C. 2005)). See also *Berger v. Medina City Sch. Dist.*, 348 F.3d 513, 520 (6th Cir. 2003); *A.K. v. Alexandria City Sch. Bd.*, 409 F. Supp. 2d 689, 692 (E.D. Va. 2005) (citing multiple case precedent), rev'd on other grounds, 484 F.3d 672 (4th Cir. 2007).

Department of Education, 471 U.S. 379 (1985). The program may be appropriate given the analysis below.

Tuition reimbursement is an available remedy for parents to receive the costs associated with a child's placement in a private school where it is determined that the program offered by the public school did not provide FAPE, and the private placement is proper. *Florence County School District v. Carter*, 510 U.S. 10 (1993); *School Committee of Burlington v. Department of Education*, 471 U.S. 359 (1985). Equitable considerations are relevant to making such a determination. *Id*. However, the parents' choice of private placement need not strictly satisfy the IDEA requirements in order to qualify for reimbursement. *Carter*. The standard is whether the parental placement was reasonably calculated to provide the child with educational benefit. *Carter; David P. v. Lower Merion School District*, 27 IDELR 915 (E.D.Pa. 1998).

The PRIVATE SCHOOL is for students with learning differences, and the teachers are trained in the Orton-Gillingham reading method (NT 326). The Parents have not received any special funds or tuition break from the PRIVATE SCHOOL (NT 373). The Parents are also seeking transportation to the school (NT 16).

Why might it be an appropriate placement? The PRIVATE SCHOOL is designed to work with students who have learning disabilities (NT 325–326) in a small class size (NT 326).

It has already determined that the District did offer FAPE for the 2019–2020 school year. After a review of the record, the private placement would be an appropriate one if the District's placement were not. The private school is a small one that could address A.'s needs. His schedule includes intensive programming in small classes at the PRIVATE SCHOOL. In sum, the program at the private school could address A.'s identified educational needs and is clearly appropriate under the applicable standard.

Equities Do Not Favor Reimbursement

The District stated correctly as a part of their closing arguments that the balance of the equities do not favor reimbursement.

The IDEA 2004 specifies that reimbursement may be reduced or denied if

(aa) at the most recent IEP meeting that the parents attended prior to removal of the child from the public school, the parents did not inform the IEP Team that they were rejecting the placement proposed by the public agency to provide a free appropriate public education to their child, including stating their concerns and their intent to enroll their child in a private school at public expense; or

(bb) ten business days . . . prior to the removal of the child from the public school, the parents did not give written notice to the public agency of the information described in division (aa); . . .

20 U.S.C. §1412(a)(10)(C)(iii). The District does not need to show prejudice by lack of timely notice.[10] Rather, as in *Bernardsville*, 42 F.3d at 156–58, the parents bear the burden of showing circumstances justifying relief from the notice requirement. The statute, however, provides very specific and limited circumstances in which notice is excused. 20 U.S.C. § 1412(a)(10)(iv) (providing exceptions from notice if the LEA prevented parents from providing notice, parents did not receive procedural safeguards, or providing notice would risk harm to the student, and in some circumstances, if parents are illiterate).

The Parents did not give a timely notice of their request for tuition reimbursement.

---

[10] *Pollowitz v. Weast*, 90 Fed. Appx. 438, 2001 WL 390035, 34 IDELR 171 (4th Cir. 2001) (*per curium*).

Order

In accordance with the foregoing findings of fact and conclusions of law, it is hereby **ORDERED** the ##### School District is not obligated to reimburse the Parents of A. for the tuition to the PRIVATE SCHOOL for the 2019–2020 school year.

_____   _____
Date   Hearing Officer

Appendix C

Letter from a Hearing Officer to Parent

NAME

ADDRESS HERE

DATE

PARENTS' NAMES
   re: FILE NAME

Dear Mr. and Mrs. PARENTS' NAME:

I have been assigned to the due process hearing concerning STUDENT NAME and the School District of NAME HERE. A hearing is scheduled in this matter for DATE HERE at TIME.

Since you are proceeding without the benefit of an attorney, I want to explain some of the events that will occur in advance so that you are aware of what will transpire. In a hearing such as this, the hearing officer is charged with the responsibility of determining whether or not the school district has acted as the Individuals with Disabilities Education Act (better known as IDEA) requires. A hearing officer only deals with the information that is presented to him or her during the hearing. So it is very important that you make sure I am aware of anything you think I should know while the hearing is in progress. I cannot accept any information from you or any party before or after the hearing.

Thirty minutes before the hearing actually begins, I will meet with you and the ATTORNEY FOR THE SCHOOL DISTRICT in a private meeting to determine the issues that will be considered in the hearing. Once the hearing begins, I will not allow any other issues to be considered unless there are very unusual circumstances. You can help me with this task if you will please write me a letter telling me what you would like this hearing to accomplish. Please be as specific as you can. If you believe there is something the district did and it should not have done or something which the district did not do and should have done, please tell me what these things are. If you believe there was information that was not considered, please tell me what that information might be. I would like you to send this letter to me by DATE HERE. An email or letter is appropriate.

After the private session is completed, we will begin the actual hearing. The school district has the burden of showing that the program it has provided for NAME HERE is appropriate. At the start of the hearing, each side has an opportunity to make an opening statement. In that statement, you should tell me what it is that you would like to see as a result of conducting this hearing. The district gives its opening statement first and then you make your opening statement.

Once the opening statements are complete, the district presents its witnesses. The attorney who represents the school district will ask the witness questions. When the attorney is finished, you may ask the witnesses any questions you want that will show me how the district did or did not do something. When the district has questioned all of its witnesses, you will be given a chance to present witnesses who can provide information that you believe will help me understand the situation NAME HERE faces. You must tell ATTORNEY FOR THE DISTRICT who your witnesses will be by DATE HERE. You must also provide her a list of all exhibits you intend to use by that same date.

When all of the witnesses have testified, each party will get the chance to make a closing statement. In the closing statement each party tries to tell me what the information has shown and how it applies to this case. Closing statements are not evidence and I cannot consider anything said at this time in reaching my decision.

Parents who have no legal representatives often misunderstand the role of the hearing officer. My role is to determine the facts and make a decision based on the facts. If you contact me in writing (or fax), you must send a copy of anything you send to me to NAME OF SCHOOL DISTRICT ATTORNEY, ADDRESS HERE. If you contact me by telephone, I can only discuss the procedures that will be followed in the hearing. I cannot provide legal advice to you. If you need advice, you can contact the STATE COORDINATING BODY FOR DUE PROCESS HEARINGS.

Should you have any questions concerning anything in this letter, I can be reached at my home, NUMBER HERE. Leave a message if I am not available.

Thank you in advance for your cooperation.

Sincerely,

NAME
Hearing Officer

cc: ATTORNEY FOR SCHOOL DISTRICT
      Office FOR DUE PROCESS HEARINGS

Appendix D

Opening Statement of Hearing Officer

Opening Statement

My name is #####, the hearing officer assigned by the STATE OFFICE OF DUE PROCESS HEARINGS to conduct this hearing.

The purpose of this hearing is to present evidence to determine if the student has been receiving an appropriate educational program.

The issues in this hearing are:

1.

2.

3.

4.

In an administrative hearing such as this, it is important to keep in mind that following the decision both parties will need to work together to implement that decision. I would hope that the atmosphere this morning will be conducive to subsequent cooperation. At times the relevancy of testimony might be questioned. Sometimes the hearing officer allows that testimony or evidence to be presented, but may disregard it when writing the decision because it becomes clear at that time that the testimony or evidence is, in fact, irrelevant.

In an open hearing, anyone from the public may attend and the decision, with the student's name but not the transcript and other materials from the hearing may be released and made available to interested persons.

In a closed hearing, only the parents, the student, the parents' representative, others designated by the parents, school officials and the IU representatives, witnesses to be called upon to testify, the hearing officer and recorder may attend. The decision will be released in an identifiable form only to the parties to the hearing and those persons who must implement the decision.

What type of hearing do the parents prefer?

In this hearing, the school district will present its case first. As witnesses are called by the district, the district will first ask questions. Following this, the parents will have the opportunity to question the witness. All questions should be asked of the witness when the witness is first called as the witness will only be called once in this proceeding. Questions should be asked in a manner so that the witness clearly understands what is asked and can answer the question. On cross examination, the parties may ask any questions they believe will aid the hearing officer in understanding the testimony of the witness.

When the district has completed calling its witnesses, the parents may call witnesses for direct testimony. The district has the right to cross examine the witness. Following the testimony from both sides, both parties will have the opportunity to make a closing statement. Such statements should summarize the information each party has presented that addresses the issues in the case.

QUERY THE REPS ABOUT WHO IS IN THE ROOM AND THEIR RELATION TO THE CHILD

The court reporter at this hearing will take a verbatim transcript of anything that is said in this proceeding. The court reporter will also swear in any witnesses. It is important for all parties to speak clearly and distinctly so that the stenographer can hear and record all comments. It is best if the witnesses face the stenographer and speak directly to the stenographer. This proceeding differs significantly from those that many educators are accustomed to attending. It is not an exchange of information but a presentation of the facts so that the hearing officer can make a determination. It should be evident that only one person can speak at one time so that the court reporter can record what is said. Please remember this point as the hearing progresses.

Have both parties provided a list of evidence and testimony to be presented at least five days prior to the hearing and have all requests to review the evidence been honored?

I would inform you of your right to appeal the decision. I am handing out to both parties copies of the procedures for appealing my decision, and am marking it as hearing officer exhibit 1.

I am also submitting into the record copies of correspondence between myself and both parties that were exchanged prior to the hearing. I am marking that correspondence as hearing office exhibit 2.

Both parties are entitled to a copy of the transcript if they desire. Please communicate with the court reporter during break about the form you wish, either electronically or paper, and the address to where the transcript should be sent.

Before the opening statements are there any facts or evidence to which the parties are willing to stipulate? This procedure may shorten the hearing and provide for speedier resolution of the issues.

Before we make opening statements, are there any stipulations that both parties are willing to make?

At this time each party may present an opening statement to specify the issues. The school district should explain why it believes it recommendations are appropriate. Then the parent should state why they asked for the hearing and what areas of disagreement exist, why the school district proposal is not appropriate and may present what they feel is appropriate. Opening statements are not evidence and a hearing decision may not be based upon these remarks.

The school district may present its opening statement.

The parents may present their opening statement.

The school district will call its first witness.

The parent's representative may call her first witness.

At this time we may have closing statements to sum up what the parties feel the evidence has shown. These statements should relate to material presented in the record. As with opening statements, these remarks are not evidence and a hearing decision may not be based upon them.

The School district may give its closing statement.

The parents' representative may make their closing statement.

At this time, I will distribute copies of the procedure to object to the decision of a hearing officer.

The transcript for the hearing will be made available within five business days.

Please provide the address to which the decision should be mailed

Parents' attorney

District's attorney

The decision will be mailed within fifteen days of the hearing.

Thank you for your working to provide the student a free appropriate public education.

This hearing is completed.

Glossary of Legal Terms for Hearings

Special education due process hearings involve a set of concepts and terminology unique to litigation and not often related to providing instruction or being a parent. Other chapters define the attributes and give examples of relevant concepts and terminology. Terms that you can expect to hear include offer of settlement (a.k.a., ten-day letter), five-day notice, subpoena, burden of proof, plus many other terms. They are described below as a means of facilitating understanding. We have provided detailed description of some of the most unique terms, with cursory description of the others.

Five-Day Notice For both parties to present a thorough argument, they need to prepare their cases and be able to rebut their opponent's case. The five-day rule mandates parties share with each other, no later than five days prior to the hearing, a list of potential witnesses and the documents to be submitted into evidence (some states use calendar days while others use working days). To prevent problems, both sides should err on the side of listing every possible witness or document, even if they are fairly certain that they won't use them. Not doing so may preclude their use in the hearing.

In preparation for the hearing the school district should be sure to have enough copies of all of their documents including copies for the parents, their attorney, the school district attorney, and a copy to be used during testimony in front of the witness, and finally a copy to be placed into the record as an evidentiary exhibit. The vast majority of due process hearings are held in school district buildings; therefore, it is recommended that a copy machine be made available for in any all necessary copies that need to be made.

Ten-Day Letter See offer of settlement.

Forty-Five-Day Hearing Rule Due process hearings are to be completed within forty-five calendar days of the request for the hearing. The purpose is to address the perceived problems relating to the student's education quickly. Within this forty-five-day period, the hearing officer has fifteen days to issue a ruling after testimony is completed. Consequently, the presentation of evidence, interrogatories, and cross-examination should be completed within thirty days. In reality, this timeline is frequently overlooked (see continuances below).

Appeal Timely procedure by an unsuccessful party in a lawsuit or administrative proceeding to an appropriate superior court empowered to review a final decision seeking to reverse or modify a judgment or final order of a lower court or administrative agency on the grounds that the decision misinterpreted or misapplied the law.

Brief A written document authored by a party in a lawsuit that includes the: (1) issue(s); (2) facts; (3) laws that can affect the issue(s); and (4) arguments explaining how the law applies to the particular facts.

Burden of Proof As indicated in other text chapters, the LEA carries the burden of proof in a due process hearing. Depending on the claims of the parent or guardians, or the issues being raised by the agency personnel, the LEA will have to demonstrate it has met the procedural as well as the substantive aspects of the law. The LEA will have to provide evidence that it has offered the student a program in the least restrictive environment that enables the student to make appropriate progress in light of their unique circumstances. This is why it is so important to follow the steps outlined in the chapter on district preparation for a due process hearing prior to the request for the hearing.

Case law Decisions issued by courts.

C.F.R. Code of Federal Regulations. For special education it the regulations promulgated by the United States Department of Education.

Class action A civil action filed in a court on behalf of a named plaintiff and on behalf of other individuals similarly situated. Due process hearings involve only one child; therefore, there are no class-action due process hearings.

Collateral Estoppel Commonly known as issue preclusion. The doctrine prevents a person from relitigating an issue once a hearing officer or court has previously decided the issue.

Complaint For due process hearings the first written statement of the issue(s) that begins the due process timelines.

Consent Under IDEA a school district must ask for consent at these times:

- Before the district conducts an initial evaluation or a reevaluation of the child.
- Before the school district provides special education services to the child for the first time through an IEP.
- Before inviting non-school agencies to participate in IEP meetings to discuss the child's transition to adult life.
- Parents must give permission in each situation above. States may have requirements relating to informed consent at other times, as well.

Informed Consent The parents have been fully informed about what the school wants to do. This is typically done in a letter or document describing what will happen in detail, often referred to as prior written notice. The parents understand and agree in writing. The school district requires parent signature.

Parents need to be made aware that consent is voluntary and you can be withdrawn or denied at any time. This is clarified in the procedural safeguards notice.

Consent Refusal School districts can try to use dispute resolution options like mediation or due process to obtain consent. This only applies to evaluations.

School districts do not have the ability to use due process procedures if the parent decides not to allow special education services to the child.

Informed Consent Not Required

* School districts can give tests that are given to all children, including standardized tests
* Review the results of previous evaluations
* Once parents' consent in writing to special education services for the first time, the school does not need consent again to implement an IEP.

Continuances Due process hearings are to be scheduled at the convenience of the parents or guardians and with consideration of the requirements of the LEA to arrange for staff to be available. If there are problems in scheduling a mutually convenient time and date, then a continuance or extension may be granted at the hearing officer's discretion. Often, scheduling issues are a function of attorneys' schedules. Neither party unilaterally or jointly has the authority to grant a continuance-only the hearing officer. To accommodate work schedules, the hearing officer may decide to take testimony in evenings or by Zoom/Facetime/Google Hangout. This is necessary because the hearing is supposed to be completed within forty-five days. Extensive use of continuances prevents resolution for the child regarding their educational services.

Controlled substance A drug or other substance identified under schedules I, II, III, IV, or V of the Controlled Substances Act. It does not include any substance legally possessed or used under the supervision of a licensed health care provider.

Cumulative file (a.k.a. cum file) File maintained by a school district containing evaluations, report cards, IEPs, grades, attendance, discipline, standardized assessment reports, and other information from a student's educational career and other information related to special education placement. Parents have a right to inspect the file and have copies of any information contained in it.

Damages Damages are not generally available under the IDEA.

Day There are several definitions of day. (1) Business Day referring to Monday through Friday, except for federal and state holidays (unless holidays are specifically included in the designation of business day). (2) School Day referring to any day, including a partial day, that children are in attendance at school for instructional purposes. The term "school day" has the same meaning for all children in school, including children with and without disabilities. (3) Calendar Day means each day shown on the calendar, including Saturdays, Sundays and holidays.

Discovery Obtaining evidence in advance of a hearing or trial. This can include depositions and review of documents.

Dismissal A hearing officer can dismiss with prejudice or without prejudice. When a suit is dismissed with prejudice, the plaintiff may not refile the same claim. The suit is permanently ended. When a suit is dismissed without prejudice, the plaintiff may subsequently bring the refile the claim

Education records (see cumulative file) All records about the student that are maintained by a school district. It can include instructional materials, teacher's notes.

Educational consultant An individual called upon to provide consultation services. The person is often familiar with school curriculum and requirements at various grade levels.

Educational Surrogate Parent A person who is assigned to act in place of parents or guardians when a student's parents or guardians are unknown or are unavailable, or when a student is a ward of the state. This person has the same responsibilities and functions as parent or guardian.

FERPA Family Educational Rights and Privacy Act; statute about confidentiality and access to education records. It stipulates who may view or amend the records, which include grades, enrollment, and billing.

IEE Independent educational evaluation means an evaluation conducted by a qualified examiner who is not employed by the LEA responsible for the education of your child. IEE's conducted at public expense means the LEA either pays for the full cost of the evaluation or ensures the evaluation is otherwise provided at no cost to the parent.

Parent Right to Evaluation at Public Expense Parents have the right to an IEE of their child at public expense if they disagree with an evaluation of their child obtained by your LEA, subject to the following conditions:

- If you request an IEE of your child at public expense, your LEA must, without unnecessary delay, either: (a) File a due process complaint to request a hearing to show that its evaluation of your child is appropriate; or (b) Provide an IEE at public expense, unless the LEA demonstrates in a hearing that the evaluation of your child that you obtained did not meet the LEA's criteria.
- If your LEA requests a hearing and the final decision is that your LEA's evaluation of your child is appropriate, you still have the right to an IEE, but not at public expense.
- If you request an IEE of your child, the LEA may ask why you object to the evaluation of your child obtained by your LEA. However, your LEA may not require an explanation and may not unreasonably delay either providing the IEE of your child at public expense or filing a due process complaint to request a due process hearing to defend the LEA's evaluation of your child.
- You are entitled to only one IEE of your child at public expense each time your LEA conducts an evaluation of your child with which you disagree.

LEA criteria If an IEE is at public expense, the criteria under which the evaluation is obtained, including the location of the evaluation and the qualifications of the examiner, must be the same as the criteria that the LEA uses when it initiates an evaluation (to the extent those criteria are consistent with your right to an IEE). Except for the criteria described above, an LEA may not impose conditions.

Independent Educational Evaluation See IEE.

Interrogatories Written questions served on a party that must be answered under oath before the due process hearing, method of discovery.

Judgment Order by a hearing officer or court.

LEA Local education agency. The school district. In some IEP meetings the individual referred to as the LEA or LEA representative is defined as:

i.   is qualified to provide, or supervise the provision of, specially designed instruction to meet the unique needs of children with disabilities.
ii. is knowledgeable about the general education curriculum; and
iii. is knowledgeable about the availability of resources of the public agency. (34 CFR 300.321(a)(4))

Motions A motion is a request by a party for a favorable order or remedy as a part of the hearing. Motions can be made at any time as a part of the hearing. They can be either written or verbal.

Notice Mandatory written notice provided to parents before the school's proposal or refusal to initiate or change the student's identification, evaluation, or educational placement. It is important that notices be provided in the parent's native language in advance of any meetings on the student's program or placement.

Offer of Settlement-Ten-Day Letter School districts may limit exposure by extending a "ten-day offer" in which it makes an offer of settlement to the parents at least ten days before an administrative due process hearing. If the parent rejects the ten-day offer, the parent may only recover attorney's fees for work done after the time of the offer if (1) the hearing leads to more favorable relief than the offer included, or (2) the parent was substantially justified in rejecting the offer. This ten-day letter involves sending to the family (or their attorney) a letter that includes a clear and cogent offer of settlement. If parents or guardians accept the terms defined in the offer of settlement, then, the terms and conditions should be defined in a written settlement agreement. Both parties should then notify the hearing officer to cancel the hearing. The hearing offer will then relinquish jurisdiction and cancel the hearing. Both parties need to remember the hearing officer needs to officially cancel the hearing as neither party has the authority to unilaterally or jointly cancel the hearing.

While there is negotiation on the ten-day letter, school district personnel should continue to work through any procedural activities within the prescribed timelines while awaiting a reply to the offer of settlement and ultimate cancellation of the hearing.

An advantage to offering a settlement is the district demonstrates a good faith effort to resolve differences. If the hearing officer rules in favor of the LEA in part or whole and the documentation of the offer of settlement will aid in refuting any claim for the parent's attorney's fees.

Objection A formal protest raised in a hearing or trial indicating that the objecting attorney seeks to have the hearing officer or judge disallow certain testimony or evidence. The hearing officer or judge may sustain or overrule the objection.

Open v. Closed Hearings Due process hearings are classified as either open or closed. In an open hearing the proceedings are open to the public. In some states the hearing officer's ruling with the student's name included is public information. The transcript of the hearing is typically not available to the public. In a closed hearing, only those individuals who are party to the action, designees of the parents or guardians, officials of the hearing (e.g., hearing officer, court reporter, etc.), or witnesses can attend the evidentiary sessions. Only the parent or guardian can determine whether the hearing will be open or closed. In a closed hearing the decision is released with the student's name only to the parties to the hearing and those persons who must implement the decision. As a part of their opening statement, the hearing officer will ask the parents to state on the record whether they want an open or closed due process hearing. Even if the hearing is closed, the parents can bring whomever they want to the hearing.

Opinion Formal written decision by a hearing officer, judge, or court. The opinion contains the legal principles and reasons upon which the decision was based.

Order Probably the first thing parties to the hearing will do when they receive a copy of the hearing officer's ruling will be to go to the end of the ruling to the section labeled "Order." This section delineates what needs to be done by the parties within a prescribed timeline. An order is often written or may be made as a part of the record at the hearing. Orders typically direct the school district or parent to comply with a ruling that relates to the issue(s) that was presented. For example, the hearing officer may order the school district to start providing individualized transportation for the student, or to reimburse the parents for the tuition to a private placement. For parents the order may direct them to make the student available for the evaluator. It does not matter whether the district agrees to the order, they are obligated to carry it out—unless there is an appeal. Both parties may choose to appeal the hearing officer's decision to court of competent jurisdiction, or the second-tier appeals panel whatever is the method in the state.

Parent A parent is a biological or adoptive parent of a child; a foster parent; a guardian generally authorized to act as the child's parent or authorized to make educational decision for the child; an individual acting in the place of a biological or adoptive parent (including a grandparent, stepparent, or other relative) with whom the child lives, or an individual who is legally responsible for the child's welfare; or a surrogate parent.

Pendency Pendency, often referred to as "stay-put" or "status-quo," means the educational placement for the eligible child during a due process hearing or appeal.

    Preschool Pendency The preschool child will stay in his or her current placement during any hearing or appeal, unless the parent and the district agree in writing to other arrangements, except for discipline reasons. The child who has received early intervention services and is now of preschool age may, during a due process hearing and appeals, receive the same early intervention special education program that was last agreed upon by both parties. If the preschool child is currently not receiving special education services and programs and the dispute related to eligibility or programming, the child may receive special education services and programs if the parent and the school district agree.

    School-Age Pendency During any due process hearing or appeal, except one related to an automatic forty-five-day removal, the school-age child will stay in their current school placement, unless the parent and the school district agree in writing to other arrangements. If the due process proceeding concerns consent for an initial evaluation, the child will not be evaluated while the proceeding is pending. If the dispute relates to the level of services, the child will stay at the last agreed upon level of services as they progress up the grades. For example, an eligible child in fifth grade would naturally progress to sixth grade but stay at the same level of special education services that were provided in fifth grade. They would not stay in fifth grade awaiting the results of the dispute.

Precedent A court or hearing officer decision that is cited as an example or analogy to resolve similar questions of law in later cases.

Prior written notice Required written notice to parents when school proposes to initiate or change, or refuses to initiate or change, the identification, evaluation, or educational placement of the child.

Pro se Representing oneself without assistance of legal counsel. When a parent represents themselves in a due process hearing and does not have an attorney present.

Procedural safeguards notice Schools must provide full explanation of procedural safeguards describing the parent's right to an independent educational evaluation, to examine records, procedures related to discipline hearings, procedures related to private school reimbursement, and the procedure to request mediation, due process, and how to file a state complaint.

Res Judicata A matter that has been adjudicated by a hearing officer or court, and may not be pursued further by the same parties.

SEA State education agency (state department of education).

Statutory rights Statutory rights are a right granted under a statute, whether federal or state. These rights emanate from laws enacted by a legislature or other governing body. The written statutes can be used as authority to govern resolving the disputes they address in many cases, rather than case law or judge-made law, constitutional law, contract law, etc. These are different than constitutional rights that are protected by the Constitution.

Statute of limitations Time within which a legal action must be commenced. Typically in special education due process hearings the statute of limitations is two years.

State education agency (SEA) State departments of education.

Statutory law State or federal laws that were written by the appropriate legislature.

Stipulations A stipulation is specifying something that is agreed to by both parties. Stipulations can range from that the student is a resident of the district to who attended a certain meeting, to the information contained in a test report. Hearing officers try to obtain a set of stipulations to identify facts in the case that are not in dispute to help reduce time spent presenting evidence. Then, the parties can spend their time focusing on the facts that are disputable. The effect is citing stipulations helps to expedite the proceedings.

Subpoena A subpoena is an official directive to have a witness attend a hearing or for a party to provide a document. Given that due process hearings are adversarial, it is good practice to subpoena individuals from other agencies to ensure participation. Subpoenas may be necessary if potential witnesses are reluctant to appear on their own. Some agencies may also be reluctant to provide confidential documents and a subpoena may be necessary to procure copies.

Testimony Oral evidence given by a person under questioning from an attorney during a hearing or court case. This is different than evidence from writings and other sources.

Transcripts A due process hearing is a legal proceeding. There will not be transcripts from a mediation. A court reporter makes a verbatim transcript of the hearing. The transcript is available to both parties and the hearing officer. The transcript is also necessary for all appeals. What we are describing here describes the first level of due process hearing. That is, a hearing is held with witnesses giving testimony and documents being submitted as evidence. For all appeals the necessary information is the documents introduced into evidence in the hearing, the transcript, and the hearing officer's ruling. These items constitute the "record" of the hearing. The transcript is used to construct the appeal decision. It is because of the potential uses of the transcripts that either party will want to have certain statements or documents in the "record." As a part of the session in a due process hearing, the parties and/or the hearing officer will want to have a conversation "off the record." These conversations may relate to whether a witness is relevant, or how long to break for lunch. During this conversation or discussion, the court reporter does not enter the conversation into the transcript. Both parties should know that if statements are not entered into the transcript or record, they may not be available for any appeal.

U.S.C. United States Code. The laws of the United States at the federal level.

Witnesses A witness is an individual who will be called on to testify to clarify either what has occurred, what might be written in a document, or to offer an opinion about services. Parents often rely on the school district personnel to tell the story necessary to obtain a favorable ruling. However, if you have others who can substantiate your case, it is important to call them. Make sure they have reviewed the files, they have qualifications relating to their opinions (i.e., they have a master's degree in education and have worked with students like yours), they have observed the child, and they can substantiate your case. Before the hearing begins, keep them informed of the status, the dates, and when they might be called to testify.

References

A.R. v. New York City Department of Education, 407 F.3d 65 (2nd Cir. 2005).

Amanda J. v. Clark County School District, 260 F.3d 1106 (9th Cir. 2001).

Arlington Central School Dist. Bd. of Ed. v. Murphy, 548 U.S. 291 (2006)

Bateman, B. D. (2017). Individualized education programs. In J. M. Kauffman, D. P. Hallahan, & P. C. Pullen (Eds.), *Handbook of Special Education* (2nd ed.). Routledge.

Bateman, D. F., & Cline, J. L. (2019). *Special Education Leadership: Building Effective Programming in Schools*. Routledge/Taylor and Francis Group.

Berney, D. J., & Gilsbach, T. (2017). Substantive vs. procedural violations under the IDE. Retrieved January 11, 2020 from http:/www.berneylaw.com/2017/11/12/substantive-vs-procedural -violations-idea/.

Beth V. v. Carroll, 87 F.3d 80 (3rd Cir. 1986).

Blue-Banning, M., Summers, J. A., Frankland, H. C., Nelson, L. L., & Beegle, G. (2004). Dimension of family and professional partnerships: Constructive guidelines for collaboration. *Exceptional Children, 70*(2), 167–184.

Board of Education v. Rowley (1982). 458 U.S. 176 (1982).

Board of the Hendrick Hudson Central School District v. Rowley, 458 U.S. 176 (1982).

Burch, S. (2009). *Encyclopedia of American Disability History*. Infobase Publishing.

CADRE (2014). The center for appropriate dispute resolution in special education. Document available at https://www.cadreworks.org/sites/default/files/resources/Resolution%20Meeting%20Parent%20Guide%202014_0.pdf.

Center for Appropriate Dispute Resolution in Special Education (CADRE; 2014). *IDEA Special Education Written State Complaints*, Available at https://www.cadreworks.org/sites/default/files/resources/Written%20State%20Complaint%20Parent%20Guide%202014_0.pdf

Champagne, J. F. (1993). Decisions in sequence: How to make placements in the least restrictive environment. *EdLaw Briefing Paper, 9 & 10*, 1–16.

Clark County School District, 113 LRP 52613 (SEA NV 2013).

Code of Virginia, Section 22.275.3 (1973).

Conroy, T., Yell, M. L., & Katsiyannis, A. (2008). *Schaffer v. Weast*: The Supreme Court on the burden of persuasion when challenging IEPs. *Remedial and Special Education, 29*(2), 108–117. doi: 10.1177/0741932508317273.

Council of Parent Attorneys and Advocates (COPAA), (N.D.). Reinstate prevailing parents' right to expect prevailing witness fees. Available from https://www.copaa.org/page/ExpertWitness.

Crockett, J. B. Billingsley, B., & Boscardin, M. L. (2019). *Handbook of Leadership and Administration for Special Education*. Routledge.

D.R. v. East Brunswick Board of Education, 109 F.3d 898 (3rd Cir. 1997). Available at https://casetext.com/case/dr-v-east-brunswick-bd-of-educ.

Endrew F. v. Douglas County School District Re-1, 580 U.S. __ (2017).

Endrew F. v. Douglas County School District, 137 S. Ct. 988; 580 U.S. ___ (2017).

Family Educational Rights and Privacy Act (FERPA), 34 C.F.R Part 99.

Federal Register, (2006), Vol. 71, n. 156, p. 46664.

Federal Register, v. 71, n. 156, p. 46700 (2006).

Federal Register, v. 71, n. 156, p. 46704, 2006.

Federal Register, Vol. 71, No. 156, 46, 700 to 46, 710 et seq., 2006.

Federal Register, Volume 71, 46600, (2006).

Federal Rules of Evidence. Available from the Cornell Legal Institute at https://www.law.cornell.edu/rules/fre.

Florence County School District Four v. Carter, 510 U.S. 7 (1993).

Forest Grove School District v. T.A., 557 U.S. 230 (2009).

Francis, G. L., Hill, C., Blue-Banning M., Turnbull, A. P., Haines, S. J., & Gross, J. (2016). Culture in inclusive schools: Parental perspectives on trusting family-professional partnerships. *Education and Training and Autism and Developmental Disabilities*, *31*(1), 281–293.

Friend, M. (2007). The co-teaching partnership. *Educational Leadership*, *64*(5), 48–52.

Gerber, M. M. (2017). The history of special education, in J. M. Kauffman, D. P. Hallahan, & P. C. Pullen (Eds.), *Handbook of Special Education* (2nd ed.). Routledge.

Gerl, J. (2014). Hot button issues in special education law. Presentation at the annual Tri-State Special Education Law Conference. Omaha, NE.

G. L. v. Ligonier Valley Sch. Dist. Authority, 802 F.3d 601 (3rd Cir. 2015)

Goss v. Lopez (1975). 419 U.S. 565 (1975).

Granelli, L. J., & Sims, B. L (2018). Special education disputes litigate or settle: That is the question. Annual pre-convention school law seminar. Available at https://www.nyssba.org/clientuploads/nyssba_pdf/Events/precon-law-2018/06-special-ed-disputes-outline.pdf.

Granelli, L. J., & Sims, B. L. (2018). Special education disputes litigate or settle: That is the question. Pre-conference workshop at the 22nd Annual School Law Conference, New York. Available at https://www.nyssba.org/clientuploads/nyssba_pdf/Events/precon-law-2018/06-special-ed-disputes-outline.pdf.

Hall v. Memphis City Schools, 764 F.3d 638 (6th Cir. 2014)

H. C. v. Colton-Pierrepoint Central School District, 341 F. App'x 687 (2nd Cir. 2009). Available at https://casetext.com/pdf-downloaded?download_redirect=hc-v-colton-pierrepont-central-sch&utm_source=Iterable&utm_medium=email&utm_campaign=prospecting-emails&content=finalday&term=long.

Honig v. Doe, 479 U.S. 1084 (1988).

IDEA Regulations, 34 C.F.R. § 300 et seq. (2006).

IDEA Regulations, 34 C.F.R. § 300.01 et seq.

IDEA Regulations, 34 C.F.R. 300.1 et seq., 2006.

IDEA, 20 U.S.C. § 14.01 et seq., 2004.

Individuals with Disabilities Education Act Regulations, 34 C.F.R. § 300.1 et seq. 2006.

Individuals with Disabilities Education Act Regulations, 34 C.F.R. § 300 et seq.

Individuals with Disabilities Education Act, 20 U.S.C. § 1401 et seq., 2004.

Johnson v. District of Columbia, 190 F.Supp.2d 34 (D.D.C. 2002).

Katsiyannis, A., & Klare, K. (1991). State practices in due process hearings: Considerations for better practice: *Remedial and Special Education, 12,* 54–58, doi:10.1177/074193259101200210.

Kirby v. Cabell County Board of Education, 46 IDELR 149 (S.D WV 2006).

Lake, B. J., Billingsley, B., & Stewart A. (2019). Building trust and responding to parent-school conflict. In J. B. Crockett, B. Billingsley, & M. L. Boscardin, *Handbook of Leadership and Administration for Special Education* (pp. 265–278). Routledge.

Lake, J. F., & Billingsley, B. (2000). An analysis of the factors that contribute to parent-school conflict in special education. *Exceptional Children, 21*(4), 240–251.

Lake, S. E. (2019). *What Do I Do When . . . The Answer Book on Special Education Practices and Procedures* (2nd ed.). LRP Publications.

Letter to Anonymous, 19 IDELR 277 (OSEP 1992).

Letter to Chief State School Officers, 2000.

Letter to Walker, 59 IDELR 262 (OSEP 2012).

Light v. Parkway School District, 41 F .3d 1223 (8th Cir. 1994).

M.C. v. Antelope Valley Union High, 858 F.3d 1189 (9th Cir. 2001).

Marinette School District, Wisconsin State Educational Agency. (2007) 114 LRP 27793

Martin, E. (2013). *Breakthrough: Special Education Legislation 1965–1981.* Bardolf & Company.

Martin, E. W., Martin, R., & Terman, D. L. (1996). The legislative and litigative history of special education. *The Future of Children: Special Education for Students with Disabilities, 6* (1), 25–39.

Martin, J. L. (2001). *Effective Strategies to Resolve Special Education Disputes Without Due Process.* LRP.

Matthews et al. v. Douglas County School District RE1, No. 1:2017cv03163— Document 40 (D. Colo. 2018).

McClendon v. School District of Philadelphia, Civil Action No. 04-1250 (E.D. Pa. Oct. 29, 2004). Available at https://casetext.com/case/mcclendon -v-school-district-of-philadelphia-2.

McFeatters, A. C. (2006). *Sandra Day O'Connor: Justice in the Balance.* University of New Mexico Press.

McNabb v. United States, 318 U.S. 332 (1943).

Meiner v. Missouri, 673 F.2d 969 (8th Cir. 1986).

Mills v. Board of Education of the District of Columbia, 348 F. Supp. 866 (D.D.C. 1972).

Neosho R-V School District v. Clark, 315 F.3d 1022 (8th Cir. 2003).

New Jersey Protection & Advocacy, Inc. v. New Jersey Department of Education, 563 F. Supp. 2d 474 (D.N.J. 2008).

Office of Special Education Programs (2000). Letter to Chief State School Officers, 33 LRP 6364.

Office of Special Education Programs (2008). Letter to Baglin, 53 53 IDELR 164.

Office of Special Education Programs (2009). Questions and answers on procedural safeguards and due process procedures for parents and children with disabilities. https://www2.ed.gov/policy/speced/guid/idea/procedural-safeguards-q-a.pdf.

Pennsylvania Association for Retarded Citizens (PARC) v. Commonwealth of Pennsylvania, 343 F. Supp. 279 (E.D. Pa. 1972).

Schaffer v. Weast, 546 U.S. 49 (2005).

School Committee of the Town of Burlington v. Department of Education of Massachusetts, 471 U.S. 359 (1985).

Shrybman, J. A. (1982). *Due Process in Special Education*. Aspen.

South Carolina Department of Education, Office of Special Education Services (2022). Facilitated Individual Education Program (FIEP) team meeting. Available at https://ed.sc.gov/districts-schools/special-education-services/parent-resources/dispute-resolution-information/facilitated-individualized-education-program-fiep-team-meeting/.

South Kingstown School Committee v. Joanna S., (D. RI, 2013). Available at https://casetext.com/case/s-kingstown-sch-comm-v-joanna-s.

South Kingstown School Committee v. Joanna S., 773 F.3d 344 (1st Cir., 2014). Available at https://casetext.com/case/s-kingstown-sch-comm-v-southern-ex-rel-pjs.

Spencer v. District of Columbia, 416 F. Supp 2d 5 (2006).

Stafford, R. T. (1978). Education for the handicapped: A senator's perspective. *Vermont Law Review*, 3, 71–82.

Stoner, J. B., Bock, S. J., Thompson, J. R., Angell, M. E., Heyl, B. S., & Crowley, E. P. (2005). Welcome to our world: Parent perspectives of interaction between parents of young children with ASD and education professionals. *Focus on Autism and Other Developmental Disabilities*, 20(1), 39–51.

Tatgenhorst A., Norlin, J. W., & Gorn, S. (2014). *What Do I Do When . . . The Answer B ook on Special Education Law* (6th ed.). LRP Publications.

Tchao, A. K. (1999). Special education settlement agreements pose challenges. *School Law Advisory*, 271, 1. Available at https://schoollaw.com/wp-content/uploads/pdf/271.pdf.

Turnbull, A., Turnbull, H. R., Francis, G. L., Burke, M. M., Haines, S., Gershwin, T., Shepard, K. Holdren, N., & Singer, G. H. (2021). *Families and Professionals: Trusting Partnerships in General and Special Education* (8th ed.). Pearson.

U. S. Department of Education, Office of Special Education (2007). Letter to Shaw. Available at https://sites.ed.gov/idea/files/idea/policy/speced/guid/idea/letters/2007-4/shaw121207dph4q2007.pdf.

U. S. Department of Education, Office of Special Education Programs (2013). Questions and answers on IDEA Part B dispute resolution procedures (Revised 2013). Available at https://sites.ed.gov/idea/files/idea/policy/speced/guid/idea/memosdcltrs/acccombinedosersdisputeresolutionqafinal memo-7-23-13.pdf

United States Code Congressional and Administrative News 1975 (U.S.C.C.A.N. 1975).

Vacca, R. S. (2017). Student discipline hearings and due process. In J. R. Decker, M. M. Lewis, E. A. Shaver, A. E. Blankenship-Knox, & M. A. Paige (Eds.). *The principal's legal handbook* (6th ed.). (pp. 1–14). Education Law Association.

Washington Township Board of Education, New Jersey State Educational Agency (2007), 107 LRP 38312.

Wettach, J. R. (2009). Preparing for special education mediation and resolution sessions. The Advocacy Institute and the Duke Children's Law Clinic. Document available from https://www.advocacyinstitute.org/resources/Preparing.for.SpEd.Mediation.Resolution.Sessions.pdf.

Wyner, S., & Tiffany, M. (2010). *Demystifying settlement agreements*. Available at https://www.wrightslaw.com/law/art/wyner.tiffany.agreement.pdf.

Yell, M. L. (2017). *The Law and Special Education* (5th ed.). Pearson.

Yell, M. L., Bateman, D. F., Shriner, J. G. (2021). *Developing Educationally Meaningful and Legally Correct IEPs*. Rowman and Littlefield.

Zettel, J. J., & Ballard, J. (1982). The Education for All Handicapped Children Act of 1975 (P.L. 94–142): Its history, origins, and concepts. In J. Ballard, B. Ramirez, & F. Weintraub (Eds.), *Special Education in America: Its Legal and Governmental Foundations* (pp. 11–22). Reston, VA: Council for Exceptional Children.

Zirkel, P. A. (2008). Legal boundaries for the IDEA complaint resolution process. *West's Education Law Reporter, 237*, 565–570.

Zirkel, P.A. (2016). A comparison of IDEA's complaint resolution processes: Complaint resolution and impartial hearings. *Education Law Reporter, 326*, 1–8.

Zirkel, P.A. (2020). Questionable initiations of both decisional dispute resolution processes under the IDEA: Proposed regulatory interpretations. *Journal of Law and Education, 49*(1), 99–109.

Zirkel, P. A., & Hetrick, A. (2017). Which procedural parts of the IEP are most judicially vulnerable? *Exceptional Children, 83*(2), 219–235. DOI: 10.1177/00ll665l849.

Zirkel, P. A., & McGuire, B. L. (2010). A roadmap for legal dispute resolution for students with disabilities. *Journal of Special Education Leadership, 23*(2), 100–112.

Index

About the Authors

David F. Bateman, PhD, is principal researcher at the American Institutes for Research (AIR.org). He was a professor at Shippensburg University in the Department of Educational Leadership and Special Education where he taught courses on special education law, assessment, and facilitating inclusion. He is a former due process hearing officer for Pennsylvania where he was involved with 580 hearings. He uses his knowledge of litigation relating to special education to assist school districts in providing appropriate supports for students with disabilities. His latest area of research has been on the role of principals in special education. He has been a classroom teacher of students with learning disabilities, behavior disorders, intellectual disability, and hearing impairments, and a building administrator for summer programs. Dr. Bateman earned a PhD in special education from the University of Kansas. He has recently co-authored the following books: *A Principal's Guide to Special Education, A Teacher's Guide to Special Education, Charting the Course: Special Education in Charter Schools, Current Trends and Legal Issues in Special Education,* and *Developing Educationally Meaningful and Legally Sound IEPs.* Drs. Yell and Bateman are the editors of the Special Education Law, Policy, and Practice series published by Rowman & Littlefield.

Mitchell Yell, PhD, is the Fred and Francis Lester Palmetto Chair in Teacher Education and professor in special education at the University of South Carolina. He earned his PhD in special education from the University of Minnesota. His professional interests include special education law, IEP development, progress monitoring, and parent involvement in special education. Dr. Yell has published 136 journal articles, 6 textbooks, 36 book chapters, and has conducted numerous workshops on various aspects of special education law, classroom management, and progress monitoring. His textbook, *Special Education and the Law,* is in its fifth edition. He co-authored the text *Developing Educationally Meaningful and Legally Sound IEPs.* Dr. Bateman and Dr. Yell are the editors of the Special Education Law, Policy, and Practice series published by Rowman & Littlefield. In 2020, he was awarded the Researcher of the Year from the Council for Exceptional Children. Dr. Yell also serves as a state-level due process review officer (SRO) in South Carolina and is on the board of directors of the Council for Exceptional Children. Prior to working in higher education, Dr. Yell was a special education teacher in Minnesota for twelve years.

Jonas Dorego, MEd, is a retired compliance officer for the Guam Department of Education. She has an MEd in special education from the University of Guam. Ms. Dorego has worked as a compliance officer for the last twenty years managing the Guam Department of Education's General Supervision System, including managing special education disputes. Her experience includes providing direct technical assistance to school teams on how to develop legally defensible IEPs, preparing school administrators on how to avoid special education disputes with parents, assisting the DOE on how to resolve disputes without going to hearing, preparing school teams to prepare for the actual hearing, and how to implement hearing outcomes.